EXAM Pro
Wills, Trusts, and Estates

What is *Exam Pro?*

Exam Pro is a study aid that helps law students prepare to take their Wills, Trusts, and Estates exams. Taking the sample exams and using the corresponding answers and analysis provides students with a more thorough understanding of Wills, Trusts, and Estates and a better understanding of how to take exams.

What *Exam Pro* offers you:

Exam Pro contains 8 Wills, Trusts, and Estates exams.

Each *Exam Pro* contains 25 detailed problems.

Tear out answer sheets create simulated exam conditions.

Detailed and thorough **Answer Keys** explain the best possible choice, why other answers are not the best choice, and provide complete and accurate responses.

Why *Exam Pro* will work for *you:*

Exam Pro Wills, Trusts, and Estates answers provide detailed analysis to help you recognize similar issues on your exams, and provide complete and accurate responses.

A **Table of Topics** helps you to locate specific topic areas in the exams that allow you to focus on the substantive areas you know you need to master.

Exam Pro expands your scope of learning and understanding beyond the sample questions by providing citations to pertinent authority.

Exam Pro
from Thomson West

WILLS TRUSTS AND ESTATES

By

PATRICIA A. CAIN
Aliber Family Chair in Law
Vice Provost
University of Iowa College of Law

and

E. GARY SPITKO
Professor of Law
Santa Clara University School of Law

Exam Pro

THOMSON
✳
WEST

"For Jean."
- PAC-

"To my parents Edward and Marjorie Spitko."
-EGS-

© 2006 Thomson/West
    610 Opperman Drive
    P.O. Box 64526
    St. Paul, MN 55164-0526
    1-800-328-9352

Printed in the United States of America

ISBN-13: 978-0-314-23947-1
ISBN-10: 0-314-23947-2

TEXT IS PRINTED ON 10., POST CONSUMER RECYCLED PAPER

ME

WILLS, TRUSTS AND ESTATES
PREFACE

Dear Law Students:

This study aid contains eight separate multiple-choice practice exams, each of which includes twenty-five questions. All 200 questions are answered and explained in detail. We believe that students in typical Trusts and Estates courses will benefit greatly from studying these questions and the answers to them.

Most of the questions in these exams are based on actual exam questions that both of us have given in final exams we have administered over the years. We have taught the course in Trusts and Estates or a related course (sometimes called Wills and Estates, or Gifts, Wills and Trusts) at ten different law schools during our combined tenure as law professors. We have taught the course using different casebooks in different years. Thus, we have gained a sense of the topics that form the core of the basic course in Trusts and Estates at a wide variety of law schools. Sometimes these courses are taught for three hours of credit and sometimes for four hours. Sometimes they emphasize community property planning issues and sometimes they omit all discussion of community property. Some courses include federal gift and estate tax considerations, while others do not. And some include coverage of the rule against perpetuities, while others do not. We realize that every course is different. Thus, some of the topics that we teach and test on may not be included in your course. Conversely, your professor may cover material that we omit from these sample exams.

Our approach has been to include a wide array of questions that test a basic knowledge of the concepts at the core of the Trusts and Estates course. We also include complex fact situations that challenge the student to choose the best outcome, applying general principles of common law or the Uniform Probate Code ("UPC"), as directed. We agree that a good multiple-choice test should include a combination of questions that are straightforward and relatively easy and questions that are more complex and difficult. Thus, we have arranged the eight practice exams to include a certain number of easier basic questions and a certain number of more advanced questions. Because not all courses include tax material or the rule against perpetuities, we have omitted detailed questions on those materials in the first four exams. We have included questions relating to both of these substantive areas, however, in the last four exams.

Using this study aid to help you review the specific subject matter of the course is only one of the benefits of this aid. Because it is based on sample multiple-choice questions from real exams, the aid can also help you practice taking multiple-choice question exams. More and more law professors are using multiple-choice

ORGANIZATION OF MATERIAL _____

questions in courses on Trusts and Estates. In addition, the multistate bar exam includes multiple-choice questions on some areas of property law that are covered in Trusts and Estates. We provide the following four pointers as good practices to follow when taking multiple-choice questions, either in law school or as part of a bar exam:

1. Always read the question carefully and be sure that you answer the question that is asked. This can be somewhat difficult when the question asks something like: Which of the following is not true? We suggest that in cases such as this you jot down a note to yourself to clarify that you are being asked to identify the statements that are false. Then go through each statement and mark whether it is true or false. The best answer will be the option that includes the false statement. Sometimes, however, the options include more than one false statement. Be sure to pick the option that includes all of the false statements in this type of question.

2. Remember that multiple-choice tests do not necessarily ask for the correct answer. Rather they ask for the best answer. Sometimes there may be two options that appear to be correct. Unless you are provided with an answer that allows you to pick both options, you must decide which of the two is the better answer. In a case where the law is unsettled, the better answer may reflect the modern trend.

3. Apply the appropriate law. In this set of practice exams, unless otherwise instructed, you should apply the most recent version of the UPC. In some questions, however, the instruction is to apply the common law. Since the UPC is statutory law such an instruction would mean that you ignore the UPC. If you are provided with a particular law in a question, then apply the law that is provided.

4. Always read all the options offered as possible answers to a question. Never stop at option B and mark it solely because it sounds right. If you read on, you may discover that option C is also right and that a later option, say option D, allows you to choose both B and C.

We wish you well in your study of the law of trusts and estates and hope that this set of practice exams will benefit you in that study.

Sincerely,
Patricia A Cain
Aliber Family Chair in Law and Vice Provost
University of Iowa

E. Gary Spitko
Professor of Law
Santa Clara University

July 2006

WILLS, TRUSTS AND ESTATES
ABOUT THE 'AUTHORS

Patricia A. Cain

Professor Cain has been in law teaching for over 30 years and has been teaching Trusts and Estates since 1977. She has taught as a tenured member of the law faculty at the University of Texas and at the University of Iowa. In addition, she has taught as a visiting professor at numerous law schools around the country, including the University of Wisconsin, the University of Southern California, Tulane University, the University of San Francisco, and Washington University in St. Louis. She is a member of the ALI and a member of the consultative group on the Restatement (Third) of Property: Wills and Other Donative Transfers.

E. Gary Spitko

Professor Spitko has taught Trusts and Estates as a member of the law faculties at Santa Clara University and Indiana University at Indianapolis, and also as a visiting professor at the Ohio State University College of Law. Presently, he serves as Chair of the Association of American Law Schools Section on Donative Transfers, Fiduciaries and Estate Planning.

WILLS TRUSTS AND ESTATES
ORGANIZATION OF MATERIAL

Table of Exam Topics

WILLS, TRUSTS AND ESTATES
TABLE OF CONTENTS

EXAM I

Wills, Trusts, and Estates

Exam One

1.   T's purported will was all on a single sheet of paper. The purported will contained three typewritten paragraphs identified as a will and making numerous bequests 1 through 9. This typewritten portion was undated, unsigned, and unwitnessed. After the three typed paragraphs was one paragraph in the handwriting of the deceased, dated and signed, which read   my brother, James, I give $10 only. This will, which shall incorporate the typed matter above, shall be complete unless hereafter altered." May the court give effect to devises 1 through 9. Assume a jurisdiction that recognizes holographic wills.

    (a)   Yes, under the doctrine of integration.

    (b)   Yes, under the doctrine of incorporation by reference.

    (c)   Yes, under the doctrine of republication by codicil.

    (d)   A, B, and C.

    (e)   No.

2.   D dies domiciled in California. All of D's property will pass by intestacy. The bulk of D's estate consists of personal property located in Nevada. D also owns real property in Georgia. The law of which state will govern the passing of D's property?

    (a)   California, Nevada, and Georgia.

    (b)   California and Nevada.

    (c)   California and Georgia

    (d)   California.

    (e)   Nevada.

3.   Under the Uniform Probate Code's intestacy provisions, if an intestate decedent "D" and the surviving spouse have children, and all of the children are "joint children" (that is, are children of both D and the surviving spouse), the spouse takes all of the intestate estate. The children do not take any portion of the intestate estate. What is the policy behind this UPC provision?

    (a)   Empirical studies have demonstrated that, except in the case of very wealthy individuals, people strongly prefer that, if they die intestate, their surviving spouse take their entire estate, even if the decedent were to leave joint children or parents surviving.

    (b)   It is thought that the surviving spouse will use the property for the benefit of the children as well as for the benefit of him/herself.

    (c)   Under the conduit theory, it is hoped and believed that the surviving spouse will use the property for the benefit of D's children as well as for D's stepchildren.

    (d)   A and B.

    (e)   A, B, and C.

4.   Which of the following doctrines could be used to validate a pour-over will at common law?

    (a)   Republication by codicil.

    (b)   Acts of independent significance.

    (c)   Incorporation by reference.

    (d)   B & C.

    (e)   None of the above.

5.   T devises "1,000,000 to be divided among my three children. " Which of the following statements is true with respect to this gift?

    (a)   This gift is presumed to be a class gift.

    (b)   This gift is presumed to not be a class gift.

    (c)   This gift is a class gift if T so intended and sufficient proof of such intent exists.

    (d)   A & C.

    (e)   B & C.

6. T devises "My house to my sister Susan. The residue of my estate to my brother Jeff." At the time of the will's execution, T lives at 1307 W. James St. One year later, T sells that house and buys and moves into a new house at 11 Shawnee Lane. One year later, T dies. Who gets the house at 11 Shawnee Lane in a jurisdiction that adheres to the identity theory of ademption?

    (a)   Susan.

    (b)   Jeff.

    (c)   T's heirs.

    (d)   We cannot tell from the facts given.

    (e)   None of the above.

7. In 2003, T executes a will leaving her estate to Marc. In 2004, T plans to execute a new will revoking the gift to Marc and leaving her estate to Fred. Jake learns of this and, because he does not like Fred, fraudulently prevents T from revoking her first will and executing the second will. Thus, if the first will is probated and given effect as written, T's property will pass to Marc, who is wholly innocent of any fraud. At T's death, the court should

    (a)   Probate the first will and allow the wholly innocent Marc to take T's property.

    (b)   Find that T died intestate and allow T's heirs to take T's property.

    (c)   Probate the first will but impose a constructive trust on the wholly innocent Marc for the benefit of Fred.

    (d)   Find that T died intestate but impose a constructive trust on T's heirs for the benefit of Fred.

    (e)   Probate the second will and allow Fred to take T's property.

8. BW is unrelated to T and is one of two necessary witnesses to T's Will #1, and Will #2, which wholly revokes Will #1. Will #1 devises to BW $170,000 in Google stock. Will #2 devises to BW $70,000 in real property. What, if any, of T's property does BW take in a jurisdiction that has a modern purging statute (purges excess gain)?

   (a)   BW takes nothing because T dies intestate as his wills lack the necessary two witnesses.

   (b)   BW takes nothing as the purging statute purges his excess gain.

   (c)   BW takes $70,000 in Google stock.

   (d)   BW takes $70,000 in real property.

   (e)   BW takes $170,000 in Google stock and $70,000 in real property.

9. The State of Nirvana has adopted the harmless error principle *(see* UPC § 2-503). The Nirvanan probate code does not recognize or even mention holographic wills. T handwrites a document that he intends to be his last will. T titles the document "My last will and testament", dates the document, and signs the document. The document remains unwitnessed at T's death. Should the Nirvanan probate court probate the will?

   (a)   Yes, if it concludes that the material provisions of the will are in T's handwriting.

   (b)   No, because the Nirvanan probate code does not recognize holographic wills.

   (c)   Yes, if it concludes that there is clear and convincing evidence that T substantially complied with the formalities for execution of a will.

   (d)   Yes, if it concludes that there is clear and convincing evidence that the testator intended the document to be his will.

   (e)   None of the above.

10. O creates a trust giving A income for life, remainder to B. The corpus is principally comprised of several apartment buildings located within walking distance of one another, which the settlor in the trust instrument forbids the trustee from selling within the 20 years of the time the trust was created. After a certain period of time, the apartment buildings start declining in value because of a general deterioration of the neighborhood. Upon petition of the trustee, should the court allow the trustee to sell the buildings if it finds that the purpose of the trust would be frustrated by retention of the buildings?

    (a) No, so long as the buildings are producing a sufficient income for the life tenant.

    (b) Yes, under the Claflin doctrine.

    (c) No, as this would defeat the intent of the settlor.

    (d) Yes, under the doctrine of administrative deviation.

    (e) None of the above.

11. T wishes to revoke her will. She directs Mark, who is in her presence, to mark an X on each page of a copy of her will and to make certain that each X touches the words of the will. Mark so marks the copy of T's will.

    (a) T's will is not revoked.

    (b) T's will is revoked.

    (c) T's will is revoked only if the jurisdiction allows partial revocation by physical act.

    (d) T's will is revoked only if Mark is an attorney.

Use the following fact pattern to answer questions 12-14:

Scott and Zelda were married to each other in 1995. Scott and Zelda died in 2002 from injuries suffered in an automobile accident. Scott predeceased Zelda by 72 hours. Zelda was survived by two children, Victor and William, from a previous marriage. They remain alive today. Scott had three children from a previous marriage — Anna, Bob, and Charlie. Anna, Bob and Charlie all died in a plane crash in 1996. Anna left two children – Ed and Fred. Bob left three children - Gary, Harry and Ida. Charlie left two children — John and Kennedy. In 1997, Ed died in a train crash survived by his children Larry and Moe. Upon hearing this news Fred committed suicide. In 1998, Gary died in a boating accident without any children surviving him. In 1999, Kennedy died surfing survived by his daughter Rhoda. Today, Harry is alive and has one child — Nancy. Ida is alive and has one son Omar. John is alive and has two children — Paul and Quincy. Assume the jurisdiction has adopted the Revised Uniform Simultaneous Death Act.

12.   If Scott dies intestate, who takes his probate estate in a classic per stirpes (also known as a strict per stirpes) jurisdiction?

      (a).   1/4 to V, 1/4 to W, 1/12 to L, 1/12 to M, 1/12 to H, 1/12 to I, 1/12 to J, 1/12 to R

      (b)   1/10 to L, 1/10 to M, 1/5 to H, 1/5 to I, 1/5 to J, 1/5 to R

      (c)   1/6 to L, 1/6 to M, 1/6 to H, 1/6 to I, 1/6 to J, 1/6 to R

      (d)   2/15 to L, 2/15 to M, 1/5 to H, 1/5 to I, 1/5 to J, 2/15 to R

      (e)   None of the above.

13.   If Scott dies intestate, who takes his probate estate in a modern per stirpes (also known as a per capita with representation) jurisdiction?

      (a)   1/4 to V, 1/4 to W, 1/12 to L, 1/12 to M, 1/12 to H, 1/12 to I, 1/12 to J, 1/12 to R

      (b)   1/10 to L, 1/10 to M, 1/5 to H, 1/5 to I, 1/5 to J, 1/5 to R

      (c)   1/6 to L, 1/6 to M, 1/6 to H, 1/6 to I, 1/6 to J, 1/6 to R

      (d)   2/15 to L, 2/15 to M, 1/5 to H, 1/5 to I, 1/5 to J, 2/15 to R

      (e)   None of the above.

14. If Scott dies intestate, who takes his probate estate in a per capita at each generation jurisdiction?

    (a)   1/4 to V, 1/4 to W, 1/12 to L, 1/12 to M, 1/12 to H, 1/12 to I, 1/12 to J, 1/12 to R

    (b)   1/10 to L, 1/10 to M, 1/5 to H, 1/5 to I, 1/5 to J, 1/5 to R

    (c)   1/6 to L, 1/6 to M, 1/6 to H, 1/6 to I, 1/6 to J, 1/6 to R

    (d)   2/15 to L, 2/15 to M, 1/5 to H, 1/5 to I, 1/5 to J, 2/15 to R

    (e)   None of the above.

15. Doug executes a will devising "90% of my estate to my wife Erica and 10% of my estate to my alma mater State U." Erica predeceases Doug. Doug dies survived by his two children Sophia and Elizabeth, who are also children of Erica. The relevant anti-lapse statute applies only to devises to a testator's predeceasing issue. The statute names as the substitute takers the issue of the predeceasing beneficiary. The jurisdiction has abolished the no-residue-of-a-residue rule. Who takes Doug's estate?

    (a)   We cannot say on these facts.

    (b)   Sophia and Elizabeth will split the estate 50/50.

    (c)   State U.

    (d)   10% to State U and 90% to the estate of Erica.

    (e)   10% to State U and 90% split between Sophia and Elizabeth.

16. Which of the following are reasons why a legatee or heir might disclaim her inheritance?

    (a)   To avoid adverse estate and gift tax consequences, and to avoid having the heir's or legatee's creditors seize the property.

    (b)   To avoid adverse estate and gift tax consequences, and to avoid ineligibility for public assistance.

    (c)   To avoid adverse estate and gift tax consequences, to avoid ineligibility for public assistance, and to avoid having the heir's or legatee's creditors seize the property.

    (d)   To avoid ineligibility for public assistance, and to avoid having the heir's or legatee's creditors seize the property.

17.   Which of the following is not true of the Uniform Prudent Investor Act?

      (a)   Forbids the trustee from delegating the discretionary duty of investing.

      (b)   Evaluates the investment portfolio as a whole rather than evaluating each investment in isolation.

      (c)   Abandons the view that the trustee must avoid "speculative" investments.

      (d)   A and C.

      (e)   None of the above.

18.   In the United States, the usual remedy with respect to a semi-secret trust is

      (a)   A secret trust in favor of the intended beneficiaries.

      (b)   A resulting trust in favor of the testator's heirs or residuary takers.

      (c)   A precatory trust in favor the trustee.

      (d)   An honorary trust in favor of the beneficiaries otherwise unable to enforce the trust.

      (e)   A constructive trust in favor of the intended beneficiaries.

19.   Which of the following future interests may be created in the transferor?

      (a)   Reversion.

      (b)   Vested remainder.

      (c)   Contingent remainder.

      (d)   Executory interest.

      (e)   All of the above.

20. 011ie transferred Blackacre by deed in 1990 to Andy for life, then to Ben and his heirs, but if Ben dies without issue surviving him, then to Carol and her heirs. In 2005, Ben died survived by his oldest son, Seth. Andy is still alive. At Ben's death, who has what interests in Blackacre? Apply general principles of common law.

    (a)   Andy has a life estate, Ben's estate has a vested remainder.

    (b)   Andy has a life estate, Seth has a vested remainder.

    (c)   Andy has a life estate, Ben's estate has a vested remainder subject to divestment and Carol has a shifting executory interest.

    (d)   Andy has a life estate, Seth has a contingent remainder, Carol has an alternative contingent remainder, and 011ie has a reversion.

    (e)   Andy has a life estate, Carol has a contingent remainder, and 011ie has a reversion.

21. Assume basically the same facts as in the prior question, except that 011ie transfers the interests in Blackacre by will. The will provision says: "I leave Blackacre to Andy for life, then to Ben, but if Ben dies without issue surviving him, then to Carol." 011ie's will also contains a residuary clause that provides: "I leave the rest of my property to Carol. " Ben dies in 2005 survived by his oldest son Seth. Then Andy dies. Under the UPC:

    (a)   Ben's estate is entitled to Blackacre because there was no express condition of survivorship.

    (b)   Seth is entitled to Blackacre as a substitute taker for Ben.

    (c)   Seth is entitled to Blackacre because there is an implied condition of survivorship.

    (d)   Carol is entitled to Blackacre under the residuary clause.

    (e)   Both B and C are true.

22.   Linda and Brent have been best friends since childhood. They are now in their late 50s. Brent has been diagnosed with a terminal illness. His primary physician predicts that he will die within 9 months. Brent, terrified of the pain he will likely endure, begs Linda to help him end his life. She agrees and saves up a large dose of her sleeping medication which she gives to him. Brent's will, executed after she agreed to help him, but without her knowledge, leaves his entire estate to Linda and names her executor. On January 22, 2006, he takes a lethal dose of the sleeping medication. After Brent's death, his brother, Ben, learns of Linda's participation in Brent's suicide and moves to have himself substituted for Linda as executor of his brother's estate. He claims that the gift to Linda in the will must be voided and that he, as the next of kin, will be entitled to the entire estate. His best argument for this position is:

(a)   Brent and Linda colluded to prevent Ben from inheriting what was rightfully his.

(b)   Brent, due to his terminal illness, did not know the natural objects of his bounty and thus did not have the mental capacity required to execute a valid will.

(c)   Linda committed a wrongdoing in providing Brent with the lethal dose and she should not be allowed to benefit from the wrong.

(d)   Under the UPC Linda will not be able to take because her actions are sufficient to constitute an intentional killing.

23.   Arthur's will leaves his entire estate to his second wife, Mary, and names Lucas, his grandson, as the Executor. At Arthur's death, the fair market value of property in his probate estate is approximately $1.0 million. Mary also takes as beneficiary of his life insurance ($1.5 million) and as the surviving joint tenant on realty ($1.0 million) and joint bank and stock accounts ($1.0 million). Mary is thinking of not probating the will, in which case, Arthur's estate would pass half to Mary and half to his grandson, Lucas, son of a deceased daughter from his first marriage. If Mary fails to probate the will:

   (a)   She can be penalized because anyone entrusted with the custody of a will is under an affirmative obligation to offer the will for probate.

   (b)   She will be treated as having made a taxable gift of $500,000 to Lucas.

   (c)   The executor must probate the will because the estate is too large to administer informally.

   (d)   Arthur's creditors are "interested parties" and so can force a probate of the will in order to force an administration of the estate.

   (e)   None of the above.

24.   Harold and Elizabeth have been married for 20 years. They have two children, Kate (age 16) and Kim (age 12). Harold also has a son, Ronald, from a prior marriage. Ronald's mother (Harold's first wife) died when Ronald was 2 and he was raised by Harold and Elizabeth. If Harold dies intestate, what will be Elizabeth's share of his estate?

   (a)   She will receive the entire estate provided its value is under $200,000.

   (b)   She will receive the entire estate provided its value is under $150,000.

   (c)   She will receive the entire estate provided its value is under $100,000.

   (d)   She will receive the entire estate.

   (e)   None of the above.

25.   Thomas wants to be sure that his brother, Ned, gets no part of his estate. Thomas has two sisters, Sally and Serena. Both of his parents are dead and he has no spouse or issue. Under the intestacy law, if Thomas dies intestate, his estate will be split equally among his three siblings. Ned lives in a UPC state. The only way that he can disinherit his brother is:

(a)   To execute a valid will that leaves everything he owns to someone other than Ned.

(b)   To execute a document with wills formalities and testamentary intent that says "If my brother Ned survives me, I want him to take nothing from my estate."

(c)   To execute a will that gives Ned $1, and the rest to someone else and contains a no-contest clause that says Ned will lose the bequest if he challenges the will.

(d)   To put all of his property into joint tenancy with right of survivorship with his sisters.

(e)   Both A and B.

EXAM 2

Wills, Trusts, and Estates

Exam Two

1. T executed Will #1 in 2004. T executed Will #2, which expressly revoked Will #1, in 2005. In 2006, T revoked Will #2 by physical act believing that this revocation would revive Will #1. In 2007, T died. The legatees under Will #2 argue in court that the court should nevertheless probate Will #2 under the doctrine of dependent relative revocation. The court agrees. What approach to revival does this jurisdiction employ?

    (a) Will #1 was never revoked because Will #2 is not effective until T's death. (#2 just covered up #1).

    (b) **Will #1 cannot be revived unless re-executed with** testamentary formalities.

    (c) Upon revocation of Will #2, Will #1 is revived if T so intends.

    (d) One cannot say from just the facts given.

2. T devises "My house at 1307 W. James St. to my sister Susan. The residue of my estate to my brother Jeff." At the time of the will's execution, T lives at 1307 W. James St. One year later, T sells that house and buys and moves into a new house at 11 Shawnee Lane. One year later, T dies. At T's death, to what is Susan entitled under UPC § 2-606 (the intent theory of ademption)?

    (a) The difference in value between the two houses.

    (b) Presumptively nothing.

    (c) The value of the house at 1307 W. James St. at the time is was sold.

    (d) Presumptively the house at 11 Shawnee Lane.

    (e) None of the above.

3. T devises "$100,000 to A, to be paid from the sale of my home, or from other sources if the sale is insufficient. " After T's death, T's executor sells T's home for $500,000. If A's gift is subject to abatement, A's gift will abate with

    (a) the residuary gifts.

    (b) the general gifts.

    (c) the specific gifts.

    (d) the class gifts.

    (e) None of the above.

4.   Which of the following is not part of the augmented estate under the UPC's elective share provisions as modified in 1993?

     (a)   Property passing from the decedent to one other than the surviving spouse by a payable-on-death account.

     (b)   Property passing at the decedent's death from the decedent to the surviving spouse by means of an inter vivos revocable trust.

     (c)   Certain inter vivos transfers from the surviving spouse within two years of the decedent's death.

     (d)   The decedent's property passing by intestacy.

     (e)   None of the above.

5.   In year 1, T executes his will, which does not mention or otherwise provide for any child born after execution of the will. In year 2, T's child C is born. In year 3, T executes a codicil to his will which changes the trustee of his testamentary trust. In year 4, T dies. In a jurisdiction in which the pretermitted heir statute applies only to children born after execution of the will, should the probate court apply the doctrine of republication by codicil?

     (a)   Yes, if T has no other children.

     (b)   No, if T had other children alive at execution of the will.

     (c)   Yes, if T would have wanted to disinherit C.

     (d)   No, if T would have wanted to disinherit C.

     (e)   None of the above.

6.   Is the following a valid attempt at creation of a trust? "I give $100,000 to me as trustee to be held in trust for my benefit."

     (a)   Yes, this trust has a settlor, property, a beneficiary, and a trustee.

     (b)   Yes, a trust will not fail for want of a trustee.

     (c)   No, one person may not be a settlor, trustee and beneficiary.

     (d)   No, there has been no delivery.

     (e)   No, a trust must have at least one beneficiary who is not the sole trustee.

7.   T executes a will the first lines of which state "I am going on a long trip into the jungle. If I do not return from the jungle, my estate should be distributed as follows: " T journeys to the jungle, returns home, and two months later dies of a rare illness. Should the court probate T's will?

   (a)   No, because the condition - "If I do not return from the jungle," - was not satisfied.

   (b)   No, unless it can be shown that T contracted the rare illness while in the jungle.

   (c)   Yes, because there is no evidence that T wanted to die intestate.

   (d)   Yes, because there is no evidence that T wanted the will to be effective only if he did not return from the jungle.

   (e)   None of the above.

8.   Testator's will gives to Daniel the power to appoint Testator's property "to such person or persons as Daniel shall appoint." Daniel holds a

   (a)   Inter vivos general power of appointment.

   (b)   Testamentary special power of appointment.

   (c)   Testamentary general power of appointment.

   (d)   Inter vivos special power of appointment.

   (e)   None of the above.

9.   D had two children, Alex & Barbara. Alex predeceased D leaving three children Elaine, Francesca, and Greg. D then died intestate, survived by Barbara, Barbara's son Carlos, and Alex's three children. Barbara disclaims her inheritance. Who takes D's intestate estate under the Uniform Probate Code, which has a per capita at each generation scheme?

   (a)   Carlos, Elaine, Francesca, and Greg each take 1/4.

   (b)   1/2 to Alex, 1/2 to Carlos.

   (c)   1/2 to Carlos, 1/2 split between Elaine, Francesca, and Greg.

   (d)   We cannot tell from the facts given.

   (e)   None of the above.

10.   Mike executes a will leaving his estate to his wife Carol, if she survives
       him, and if not to his children (from a prior marriage) Greg, Peter, and
       Bobby. Carol executes a will leaving her estate to her husband Mike, if he
       survives her, and if not to her children (from a prior marriage) Marcia, Jan,
       and Cindy. Mike and Carol are involved in a car accident that ends up
       taking both of their lives. Mike dies on Tuesday, and Carol dies on
       Friday. Who takes Mike's estate in a jurisdiction that has adopted the
       Revised Uniform Simultaneous Death Act?

           (a)   Carol's estate.
           (b)   Greg, Peter and Bobby will take as Mike's intestate heirs.
           (c)   Greg, Peter and Bobby will take as Mike's devisees.
           (d)   Marcia, Jan and Cindy will take as Carol's devisees.
           (e)   Alice.

11.   Under the Uniform Trust Code and in most American jurisdictions, a
       spendthrift provision in a trust is valid

           (a)   If it restrains voluntary alienation of a beneficiary's
                  interest, even if it does not restrain involuntary alienation.
           (b)   If it restrains involuntary alienation of a beneficiary's
                  interest, even if it does not restrain voluntary alienation.
           (c)   Only if it restrains both voluntary and involuntary
                  alienation of a beneficiary's interest.
           (d)   A and B.

12.   Which of the following is not a trustee's defense to a claim of self-
       dealing?

           (a)   The settlor authorized the self-dealing, and the transaction
                  was fair and reasonable with respect to the beneficiaries.
           (b)   The beneficiaries consented to the self-dealing after full
                  disclosure, and the transaction was fair and reasonable with
                  respect to the beneficiaries.
           (c)   The transaction was fair and reasonable with respect to the
                  beneficiaries.
           (d)   The court approved of the transaction before hand.
           (e)   None of the above.

13.   Helen executed a will in Year 1 that provided in part that "Certain of my real and personal property shall be distributed to such person or persons as I will designate in a memorandum that I will title "Distribution of My Real and Personal Property'. Helen later drafted a memorandum so titled and from time to time revised it. In Year 5, Helen included in the revised memorandum an entry "To Ginny, my house on Dilido Island. " Helen never signed any version of the memorandum. In Year 9, Helen executed a codicil to her will changing the designation of the trustee of a testamentary trust set up by the will. In Year 10, Helen died. Will Ginny take the home on Dilido Island under Helen's will?

   (a)   Yes, pursuant to the doctrines of incorporation by reference and republication by codicil.

   (b)   No, because the doctrine of incorporation by reference does not apply to devises of real property.

   (c)   No, because the testator did not sign the memorandum.

   (d)   No, because the memorandum designating Ginny as the taker of the home on Dilido Island was not in existence at the execution of the will.

   (e)   B & C.

14.   A remedy that orders the owner of property to transfer that property to another person is

   (a)   A precatory trust.

   (b)   A successive interest trust.

   (c)   An honorary trust.

   (d)   A resulting trust.

   (e)   A constructive trust.

15.   Testator died leaving a will devising the residue of her estate in trust to pay the income to her three children Kevin, Brian, and Danny for their respective lives. The will further provided that at the death of the last surviving beneficiary, the trust was to terminate and the residue was to be distributed to the testator's "then surviving issue." What future interest is created by this will?

      (a)   Reversion.

      (b)   Vested remainder.

      (c)   Contingent remainder.

      (d)   Executory interest.

      (e)   A & C.

16.   Klare loaned Bob $10,000 on an unsecured note two years ago and Bob used the funds to pay off an old gambling debt. At Bob's death, Klare wants to file a claim against Bob's estate for the unpaid balance of $8,000. Bob's primary asset was a ten acre tract of land valued at $150,000, held for investment, and owned by Bob and his spouse, Ellen, as joint tenants with right of survivorship. Bob created the joint tenancy five years ago. The few assets he owned individually at his death were all exempt from creditors (e.g., clothing, a funeral plot, a small life insurance policy.) Bob and Ellen were domiciled in a UPC common law property state. What is the best way for Klare to proceed?

      (a)   File a claim against Bob's estate in order to force a sale of the land.

      (b)   File a claim directly against Ellen since she is the current owner of the land.

      (c)   Write his claim off as a bad debt because joint tenancy real assets of a decedent can't be reached by creditors after death.

      (d)   Make a fraudulent transfer claim against half the joint tenancy asset now held by Ellen.

17.   In 1998, Larry Lawyer represented Ted Testator and helped him with his estate plan. Ted left his entire estate to his paramour, Pam, cutting out his wife of 40 years, Flo. Ted died in 2006. Flo sued to have the will set aside, claiming lack of testamentary capacity and undue influence. In addition, Flo asserted her statutory elective share as an alternative claim against the estate. Larry Lawyer acted as attorney for the estate and successfully defended the validity of the will. However, the court ruled in favor of Flo on her elective share claim. Pam, upset that her inheritance has been virtually cut in half, sues Larry Lawyer for malpractice.

Lawyer's best defense to this claim is:

    (a)   A spouse cannot waive her right to an elective share.

    (b)   Lawyer did not know that Ted was married for 40 years because Ted did not reveal that he had a wife on the questionnaire Lawyer asked Ted to fill in summarizing his family relationships and his property holdings.

    (c)   Lack of privity.

    (d)   It is unreasonable for Pam to recover since it is against public policy for a testator to leave his estate to a paramour.

    (e)   The six year statute of limitations has run because the will was drafted in 1998.

18.   Harold and Elizabeth have been married for 20 years. They have two children, Kate (age 16) and Kim (age 12). Harold also has a son, Ronald, from a prior marriage. Ronald's mother (Harold's first wife) died when Ronald was 2 and he was raised by Harold and Elizabeth. Elizabeth adopted Ronald when he was four, If Harold dies intestate, what will be Elizabeth's share of his estate?

    (a)   She will receive the entire estate.

    (b)   She will receive the first $200,000 and 75% of the rest.

    (c)   She will receive the first $150,000 and 50% of the rest.

    (d)   She will receive the first $100,000 and 50% of the rest.

    (e)   None of the above.

19.   Evelyn is the sole child of Testator and is named as the sole beneficiary in Testator's will. Testator's estate is worth approximately $5.0 million. Evelyn is 75 years old and is currently in a nursing home, recovering from a stroke. It is unlikely that she will ever fully recover and she may need to stay in the nursing home for the rest of her life. The costs of the nursing home are currently being paid by her private insurance, but it has a $100,000 cap, which is expected to cover her costs for the next three years. Her son, Evan, has a valid power of attorney and has consulted you about the possibility of exercising the power in order to disclaim the $5.0 million testamentary gift from Testator. What do you tell him?

    (a)   He cannot exercise the power of attorney to disclaim because disclaimers generally cannot be exercised by agents, but instead must be exercised by the principal.

    (b)   He cannot exercise the power of attorney to disclaim because it creates a conflict of interest by creating a benefit to him.

    (c)   He can exercise the power of attorney to disclaim but it will not avoid the estate tax.

    (d)   He can exercise the power of attorney to disclaim and it will avoid both estate taxes and creditors' claims.

    (e)   He can exercise the power of attorney to disclaim, but the nursing home may be able to make a claim against the estate for future costs it incurs.

20.   George's will provides that his executor shall destroy his home after his death. The rest and residue of his property, including the land on which the home sits, is left to his son, Bill. The house is in perfectly fine condition and Bill thinks the only reason his father included the provision regarding its destruction in his will is because his father had become very antisocial in his later years and never wanted to let anyone come into the house. Bill asks the executor not to follow the direction to destroy the home. Which of the following is a possible outcome of this request?

    (a)   The executor may agree to Bill's request and no one has standing to challenge it.

    (b)   If the executor and Bill litigate over this issue, a court will likely rule that the destruction shall not occur because it violates public policy.

    (c)   If the executor and Bill litigate over this issue, a court will likely uphold the provision in the will because of the strong policy supporting freedom of testation.

    (d)   Both A and B.

21.   Frank wants his family to understand clearly why his estate plan leaves some of them out. He makes a video of himself using a webcam that will explain it all. He dies two years later After his death, the video was found on his computer but no will was found. In the video, Frank appears to be reading from a set of note cards. He announces that he is of sound mind and intends for the video to serve as a recording of his testamentary intent. He then says: "To my oldest daughter, Fran, I give nothing, because she has had the bad sense to hang out with people who will take advantage of her. To my next daughter, Claire, I give the sum of $2.0 million, but she must use it to do good in the world as I know she will. To my son, Victor, I leave enough money to fly home for my funeral. Finally, to my wife, who I doubt has ever been faithful to me, I leave one year's allowance of $250,000, which should give her enough tine to find another sucker. If I have anything left over, I give it to the American Red Cross." The Red Cross wants to know whether it can collect the legacy.

   (a)   The Red Cross may be able to collect if Frank died in a state that recognizes holographic wills.

   (b)   The Red Cross may be able to collect if Frank died in a state that recognizes nuncupative wills.

   (c)   The Red Cross may be able to collect if Frank died in a state that had adopted a harmless error statute.

   (d)   The Red Cross is not likely to be able to collect.

22.   Mildred's will leaves everything to her husband, Lon, and if he fails to survive her, then to Lon's nephew, Ted. Five years later, Mildred divorces Lon. However, they remain good friends and she dies six months later, never having changed her will. Mildred died in a non-UPC state in which the applicable state statute provides: "Any gift in a will in favor of a spouse is revoked upon divorce. The property will be distributed as if the beneficiary had predeceased the testator." Mildred is survived by her mother, Mona, and by Lon and Ted. The most likely distribution of Mildred's estate is:

   (a)   Everything to Lon because that was her intent.

   (b)   Everything to Ted because the gift to Lon is revoked by statute.

   (c)   Everything to Mona because the gift to Ted should be revoked along with the gift to Lon.

   (d)   Everything to Mona because Lon did not in fact predecease Mildred and so the condition precedent to Ted's taking has not occurred.

23.   Van cares about what will happen to his body after his death. He has asked his good friend Rip to see that his body is cremated and his ashes are buried next to his dog's ashes in the field behind the farmhouse where Van currently lives. Rip told Van he'd try to carry out his wishes, but advised Van to see a lawyer. In the absence of any applicable statutory provision, which of the following do you advise Van to do:

    (a)   Van should will his body to Rip so that Rip will have the authority to request a cremation.

    (b)   Van should give Rip a power of attorney and specifically authorize Rip to arrange for a cremation.

    (c)   Van should give Rip a durable power of attorney and specifically authorize Rip to arrange for a cremation.

    (d)   Van should execute a living will that makes it clear that he wishes his body to be cremated.

    (e)   None of the above.

24.   Prince married Zoe and they had one daughter, Clarissa. Five years later, Prince died intestate. When the administration of his estate was opened, a woman named Minnie came forward and proved that she had been legally married to Prince 10 years earlier, that they had two children, and that she and Prince had never been divorced. State law provides that nonmarital children can inherit from their fathers only if their parents marry after the birth of the child. Otherwise, the state follows the intestacy scheme of the UPC. Which of the following is not true with respect to the distribution of Prince's estate?

    (a)   Minnie is the only legal spouse of Prince and is thus entitled to an intestate share.

    (b)   Clarissa will be considered an illegitimate or nonmarital child of Prince.

    (c)   Clarissa will not inherit from Prince.

    (d)   Zoe has no basis for claiming part of the estate.

    (e)   Both C and D.

25.   The State of K has a statute that protects omitted spouses by giving them an intestate share. An omitted spouse is described as someone who married the testator after the testator had executed a will. In the absence of children from another marriage, the omitted spouse would be entitled to 100% of the testator's estate as her intestate share. The State of K has another statute that allows spouses to elect against the will. This statute limits the amount that the spouse can claim to one-third of the testator's estate. What is the best explanation for the difference in these two remedies?

(a)   The elective share is derived from the law of dower which limited recovery to a life estate in one-third of the estate.

(b)   The omitted spouse provision is based on a presumption of testamentary intent and the elective share is based on a policy of protecting disinherited spouses.

(c)   The omitted spouse provision is rarely triggered whereas the elective share is often used by disinherited spouses.

(d)   The difference in distribution amounts really doesn't matter because the surviving spouse can decide which remedy is preferable.

(e)   The elective share comes off the top whereas the omitted spouse share is distributed after the payment of debts; thus, the omitted spouse's spousal share must be larger.

EXAM 3

Wills, Trusts, and Estates
Exam Three

1. For a marriage of ten years duration, the elective share percentage, as set out in the UPC's elective share provisions (as modified in 1993) is 30%. From this, we know that the drafters of the UPC's elective share have made the assumption that in a ten-year marriage,

    (a)   30% of the augmented estate is marital property.

    (b)   the survivor is entitled to 30% of the decedent's net estate.

    (c)   60% of the augmented estate is marital property.

    (d)   15% of the augmented estate is marital property.

    (e)   the survivor is entitled to 60% of the decedent's net estate.

2. Is the following a valid attempt at creation of a testamentary trust (assume a valid will)? "I devise my cattle ranch in Texas to my sister Susan, and I desire that she use the profits from the ranch to benefit my brother Jeff."

    (a)   No, because the devise lacks words of direction.

    (b)   No, because we cannot be sure that the ranch will produce any profits.

    (c)   Yes, because Susan is the trustee.

    (d)   Yes, because a testamentary trust will not fail for want of a trustee.

    (e)   None of the above.

3. Jurisdiction X has eliminated the formalities for execution of a will from its probate code. For a document to be a will in jurisdiction X, there must be clear and convincing evidence that T intended a document to be his will. Jurisdiction X is a

    (a)   Harmless error jurisdiction, such as the UPC.

    (b)   Strict compliance jurisdiction, such as a majority of American jurisdictions.

    (c)   Substantial compliance jurisdiction.

    (d)   None of the above.

<u>4.</u>   Assume you are in a jurisdiction that follows the *Claflin* doctrine. Assume further that all trust beneficiaries agree to early termination of the trust. Which of the following trusts cannot be terminated?

> 1. "Such income to A for life as is needed for A's support, remainder in principal at A's death to B."
>
> 2. "Income to H for life, and upon H's death, income to Son until he reaches the age of 35, at which time Son is to receive the principal in fee."
>
> 3. "Income to A for life, remainder in principal at A's death to B."
>
> 4. "Income to A for life to be used for A's support, remainder in principal at A's death to B."
>
> 5. "Income to A for life, remainder in principal at A's death to B. A's interest may not be assigned or attached."
>
> 6. "Income to A for life, remainder in principal at A's death to B. A's interest may not be assigned or attached." Settlor wants to terminate the trust but failed to retain a power to revoke.

    (a)   1, 2, 4, 5, and 6.
    (b)   1, 2, and 5.
    (c)   2, 4, and 5.
    (d)   2, 4, 5, and 6.
    (e)   None of these trusts is destructible.

5.   Steven possesses an inter vivos general power of appointment. He contracts with Harriet to appoint the property to Harriet's two children, who are objects of the power. Is the contract likely to be enforceable?

    (a)   No, because the donee of a power of appointment that is not presently exercisable may not contract to make an appointment.

    (b)   No, unless the court construes the contract as one to release the power and allow the property to pass in default of appointment.

    (c)   Yes, because Steven holds a power that is tantamount to ownership of the appointive property in that he has the power to vest himself of ownership at any time.

    (d)   No, because such a contract is a "fraud on the power."

    (e)   B and D.

Use the following fact pattern to answer questions 6-8:

T executes a typed will which contains a $50,000 devise to Benny but no residuary clause. Later, T crosses out the "$50,000" and writes "$60,000," signs and dates the change.

6.   After T dies, to what is Benny entitled to in a non-UPC state that allows partial revocation by physical act, recognizes holographic wills, and does not have the doctrine of dependent relative revocation?

       (a) $110,000.
       (b) $60,000.
       (c) $50,000.
       (d) $0.

7.   After T dies, to what is Benny entitled to in a state that has adopted the harmless error principle (aka the "dispensing power") *(see* UPC § 2-503), allows partial revocation by physical act, recognizes holographic wills, and does have the doctrine of dependent relative revocation?

       (a) $110,000.
       (b) $60,000.
       (c) $50,000.
       (d) $0.

8.   After T dies, to what is Benny entitled to in a non-UPC state that allows partial revocation by physical act, recognizes holographic wills, and does have the doctrine of dependent relative revocation?

       (a) $110,000.
       (b) $60,000.
       (c) $50,000.
       (d) $0.

9.   D died intestate survived by five children and no spouse. D left a net probate estate of $800,000. While D was alive, he gave Child A a $150,000 home. While D was alive, he gave Child B a $100,000 boat. While D was alive, he gave Child C a $25,000 car. D gave no large gift to his two remaining children, E and F. Assume that the gifts to A, B and C were advancements. Who takes what portion of D's intestate estate?

    (a)   Each child takes $160,000.

    (b)   E and F take the entire intestate estate.

    (c)   A takes $65,000, B takes $115,000, C takes $190,000, E and F each take $215,000.

    (d)   W cannot tell from the facts given.

    (e)   None of the above.

10.   When a person intentionally makes a misrepresentation that causes the testator to execute a will, not to execute a will, to include provision X, not to include provision X, to revoke a will, or not to revoke a will, that person has committed

    (a)   Fraud in the execution.

    (b)   Fraud in the inducement.

    (c)   Constructive fraud.

    (d)   Resulting fraud.

    (e)   Precatory fraud.

11.   The law of the marital domicile at the time personal property is acquired generally controls

    (a)   Problems related to land.

    (b)   Characterization (separate or community) of the property.

    (c)   The survivor's marital rights (such as an elective share).

    (d)   All of the above.

12.   Testator devises the residuary of her estate to the Reverend Wells in trust to be administered "in such manner as in his discretion shall appear best calculated to carry out wishes which I have expressed to him or may express to him." This donative transfer is

    (a)   An honorary trust.

    (b)   A secret trust.

    (c)   A semi-secret trust.

    (d)   A precatory trust.

    (e)   A resulting trust.

13.   Testator devises property in trust "to Elizabeth for her life and at her death to my heirs." In the absence of any applicable statutory provision, at what date is a modern court likely to determine the testator's heirs for the purposes of this devise?

  (a)   At Elizabeth's death.

  (b)   At the testator's death.

  (c)   At Elizabeth's death, if Elizabeth is the only heir of the testator.

  (d)   At the testator's death, if Elizabeth is the only heir of the testator.

  (e)   At the probating of the will.

14.   At Jerry's death, he owned the following property: a personal residence held in joint tenancy with his wife Samantha; two joint bank accounts also held with Samantha; a POD savings account naming his daughter, Jocelyn, as the beneficiary; a life insurance policy and retirement account, both acquired through his employer and naming his wife as beneficiary, various personal items, including clothing, a model train collection, and jewelry, and $20,000 worth of Rockwell stock that he inherited from his father, held in his name alone. The only debt he owed was a $10,000 mortgage balance on the personal residence. Samantha can find no will and comes to you for advice on whether she needs to begin a formal estate administration.

  (a)   She will need to institute a formal estate administration in order to clear up title to all the property owned by Jerry at death.

  (b)   She can collect the personal property by providing an affidavit that she is Jerry's only heir, but only if the daughter is not a minor.

  (c)   She does not need to institute any administration because all of Jerry's property passes outside of probate.

  (d)   She can avoid administration completely if she applies to become a universal successor.

  (e)   **She will need to institute some form of estate** administration in order to use the $20,000 worth of stock to pay off the mortgage.

15.   Jane and Larry have been married for 5 years. Larry has a $100,000 face amount life insurance policy that names Jane as the beneficiary and his mother, Esther, as the contingent beneficiary. Jane and Larry have no children. Both of their fathers are dead, but Larry's mother, Esther, and Jane's mother, Mildred, are both in good health. While vacationing in Florida, Jane and Larry are both killed in a freak boating accident which appears to have killed everyone on board instantaneously. The applicable state simultaneous death act provides that "when there is no sufficient evidence that two individuals died otherwise than simultaneously, each individual's property is distributed as if he or she survived the other." The insurance company should pay the $100,000 as follows:

   (a)   Under the State's Simultaneous Death Act, to Esther.

   (b)   Under the State's Simultaneous Death Act to Jane's estate.

   (c)   Under the State's Simultaneous Death Act to Mildred.

   (d)   Under the State's Simultaneous Death Act to Larry's estate.

16.   Lawrence died many years ago, leaving a will that left his entire estate in trust, with the following instruction to the trustee: "distribute all income to my wife, Maureen, for her life, and then to my stepdaughter, Dorothy, for her life, and then to Dorothy's then living issue if any, and if none, then distribute to my heirs." At Lawrence's death, he was survived by a brother, Benjamin and Benjamin's son, Luke, and by his stepdaughter, Dorothy. His wife (Dorothy's mother) had predeceased him.

Income was paid to Dorothy for 15 years until her death last year. Dorothy had no surviving issue at her death. Benjamin died 10 years ago, with a will that left everything to his wife, Millie, if she survived, and if not, to his son Luke. Millie did survive. She is still alive and so is their son, Luke, and Luke's two children, born after Lawrence's death.

In the absence of any statutory provision covering this gift, to whom should the trustee distribute the trust corpus?

   (a)   Millie

   (b)   Benjamin's estate, to be distributed to his intestate heirs.

   (c)   Dorothy's estate

   (d)   Luke

   (e)   Luke and his two children.

17. Assume the same facts as in the previous question but now assume that the UPC provision that covers this fact situation is part of the probate code of the state in which Lawrence died. In this event, the trust corpus will go to.

    (a) Maureen's estate

    (b) **Benj**amin's estate

    (c) Millie

    (d) Luke

    (e) Maureen's estate and **B**enjamin's estate

18. Harry's will leaves "everything I own to my wife, Willa, if she survives me by 30 days. If she fails to survive me by 30 days, then I leave my entire estate to Willa's sister, Stella." Harry also has an insurance policy naming Willa as beneficiary. Harry and Willa are divorced. Two years later Harry dies, never having changed his will. He has no living relatives at the time of his death. He is survived by Willa and Stella and their mother, Maude. Under the UPC:

    (a) Stella is entitled to Harry's probate estate and Willa is entitled to the insurance proceeds.

    (b) Willa is entitled to Harry's probate estate and to the insurance proceeds.

    (c) Maude is entitled to Harry's probate estate and Willa is entitled to the insurance proceeds.

    (d) The state is entitled to Harry's probate estate and Willa is entitled to the insurance proceeds.

    (e) The state is entitled to Harry's probate estate and to the insurance proceeds.

19. Truman's will provided: "I leave the contents of the drawers in my desk to Annie." At Truman's death, Annie and others go through his desk drawers. Included in the top drawer was an original gelatin silver photograph by Ansel Adams, signed by Adams, and valued at $35,000. The residuary takers under the will argue that Annie should not be entitled to the photograph. It is not clear when Truman purchased the Ansel Adams photograph. Which of the following arguments would you make on behalf of the residuary takers?

    (a) Putting a valuable photograph in a desk drawer is not an act of independent significance.

    (b) There are insufficient testamentary formalities attached to the inclusion of this photograph in the gift to Annie.

    (c) Assuming they can prove it, that Truman did not purchase the photograph until after the execution of his will.

    (d) All of the above.

    (e) Only A and C.

20. Which of the following do not have standing to contest a will that has been submitted for probate?

    (a) An adopted child of the testator who was left out of the will.

    (b) A contingent beneficiary in an earlier will that was revoked by the will submitted to probate.

    (c) A trustee named in the will.

    (d) A person, cut out of the will completely, who claims to be married to the testator at death even though it is proved that the testator had never divorced his first spouse and that the first spouse is still alive.

21. Betsy's will leaves all her property to her best friend, Will. Will predeceases Betsy, but she fails to change her will. He is survived by a son, Darwin. At Betsy's death, she is survived by Darwin and a distant cousin, Colin, who is the grandchild of her mother's great aunt, Sarah. Betsy lives in State M, which has adopted the UPC. At Betsy's death, the probate estate will go to:

    (a) Will's estate

    (b) Darwin

    (c) Colin

    (d) Half to Darwin and Half to Colin

    (e) The State of M.

22.   Harvey and Ellen are about to get married. Harvey is asking Ellen to waive her rights in his estate in exchange for a current payment of $2.0 million. He proposes to pay the $2.0 million by transferring $2.0 million worth of real estate to the two of them as joint tenants with right of survivorship. She consults you to ask whether this arrangement sufficiently protects her right to the $2.0 million. She realizes that if she dies first, she would get nothing and isn't worried about that. But she wants to be certain that she receives at least $2.0 million in value at his death. Which of the following best protects her right?

(a)   The joint tenancy with right of survivorship.

(b)   A tenancy in common backed up by a will leaving all the property to Ellen.

(c)   A tenancy by the entirety.

(d)   A deed granting the property to Harvey and Ellen for their joint lives with alternative contingent remainders to the survivor of them.

(e)   A revocable inter vivos trust naming Harvey and Ellen as co-trustees and leaving all the property to Ellen at Harvey's death.

23.   State G adopted the intestacy provisions of the Uniform Probate Code in 1999. Then the State Probate Code was amended in 2005 to provide as follows:

§ 53-2-1. Determining heirs of decedent who died without will

(a) For purposes of this Code section:

(1) Children of the decedent who are born after the decedent's death are considered children in being at the decedent's death, provided they were conceived prior to the decedent's death, were born within ten months of the decedent's death, and survived 120 hours or more after birth.

Decedent died intestate in 2006, survived by his mother and two brothers. Six months later his fiancé became pregnant using decedent's frozen sperm. If she gives birth to a healthy baby who lives for at least 120 hours, what is the most likely distribution of Decedent's estate by a State of G Probate Court?

(a)   Everything to his mother.

(b)   Half to his brothers and half to his mother.

(c)   Everything to his child.

(d)   Everything to his child, provided Decedent had signed a consent form before death, consenting to the use of his sperm.

(e)   Everything to the fiancé as guardian of the child.

24.   Gene and Frank were brothers. Before going on an extended cruise around the world, Gene transferred $100,000 from his savings account to Frank and asked Frank to purchase a ten acre tract of land close to Gene's farm that was to be auctioned off at a tax sale the next month. Frank bought the land and took title in his own name and recorded the deed, intending to transfer the property to Gene when Gene returned from the cruise. Shortly after Gene returned but before Frank transferred the property, Frank died. His will leaves everything to his daughter, Rose. Rose, as executor, has included the ten acre tract in Frank's probate estate. Gene challenges that characterization. What is the most likely outcome of this conflict?

   (a)   The court will honor record title and Rose will win.

   (b)   The court will impose a constructive trust and Gene will win.

   (c)   The court will give the property to Gene under a resulting trust theory.

   (d)   The court will presume a gift from Gene to Frank and Rose will win.

   (e)   Rose will win unless the deed indicates that Frank was acting as Gene's agent or trustee.

25.   Testator visited his lawyer to ask to change his will. The change affected only Article V, which included a list of charitable beneficiaries. The lawyer's secretary retyped Article V and inserted it in the will in place of the existing Article V. She then told the Testator that the will had been changed and there was nothing more he needed to do. At Testator's death, if someone wants to challenge the probate of the will, which of the following requirements in the law of wills is likely to be useful?

   (a)   A will must be signed by the testator.

   (b)   A will must be witnessed by two witnesses.

   (c)   The doctrine of integration.

   (d)   All of the above.

   (e)   None of the above.

EXAM 4

Wills, Trusts, and Estates
Exam Four

1.   In 2002, T duly executes a will devising all of her property to be divided equally among A, B, and C. In 2004, T duly executes a will devising all of her property to be divided equally among E, F, and G. In 2006, T duly executes a document purporting to be a will which states merely By this instrument, I hereby revoke my 2004 will. " Under the UPC, who among the following takes at least some of T's property?

      (a)   A, B and C.

      (b)   E, F, and G.

      (c)   T's intestate heirs.

      (d)   All of the above.

      (e)   Either A or C, depending on T's intent..

2.   Gary granted to Harold the power to appoint certain property by will to any or all of Oscar, Oprah, and Andrew. Gary failed to specify any takers in default. Harold died intestate. The property might pass to

      (a)   Harold's heirs.

      (b)   Oscar, Oprah, and Andrew in equal shares.

      (c)   the class of appointees in equal shares.

      (d)   B and C.

      (e)   Gary or Gary's estate.

3.   T devises "$500,000 to A, to be paid from the sale of my home, or from other sources if the sale is insufficient." After T's death, T's executor sells T's home for $100,000. If A's gift is subject to abatement, A's gift will abate with

      (a)   the residuary gifts.

      (b)   the general gifts.

      (c)   the specific gifts.

      (d)   the class gifts.

      (e)   B & C.

4.   In the State of Nirvana, persons who are equally related to the intestate decedent and who take a share of the intestate estate, take the same proportion of the estate. The Nirvanans believe that this approach best carries out the likely intent of the typical intestate decedent. Which intestacy scheme has the State of Nirvana adopted?

        (a)   Classic per stirpes

        (b)   Modern per stirpes

        (c)   Either A or B could be correct.

        (d)   Per capita at each generation.

        (e)   Either B or D could be correct.

5.   Under the Uniform Trust Code and in many American jurisdictions, certain "exception creditors" might be able to attach a beneficiary's interest in a trust notwithstanding an otherwise valid spendthrift provision. "Exception creditors" under the Uniform Trust Code and in many jurisdictions include

        (a)   One who has obtained a tort judgment against the beneficiary.

        (b)   A former spouse of the beneficiary who has a judgment or court order against the beneficiary for spousal support.

        (c)   A child of the beneficiary who has a judgment or court order against the beneficiary for child support.

        (d)   A, B and C.

        (e)   B and C.

6.   Settlor creates a revocable trust of which he is not a beneficiary. Under the Uniform Trust Code and in most American jurisdictions

        (a)   The settlor's creditors generally cannot reach the trust assets as "the power to revoke is not property."

        (b)   The settlor's creditors can reach the trust assets only if the creation of the trust involved a fraudulent conveyance.

        (c)   The settlor's creditors can reach the trust assets only if the trust does not contain a spendthrift provision.

        (d)   The settlor's creditors can reach the trust assets.

        (e)   <u>A & B.</u>

7.   Which of the following statutes is designed to be a principal limitation on testamentary freedom?

      (a)   An omitted spouse statute.

      (b)   An anti-lapse statute.

      (c)   An elective share statute.

      (d)   A, B, and C.

      (e)   A & C.

8.   Testator leaves "All of my estate to my beloved Francisco. " The devise to Francisco is

      (a)   A residuary gift.

      (b)   A general gift.

      (c)   A specific gift.

      (d)   A demonstrative gift.

      (e)   None of the above.

9.   When a will purports to make an absolute gift, but there is an undisclosed agreement between T and the legatee that the latter will hold the property in trust for another, this is

      (a)   An honorary trust.

      (b)   A secret trust.

      (c)   A semi-secret trust.

      (d)   A precatory trust.

      (e)   A resulting trust.

10.   Marc has been adjudicated incompetent to manage his property. From that fact, we can conclude

      (a)   Marc lacks the capacity to execute a will.

      (b)   Marc might have the capacity to execute a will.

      (c)   Marc necessarily lacks the capacity to execute a will unless he has a "lucid interval" during which he executes his will.

      (d)   Marc lacks the capacity to execute a will but might have the capacity to revoke a will.

      (e)   B & C.

11. The UPC and the law in most jurisdictions is grounded on the view that to best balance an interest in discouraging litigation that is without merit, family disharmony, and the defaming of the deceased testator on the one hand with an interest in not discouraging litigation that would expose fraud, undue influence, a lack of mental capacity, or other defects in the will, on the other hand, a court should

> (a) Enforce a no-contest clause only if the suit lacks probable cause.
>
> (b) Enforce a no contest clause as written only in a suit to construe the will.
>
> (c) Refuse to enforce no-contest clauses.
>
> (d) Enforce a no-contest clause strictly unless the suit alleges forgery, revocation or a provision benefitting a drafter of the will or a witness to the will.

12. At common law, which of the following types of gifts would not fall into the residue if the gift lapsed.

> (a) A residuary gift.
>
> (b) A general gift.
>
> (c) A specific gift.
>
> (d) A demonstrative gift.
>
> (e) None of the above.

13. The grantor conveys "To Susan for life, then to her son Zachary, but if Zachary does not survive Susan, to the Red Cross. " What interests has the grantor created in Zachary, and the Red Cross?

> (a) Zachary has a vested remainder subject to divestment and the Red Cross has a shifting executory interest.
>
> (b) **Zachary and the Red Cross have alternate vested remainders.**
>
> (c) Zachary has a contingent remainder and the Red Cross has a shifting executory interest.
>
> (d) Zachary and the Red Cross have alternate contingent remainders.
>
> (e) Zachary has a vested remainder subject to divestment and the Red Cross has a springing executory interest.

14. Jane and Larry have been married for 5 years. Larry has a $100,000 face amount life insurance policy that names Jane as the beneficiary and his mother, Esther, as the contingent beneficiary. Jane and Larry have no children. Both of their fathers are dead, but Larry's mother, Esther, and Jane's mother, Mildred, are both in good health. While vacationing in Florida, Jane and Larry are both killed in a freak boating accident. Larry died instantly, but Jane was rushed to a nearby hospital, where she died two days later. Under the UPC, the insurance company should pay the $100,000 as follows:

    (a)   To Jane's estate since she survived, but is now dead.

    (b)   To Esther as the contingent beneficiary under the life insurance policy.

    (c)   To Mildred as Jane's only living heir.

    (d)   None of the above.

    (e)   Either A or C at the election of the insurance company.

15. Gary died intestate survived only by the following lineal descendants: three grandchildren, all children of a deceased daughter Joan, and three great-grandchildren, Kim, Karl, and Kathy. Kim and Karl were the children of a deceased son of Joan named William. Kathy was the granddaughter of Gary's only son, Harry, who died many years ago in a boating accident that also took the lives of Kathy's parents.

Gary lives in a UPC state. The most likely distribution of Gary's estate will be:

    (a)   One-sixth to each of the surviving lineal descendants.

    (b)   One-half to be split among the three children of Joan and the other one-half to be split between Kim, Karl, and Kathy.

    (c)   One-fifth each to the three grandchildren and to Kathy, and one-tenth each to Kim and Karl.

    (d)   One fifth each to the three grandchildren and 2/15[th]s to each of the three great grandchildren.

    (e)   One-eighth each to the three children of Joan and one-sixteenth each to Kim and Karl and one-half to Kathy.

16.   Maureen's will leaves "my house at 214 Dover Street to my good friend
       Annie." It turns out that Maureen doesn't own 214 Dover Street, but she
       does own 215 Dover Street. There are three people who claim to be her
       good friend Annie. In most United States jurisdictions:

       (a)   The gift fails because there is no remedy for correcting a
              scrivener's mistake in a will.

       (b)   The court will allow parol evidence to prove which of the
              three people named Annie was the "Annie" that Maureen
              intended to give her property to.

       (c)   The court will probably give the house equally to all three
              Annies if they can all prove that they are good friends of
              Maureen's.

       (d)   The court will change 214 to 215 since this is a patent
              ambiguity.

17.   Susan created a testamentary trust in the residuary clause of her will that
       provided as follows: "All income shall be paid to my son, Thomas, for his
       life and then to his then living issue, if any. And if none, then to my then
       living heirs."

       Susan died survived by Thomas and an estranged son, Samuel. Samuel
       dies several years later, survived by a daughter, Rachel. Thomas dies some
       years later with no living issue. Rachel seeks a distribution of the trust
       assets to herself as the only living heir of Susan.

       Assuming there is no statutory provision that applies to this situation. At
       the death of Thomas, the trust corpus should be distributed to:

       (a)   The estate of Thomas.
       (b)   The estate of Samuel.
       (c)   Equally between the estates of Samuel and Thomas.
       (d)   Rachel.
       (e)   The state.

18.   Clara was in the hospital. She called her lawyer to give directions about certain changes she wanted made in the disposition of her estate under her current will. In particular, she wanted to add two sizeable legacies to her two friends, Bert and Jane. In addition, she wanted to change her residuary clause so that a larger portion would go to charity. The lawyer decided to draft a codicil to the will that would effectuate these changes. He brought the typed codicil to the hospital for Clara to review. It included a gift of $100,000 each to Bert and to Jane. And it changed the residuary from a 10% gift to charity to a 50% gift to charity, thereby cutting back the size of the residuary gift to her daughter Hallie.

Clara read the codicil and said she approved it. The lawyer went to find some hospital employees who might agree to be witnesses to her execution of the document. When he returned with two nurses, Hallie had already signed the codicil. She and the lawyer began to discuss the effect of that and whether or not the nurses could now witness the execution of the will. She said it was her signature and she would be willing to sign it again if that was necessary. She opened her bedside drawer to pull the pen back out to sign again and was suddenly overtaken by a massive coronary. She was immediately rushed out of the room and the lawyer stuffed the codicil into his briefcase. Clara survived the attack, went home from the hospital, regained her health for a while, but died six months later. The lawyer wants to probate the will, but realizes that the witnesses never signed the codicil. He signs it himself at that time and goes to the hospital to find one of the nurses who was in the room that day and gets her to sign as well.

In a state that has a UPC-style will execution statute, but no harmless error statute, a probate court will most likely:

    (a)   Disallow probate of the codicil because no one ever witnessed Clara's signature.

    (b)   Disallow probate of the codicil because the witnesses had not signed it before her death.

    (c)   Disallow probate of the codicil because it was signed by the lawyer rather than one of the intended witnesses.

    (d)   Allow probate of the codicil because the witnesses did witness Clara's acknowledgement of her own signature and ultimately signed the codicil themselves.

    (e)   Allow probate of the codicil relying on a theory of substantial compliance.

19.   Hank and Wilma have been married for over 40 years. They have two children and three grandchildren. Before Hank goes into the hospital for surgery, they agree to sign a will. They write it together, with Hank dictating out loud to Wilma who does the writing. They state that they intend for this document to serve as the will of both of them. The will provides: "Our property shall go to whichever one of us survives the other and then it shall go to our two children." They both sign at the end and when Hank goes to the hospital the next day they take it with them, show it to the receptionist, and ask her and her co-worker to sign the will as witnesses. They do. Hank dies, survived by Wilma and the two children. They probate the will and Wilma takes title to all the couple's assets.

Five years later Wilma marries Henry. At her death 2 years later, the children try to re-probate the will that she and Hank had executed years before. Henry claims that he should be entitled to Wilma's estate as her surviving husband. Under the UPC, Henry's most successful claim is:

    (a)   A joint and mutual will is insufficient to raise a presumption of a contract between Wilma and Hank.

    (b)   The will was not properly witnessed because the witnesses did not see Wilma sign the will.

    (c)   He is a pretermitted spouse and is entitled to an intestate share.

    (d)   He has the right to an elective share.

    (e)   He has no claim to the estate because the children will take everything.

20.   Constance wants to be buried in her wedding gown next to her husband who died 20 years ago. In addition, she wants all of her jewelry buried with her. The jewelry is valued at $20,000. The best way to ensure that this happens is:

   (a)   For Constance to instruct her Executor to make these arrangements in her will.

   (b)   For Constance to execute a separate document, addressed to her Executor instructing that this happen.

   (c)   For Constance to make the payment of funeral expenses under the will conditional on burial in accord with her wishes.

   (d)   For Constance to create a trust fund that provides the necessary funds for burial and includes a substantial additional sum to be paid to the named beneficiary provided her burial wishes are carried out, and if not, the gift will revert to a charity.

   (e)   For Constance to direct an attorney in fact to make these arrangements on her behalf after her death.

21.   Henry and Mary were married for 30 years. Henry started dating his secretary and tried to keep it from Mary. When Mary discovered the affair, she had a huge fight with Henry that became physical. During the fight, she picked up a heavy object in the kitchen and hit him on the head with it. Henry died two days later in the local hospital. Mary is convicted of homicide and sentenced to prison. Her children are supportive of her and are worried about her financial stability. Henry's will leaves everything to Mary, but if she predeceases him then to the children. He also has an insurance policy that names Mary as the primary beneficiary. The oldest child, Shirley, is executor of the estate and she wants to know whether she can distribute any of the assets to her mother.

   (a)   If the state has no slayer statute, then Shirley can distribute the assets to her mother.

   (b)   If the life insurance is part of an ERISA controlled pension plan, then Shirley can distribute the assets to her mother

   (c)   If Henry and Mary lived in a community property state, then Shirley can distribute all the assets to her mother.

   (d)   Both A and B.

   (e)   The safest way to ensure that Mary receives the assets in Henry's estate is for the children to distribute the assets to themselves and then gift them to Mary.

22.   Tom Testator executed a will on June 1, 2001 and provided for a specific bequest of $250,000 to be paid to the John Jones trust and distributed under the terms of that trust. The John Jones irrevocable trust was created on July 15, 2001 by Tom's brother, John, who transferred $1.0 million to the trust. The trust provided for all trust funds to be accumulated until July 15, 2021 and then distributed to the then living descendants of Tom and John. Tom died in 2006 and his will was probated. The residuary takers are attacking the specific bequest of $250,000 and argue that it should be distributed to them. The trustee of the John Jones trust argues that the $250,000 is a valid gift to the trust. The most likely outcome of this dispute, in a UPC state, is:

    (a)   The gift will fail because the creation of a trust is not an act of independent significance.

    (b)   The gift is valid.

    (c)   The gift will fail because this trust was not created by the testator.

    (d)   The gift will fail because the interests vest too remotely.

    (e)   The gift will fail because the trust was created after the will was executed.

23.   Which of the following is not true about real estate held as joint tenants with right of survivorship?

    (a)   The survivor cannot disclaim any of the property at the death of the first joint tenant.

    (b)   The real estate will not be included in the probate estate at the death of the first joint tenant.

    (c)   The joint tenancy can only be severed by agreement of all joint tenants.

    (d)   All of the above.

    (e)   Both A and C.

24. State 0 has a probate statute providing that children born outside of wedlock can inherit from their fathers provided "paternity has been determined by a court of competent jurisdiction during the life of the father." M and F were engaged to be married. They were expecting a child to be born in six months and had set the wedding date to occur one month before the birth. Two days before the wedding F died unexpectedly from congenital heart defect that had been unknown until his death. One month later, child S was born. S claims to be F's intestate heir. Which of the following is S's strongest claim:

  (a)   His parents should be considered constructively married at the time of F's death.

  (b)   It is unfair to penalize him solely because his father died before the marriage.

  (c)   S has a fundamental right to inherit.

  (d)   State 0's statute regarding inheritance by nonmarital children violates the equal protection clause of the U.S. constitution.

  (e)   F had a common law duty to support S upon S's birth and the intestacy laws must recognize that obligation.

25. John created a trust in his will for his family, naming First Bank as trustee. The trust document provided "The trustee shall distribute all income to my wife, if she survives me, and then at her death, the trustee shall distribute the income among my then living issue as my trustee in its sole discretion determines is in their best interests. Twenty-one years after the death of my wife, the trust shall terminate and the assets shall be distributed to my then living issue per stirpes." At John's death, his wife disclaims her interest in the trust in order to make the income available for younger generations. John's oldest son, Tim, asks for a distribution to help him start a new business. The Trustee declines. Tim wants to sue the Trustee for abuse of discretion. What advice do you give him?

  (a)   There is no chance of success in such a suit because the trustee has absolute discretion.

  (b)   If Tim can prove a breach of trust, he will be able to obtain the funds needed for the new business.

  (c)   While suits like this are not generally successful, Tim might win if he can prove that the trustee bank declined to distribute the income because another bank client wanted to start a similar business.

  (d)   Both B and C.

EXAM 5

Wills, Trusts, and Estates

Exam Five

Use the following fact pattern to answer questions 1 and 2:

The decedent died intestate survived only by (1) her first cousin twice removed Sonny (the grandchild of the decedent's great-great grandparents, who are the first common ancestors between Sonny and the intestate decedent) (2) her second cousin once removed Buddy (the great-great grandchild of the decedent's great grandparents, who are the first common ancestors between Buddy and the intestate decedent), and (3) her first cousin thrice removed Happy (the great-great-great grandchild of the decedent's grandparents, who are the first common ancestors between Happy and the intestate decedent).

1. Who takes the decedent's intestate estate in a jurisdiction that applies a degree of kinship (aka degree of relationship) system to this fact pattern?

    (a)   Sonny takes all.
    (b)   Buddy takes all.
    (c)   Happy takes all.
    (d)   Sonny and Buddy split the property 50-50.
    (e)   Sonny, Buddy and Happy split the property each taking ½.

2. Who takes the decedent's intestate estate in a jurisdiction that applies a parentelic system to this fact pattern?

    (a)   Sonny takes all.
    (b)   Buddy takes all.
    (c)   Happy takes all.
    (d)   Sonny and Buddy split the property 50-50.
    (e)   Sonny, Buddy and Happy split the property each taking 1/2.

3.   Testator devises his home to Anthony, $150,000 to Brittany, and all the rest of his estate to Carlos. At the testator's death, the testators obligations to creditors are such that these gifts cannot be paid in full. One of more of the gifts must abate. What is the most likely order of abatement?

    (a)   The gifts will abate equally pro rata.

    (b)   Anthony's gift will abate first, Brittany's gift will abate second, and Carlos's gift will abate third.

    (c)   Brittany's gift will abate first, Carlos's gift will abate second, and Anthony's gift will abate third.

    (d)   Carlos's gift will abate first, Brittany's gift will abate second, and Anthony's gift will abate third.

    (e)   Carlos's gift will abate first, Anthony's gift will abate second, and Brittany's gift will abate third.

4.   Settlor creates an irrevocable trust of which he is a beneficiary. Settlor's creditor seeks to attach settlor's interest in the trust. Under the Uniform Trust Code and traditional doctrine, still in effect in most American jurisdictions

    (a)   The settlor's beneficial interest is immune from the creditor's claim because the trust is irrevocable.

    (b)   The settlor's beneficial interest is immune from the creditor's claim but only if the trust contains a spendthrift provision.

    (c)   The creditor may attach the settlor's beneficial interest provided that the trust is not a discretionary trust.

    (d)   The creditor may attach as much of the trust as the trustee could distribute to or for the settlor's benefit.

    (e)   The creditor may attach all of the trust property that is traceable to the settlor.

5.   Which of the following is not true of will substitutes?

    (a)   They avoid probate.

    (b)   They are inter vivos transfers.

    (c)   They are testamentary gifts.

    (d)   A & B.

    (e)   B & C.

6. Testator devises "$10,000 each to Amanda, Lisa, and Tyler." The devises to Amanda, Lisa, and Tyler are

    (a) Residuary gifts.

    (b) General gifts.

    (c) Specific gifts.

    (d) Demonstrative gifts.

    (e) Class gifts.

7. As a general rule, which of the following trusts need not be in writing?

    (a) A testamentary trust of real property.

    (b) An inter vivos trust of real property.

    (c) A testamentary trust of personal property.

    (d) An inter vivos trust of personal property.

    (e) B and D.

8. Father died without a spouse, civil union partner, or domestic partner. Father's first will devised his entire estate to his daughter Mary, and expressly disinherited his sons Peter and Paul. Father's second will expressly revoked his first will and left one half of his estate to Mary and one half of his estate to Peter. Who might have standing to challenge the second will?

    (a) Peter, Paul, and Mary.

    (b) Peter and Paul, but not Mary.

    (c) Paul, but not Peter or Mary.

    (d) Paul and Mary, but not Peter.

    (e) Peter and Mary, but not Paul.

9. A court may properly apply the traditional cy pres doctrine only if,

    (a) The settlor had an intent to benefit charity generally.

    (b) The trust has become inefficient.

    (c) The purpose of the trust has become impossible or impracticable.

    (d) A & C.

    (e) A, B & C.

10.   Which of the following is true of most anti-lapse statutes?

      (a)   They apply to a particular gift only if the predeceased beneficiary was of a specified relationship to the testator.

      (b)   They apply to future interests created in an inter vivos trust.

      (c)   They prevent lapse of a gift where the devisee has predeceased the testator.

      (d)   All of the above.

      (e)   None of the above.

11.   Frank directs his lawyer to draft a will for him leaving his estate to Frank's girlfriend Mary. The lawyer drafts the purported will. Franks executes it complying with the formalities for the execution of a will required by the state at the time. But at the execution ceremony, Frank tells the two witnesses that he does not wish or intend to leave his estate to Mary: Rather, he is executing the will to induce Mary to sleep with him. Several years later Frank dies leaving the purported will intact. Does Mary take Frank's estate under the purported will?

      (a)   No, because Frank committed fraud in the execution.

      (b)   No, because Frank committed fraud in the inducement.

      (c)   Yes, because Frank complied with the formalities required for the execution of a will.

      (d)   Yes, if Frank changed his mind about leaving his estate to Mary in the time between the purported will execution and Frank's death.

      (e)   No, because Frank lacked testamentary intent.

12.   When a person intentionally misrepresents the contents or the character of a document, thereby causing the testator to execute the document as her purported will, that person has committed

      (a)   Fraud in the execution.

      (b)   Fraud in the inducement.

      (c)   Constructive fraud.

      (d)   Resulting fraud.

      (e)   Technical fraud.

13. Which of the following is a fiduciary relationship with respect to property in which one person manages the property for the benefit of another?

      (a) A precatory trust.

      (b) A postponement of enjoyment trust.

      (c) An honorary trust.

      (d) A resulting trust.

      (e) A constructive trust.

14. Michael conveys property in trust "to Anna for life, remainder to Jackie." Jackie dies during Anna's lifetime having devised his estate to Edward. Under general principles of common law, who takes the remainder?

      (a) Edward as the devisee of Jackie.

      (b) Michael (or Michael's estate) by way of a reversion.

      (c) Anna's estate by way of a contingent remainder.

      (d) Jackie's heirs by way of the anti-lapse statute.

      (e) The state by way of escheat.

15. Harold and Wanda were married 20 years ago in Texas, a community property state. They have lived in Texas throughout their married lives. During the marriage, they acquired a 100 acre tract of land from their own wages at a cost of $100,000 and Harold inherited some stock from his mother. At Harold's death in 2005, the land was worth $2.0 million and the stock was worth $1.0 million. Assuming no other assets, which of the following is true?

      (a) Harold's gross estate for federal estate tax purposes is $3.0 million.

      (b) Harold's gross estate for federal estate tax purposes is $1.0 million.

      (c) Harold's gross estate for federal estate tax purposes is $2.0 million.

      (d) If Harold leaves all his property to Wanda, his estate will pay no estate taxes.

      (e) Both (c) and (d) are true.

16. In most states, the signing of a self-proving affidavit will create which of the following:

    (a)   An irrebuttable presumption that the will was duly executed.

    (b)   A rebuttable presumption that the will was duly executed.

    (c)   An irrebuttable presumption that the will is valid.

    (d)   A rebuttable presumption that the will is valid.

    (e)   An irrebuttable presumption that the testator was of sound mind.

17. Harold and Maude have been married for 45 years. They have one child, Tommy, who is 40 years old and in financial difficulty. They have come to you to do a joint estate plan. They each want a simple will that will leave everything they own to each other. After the death of the survivor, if anything is left, it can go to Tommy. After you collect a list of their assets, you determine that Harold owns approximately $2.5 million in assets and Maude owns approximately $3.0 million in assets. It is 2006. Which of the following do you advise them?

    (a)   Unless their assets appreciate between now and the death of the survivor, there will likely be no estate tax liability.

    (b)   There will be no estate tax liability at the death of the first to die because of the marital deduction.

    (c)   If both of them were to die in the next three years, their combined estate would likely trigger an estate tax at the death of the survivor.

    (d)   Both A and B.

    (e)   Both B and C.

18.   Ursula's will provides as follows: "I leave the rest of my property in trust for the benefit of my grandson Amir for life, then to Amir's first child to graduate from college." Ursula is survived by Amir aged 25 and Amir's son, Sam, aged 2. How does the common law rule against perpetuities affect this gift?

(a)   The rule does not void any gifts because all of the potential beneficiaries are "lives in being" at Ursula's death.

(b)   The gift to Amir is valid, but the contingent remainder to his first child is void.

(c)   The gift to Amir is valid, but the gift to Sam will only take effect if he is in fact the first child to graduate from college.

(d)   The entire gift violates the rule.

(e)   None of the above.

19.   Assume the same facts as the previous question, except that Amir predeceases Ursula. Under common law rules, who will benefit from the trust fund?

(a)   Only Ursula's estate will benefit because no one else can take.

(b)   Amir's estate will collect the income from the gift until Sam graduates from college and then Sam will get the trust corpus.

(c)   Sam will get the trust corpus because his interest does not violate the rule against perpetuities.

(d)   Sam will not benefit because his interest violates the rule against perpetuities.

(e)   Sam will collect the trust corpus if he graduates from college.

20.   Nick's will created a trust in which he gave his son, Mick, the income from the trust for life and "then as Mick shall appoint by last will and testament." The same will gave the "rest and residue of my property to Yale University." Mick was Nick's only child. At Mick's death, his will was probated. It was a simple will that appointed his wife, Molly, as executrix and then provided "I give all of my property, of every kind and wherever situated, to my wife Molly." Molly survived Mick. Under the UPC, the trust assets will go to:

    (a)   Molly, because she was named as the residuary taker in Mick's will.

    (b)   Mick's estate because he held a general power of appointment, but he did not exercise it.

    (c)   Nick's intestate heir, Mick, because Nick had a reversionary interest in the trust assets.

    (d)   Nick's residuary taker, Yale, because his reversionary interest would pass under his residuary clause.

    (e)   The state in which Nick was domiciled because he has no living heirs to take his interest.

21.   Assume the same facts as in the prior question except that Nick's will provided that the income would be made to Mick and then the assets of the trust would be distributed "as Mick appoints by will to anyone other than himself, his estate, or his creditors." At Mick's death, under the UPC, the trust property will go to:

    (a)   Molly, because she was named as the residuary taker in Mick's will.

    (b)   Mick's estate because he held a general power of appointment, but he did not exercise it.

    (c)   Nick's intestate heir, Mick, because Nick had a reversionary interest in the trust assets.

    (d)   Nick's residuary taker, Yale, because his reversionary interest would pass under his residuary clause.

    (e)   The state in which Nick was domiciled because he has no living heirs to take his interest.

22.   Gino declared himself trustee of $1.0 million in perpetuity for the purpose of granting college scholarships out of the income of the fund to any then living issue of his top three managers. At the time of his death, he had awarded two college scholarships to qualifying children. The trust's ability to continue awarding scholarships in the future is threatened by:

      (a)   The rule against perpetuities.

      (b)   The identifiable beneficiary rule.

      (c)   The failure to name a successor trustee.

      (d)   All of the above.

      (e)   None of the above.

23.   Blanche's will left everything to her brother Bob. She kept the original will in a drawer in her bedroom. One day Blanche was rushed to the hospital after a severe stroke. She was in the hospital for weeks, but Bob never came to see her. One day when her neighbor Nellie was visiting, Blanche complained about Bob's absence. She then gave Nellie the key to her house and told her to go find the will and tear it up. Nellie did so and immediately called Blanche to tell her the will had been taken care of. Blanche died survived by her brother Bob and three sisters. When Bob learned about the will's destruction, he was very upset. He called his sisters and explained that he had called the hospital regularly to check on Blanche but hadn't visited her because he had a bad cold at the time and the nurses told him he should wait until he was over it because Blanche was very susceptible to germs.

Under the UPC:

      (a)   The will in favor of Bob can be probated under the Doctrine of Dependent and Relative Revocation.

      (b)   The will in favor of Bob can be probated because it was never revoked.

      (c)   The will in favor of Bob can be probated under the revival statute.

      (d)   Bob will take one-fourth of Blanche's estate by intestacy.

      (e)   Blanche's estate will be distributed to the three sisters in order to carry out her probable intent.

24.   In 2006, Husband tells estate planner that he wants to leave his entire $10.0 Million estate to his wife and if she fails to survive him, then to his two children. He has made no lifetime gifts. The estate planner suggests that he consider including a by-pass trust in his will and transfer at least $2.0 million to the trust. The primary reason to use a by-pass trust in this fact situation is:

      (a)   To avoid over-qualifying for the marital deduction.

      (b)   To use up his gift tax life-time exemption.

      (c)   To avoid the generation-skipping tax.

      (d)   To reduce taxes at husband's death.

25.   Uncle Marvin, age 80, has a favorite niece, Samantha. He has decided to leave his entire estate to her, but he is worried that his other nieces and nephews will challenge the will. His estate is valued at over $5.0 million, so his fears seem well founded. He has asked for your advice on how best to protect Samantha after his death from claims by his other relatives. His current will names Samantha as his sole beneficiary. You advise him to:

      (a)   Put everything he owns into joint tenancy with right of survivorship.

      (b)   Adopt Samantha.

      (c)   Add a codicil to the will that reconfirms Samantha as sole beneficiary and provides that anyone who challenges the will shall lose his intestate share.

      (d)   Transfer all his property to Samantha, but reserve a life estate for himself.

      (e)   Include a provision in his will explaining why he is disinheriting all his other heirs.

EXAM 6

Wills, Trusts, and Estates
Exam Six

1. Under what circumstances may the settlor of a revocable inter vivos trust revoke the trust while she is subject to undue influence?

    (a)   When the alleged influencer is the trustee.

    (b)   When the alleged influencer and the settlor are not in a confidential relationship.

    (c)   When the settlor is the sole beneficiary of the trust during her lifetime.

    (d)   All of the above.

    (e)   None of the above.

2. Testator devises "My house at 627 Canal View Drive" to Reuben. The devise to Reuben is

    (a)   A residuary gift.

    (b)   A general gift.

    (c)   A specific gift.

    (d)   A demonstrative gift.

    (e)   None of the above.

3. Testator, who has 2 sisters, executes a will complying with all applicable will formalities which provides "I leave my entire estate to the oldest of my sisters who shall be alive at my death."   Shortly after Testator executes the will, his oldest sister dies. Testator's other sister survives him. At Testator's death, does Testator's surviving sister take his estate?

    (a)   Yes, because she is his intestate heir.

    (b)   No, if Testator's oldest sister left issue and is within the relationship to Testator required by the jurisdiction's anti-lapse statute.

    (c)   Yes, because the older sister's death is an act of independent significance.

    (d)   No, because Testator has imposed an invalid condition on the gift to the oldest sister.

    (e)   No, because she was not Testator's oldest sister when Testator executed the will.

4. Most states have a prohibition on inheritance by slayers of the property owner. For example, California has a statute that precludes one who feloniously and intentionally kills the decedent from inheriting from the decedent. Which of the following is not a likely rationale behind such statutes?

    (a)   A desire to deter wrongful killing.

    (b)   A desire to promote the likely donative intent of the victim.

    (c)   A desire that the slayer should not profit from his wrong actions.

    (d)   None of the above.

    (e)   A and C.

5. Ademption by satisfaction applies only to

    (a)   Residuary gifts.

    (b)   General gifts.

    (c)   Specific gifts.

    (d)   Class gifts.

    (e)   None of the above.

6. A goal of the drafters of the modern Uniform Probate Code's elective share provisions was to approximate the results of a community property state at the death of a spouse. Significant differences exist, however, between the structure and results of the UPC's elective share provisions and the structure and results of community property law. In what way does the UPC's elective share differ significantly from a community property regime?

    (a)   The surviving spouse takes a greater share of the decedent's property under a community property system.

    (b)   Under the UPC's elective share, but not under community property law, a spouse's rights are conditioned on surviving the decedent.

    (c)   The UPC's elective share operates on an augmented estate, which adds together all of the couple's assets, including assets acquired before marriage and property acquired during marriage by gift or inheritance.   In contrast, community property rights do not attach to assets acquired before marriage or to property acquired during marriage by gift or inheritance.

    (d)   B and C.

    (e)   All of the above.

7. In the United States, the usual remedy with respect to a secret trust is

   (a) A semi-secret trust in favor of the intended beneficiaries.
   (b) A resulting trust in favor of the testator's heirs or residuary takers.
   (c) A precatory trust in favor the trustee.
   (d) An honorary trust in favor of the beneficiaries otherwise unable to enforce the trust.
   (e) A constructive trust in favor of the intended beneficiaries.

8. The omitted spouse doctrine is

   (a) Intended to carry out the intent of the testator.
   (b) Unconcerned with the intent of the testator.
   (c) Intended to defeat the intent of the testator.
   (d) Applicable to all wills that do not mention a married testator's spouse.
   (e) A and D.

Questions 9 through 11 relate to the following fact pattern: Dorothy had two children — John and Patty. In year 1, Dorothy devised "$1,000,000 to be divided among my grandchildren who reach the age of 21." In year 4, John had his first child Judy. In year 9, John had his second child Kathy. In year 14, John had his third child Karen. In year 15, Dorothy died survived by her son John, her daughter Patty, and her 3 grandchildren. In year 19, Patty had her first child Danny. In year 20, John died. In year 24, Patty had her second child Francis. In year 27, Judy died. In year 28, Kathy died. In year 29, Patty had her third child Greg. In year 39, Patty died. In year 50, Greg reached the age of 21. In year 50, when Greg turned 21, Karen, Danny, Francis, and Greg are alive. The jurisdiction follows the "rule of convenience."

9. In what year, does the class relating to Dorothy's class gift close?

   (a) Year 4.
   (b) Year 15.
   (c) Year 25.
   (d) Year 39.
   (e) Year 50.

10.   Assume the same fact patter as above, except that Dorothy died in year 2. In what year does the class relating to Dorothy's class gift close?

     (a)   Year 4.

     (b)   Year 15.

     (c)   Year 25.

     (d)   Year 39.

     (e)   Year 50.

11.   Assuming that Dorothy died in year 2, what if anything will Judy take?

     (a)   Nothing, because she died before the class closed.

     (b)   Nothing, because she failed to live to distribution of the gift.

     (c)   <u>A & B.</u>

     (d)   Judy will divide the $1,000,000 equally with Kathy, Karen, Danny, Francis, and Greg

     (e)   Judy will divide the $1,000,000 equally with Karen, Danny, Francis, and Greg

12.   Francis has legally adopted Carlos. Which of the following statements generally is not true in most American jurisdictions?

     (a)   If Francis dies intestate, Carlos will inherit from Francis as would a biological and legal child of Francis.

     (b)   If Carlos dies intestate, Francis will inherit from Carlos as would a biological and legal parent of Carlos.

     (c)   If Francis predeceases Carlos, Carlos will inherit through Francis as would a biological and legal child of Francis.

     (d)   B & C.

     (e)   None of the above.

13.   Wealthy Client has asked that you redo her estate plan. She owns real property in several different states and has a gross estate of over $3.0 million. She says she has heard that using a revocable trust instead of a will can save her lots of money, both in probate fees and in estate taxes. Which of the following should you tell Ms. Client?

    (a)   Yes, a revocable trust can save her lots of money in both probate fees and estate taxes.

    (b)   No, a revocable trust saves no money, but it is easier to amend than a will and so is preferable for that reason.

    (c)   She should use a revocable trust, but only for life insurance policies, because that will save her the most in estate taxes.

    (d)   The revocable trust may save her some probate fees, but no estate taxes.

    (e)   The revocable trust may save her a small amount in estate taxes, but very little in probate fees.

14.   Clarence purchased a will form while he was traveling in California. He brought it back to his home state and filled it out in his own handwriting. Then he turned to the last page, which said "Self-Proving Affidavit." He signed the line on that page that was indicated for the Testator's signature. Then he went to work and asked two of his co-workers to sign on the lines labeled "witness," but in the end only one of them signed the affidavit and neither signed the will itself. Then he found a notary public and he swore to the notary public that he and the witness had signed the document on the lines indicated. The notary signed as well at the end of the self-proving affidavit. After Clarence's death, his brother, Bob, found the will and tried to probate it. Clarence' sister, Celia, challenged since she was not named in the will, claiming that the will itself had not been signed. Her claim was based on the fact that since Clarence and the witness and the notary public had only signed the self-proving affidavit, no one had signed the will. Under the UPC, what is the most likely result?

    (a)   The will can be probated if Bob can establish by "clear and convincing" evidence that Clarence intended the document to be his will.

    (b)   The will cannot be probated because at the very least a will must be signed by the testator.

    (c)   The will can be probated as a holographic will if the state recognizes holographic wills since all of the essential terms are in Clarence's handwriting.

    (d)   The will can be probated under the doctrine of substantial compliance.

    (e)   The will can be probated under the doctrine of probable intent.

15.   Michelle's father's last testament provided as follows: "I give the family farm to my daughter, Michelle, for her to use as she pleases for her life, and at her death, the farm shall vest in fee in her children, if there are any who survive her." Michelle died in 2004, survived by two children, Bess and George. At her death the family farm was worth $1.0 million. She owns additional assets worth $5.0 million. You are responsible for filing Michelle's estate tax return. How should you treat the family farm?

      (a)   It should not be included in her gross estate because it is not property she owns at death.

      (b)   The fair market value of her life estate should be included in her gross estate.

      (c)   The value of the interests that passed to Bess and George should be included in Michelle's gross estate at their discounted value.

      (d)   The farm should not be included in her gross estate, but her estate will have to pay a generation-skipping tax on the transfer.

16.   Gary died intestate survived only by the following lineal descendants: three grandchildren, all children of a deceased daughter Joan, and two great-grandchildren, Kim and Kathy. Kim was the daughter of a deceased son of Joan named William. Kathy was the granddaughter of Gary's only son, Harry, who died many years ago in a boating accident that also took the lives of Kathy's parents.

Gary lives in a UPC state. The most likely distribution of Gary's estate will be:

      (a)   One-fifth to each of the surviving lineal descendants.

      (b)   One-half to be split among the three children of Joan and the other one-half to be split between Kim and Kathy.

      (c)   One half to be split equally among the three children of Joan and Kim (i.e., one-eighth each) and one half to Kathy.

      (d)   One-eighth to each of the three children of Joan, one-eighth to Kim and one-half to Kathy.

      (e)   Three-fourths to the children and grandchildren of Joan (divided equally) and one-fourth to Kathy.

17. Ralph deeds Whiteacre to Susan for life, then to Susan's children who reach age 25. At the time of the transfer Susan has three children, aged 25, 21, and 18. She does not intend to have any more children. Under general principles of common law, at Susan's death, Whiteacre will be vested in:

   (a)   Ralph because the future interest in Susan's children violates the common law rule against perpetuities.

   (b)   Susan because the future interest in Susan's children violated the common law rule against perpetuities.

   (c)   All three of Susan's children, or their estates if they are not then living.

   (d)   All of Susan's children who in fact reach age 25, or their estates, if they are not then living.

   (e)   Only to the child who was 25 years old at the time of the transfer because that is the only child who is vested.

18. Tim's will leaves Greenacre to his two sons, Bob and Jim, but if either of them should die without children surviving him, that son's share shall pass to the other son. At Tim's death, the state of the title is:

   (a)   Bob and Jim both have a fee simple subject to a condition subsequent and each of them has a contingent remainder.

   (b)   Bob and Jim both have a fee simple subject to a condition subsequent and each of them has an executory interest.

   (c)   Bob and Jim both have a fee simple subject to divestment.

   (d)   Bob and Jim both have a fee simple absolute.

   (e)   Bob and Jim both have a life estate, followed by alternative contingent remainders, and Tim has a reversion.

19. Trudy Trustor created an irrevocable living trust at age 60. She directed that the trustee "pay the income to my grandson, Gary, for his life, and then pay the income to Gary's first child to graduate from high school for that child's life, and at the death of that child, pay to the then living issue of Gary." At the time the trust was created, Gary was 20 years old and had a two year old son, Cliff. Cliff graduated from high school 16 years later, married Julie, and had three children. Gary died when Cliff was 60. Cliff died last year at age 97, survived by his three children. Under the common law:

   (a)   Gary's interest in the trust is valid.

   (b)   Cliff's interest in the trust is valid.

   (c)   The interest in Cliff's children is valid.

   (d)   All of the above.

   (e)   Only A and B.

20.   Assume the same facts as in the prior question. Under the UPC:

   (a)   Gary's interest in the trust is valid.

   (b)   Cliff's interest in the trust is valid.

   (c)   The interest in Cliff's children is valid.

   (d)   All of the above.

   (e)   Only A and B.

21.   Before adoption of the modern UPC rules with respect to nontestamentary transfers, which of the following gifts would have been most susceptible to attack?

   (a)   T purchases a life insurance policy and names X as the beneficiary.

   (b)   T adds X as a joint owner to T's bank account, but does not have X sign a signature card and does not tell X about this decision.

   (c)   T creates a revocable trust, naming T and X as trustees and providing that the trust income shall be paid to T during T's life and then to X. T transfers title to real estate and stock to the trustees.

   (d)   T transfers realty owned by T to T and X as joint tenants with right of survivorship and mails the deed to X with instructions to record after T's death.

   (e)   T sends X a letter and says: "**I** am giving you my dog (picture enclosed). You may come to my house and pick her up at any time." T dies before X picks up the dog.

22.   Marjorie and Nancy have lived most of their lives together as domestic partners, but they live in a state that does not recognize their relationship. Marjorie has been advised to consult an attorney to draft documents that will protect them in the event either of them becomes disabled or dies. They have discussed their desires regarding "pulling the plug" should either of them wind up on life support. They share the philosophy that life should not be prolonged and have promised each other that they'll carry out the partner's wishes should that situation arise. They know they need wills, but wonder what other documents they need. You advise them:

(a)   They need to create a life insurance trust if they plan to name each other as beneficiaries on a life insurance policy.

(b)   They should execute either a living will or a durable power of attorney for health care, but they don't need both.

(c)   They should execute a living will and a durable power of attorney for health care.

(d)   A and B.

(e)   A and C.

23.   Paula's will provided as follows: "The rest and residue of my estate shall be held in trust for the benefit of my son Clarence, for his life, and then to his then living issue, if any, and if none, then as Clarence appoints among the then living lineal descendants of my grandparents." Clarence does not have any children. He wants his longtime domestic partner, George, to be supported if Clarence should die first, but Clarence's only source of support is the income from Paula's trust. The issue of Paula's grandparents who are now alive include a cousin Shelley and a niece, Karen, who has a son, Charles. Clarence consults you for advice. You tell him:

(a)   He should let the power of appointment lapse. Since there are no default takers the property will revert to Paula's estate and it looks like Clarence is the only heir entitled to take. He should execute a will that leaves all of his property to George.

(b)   He should make a side deal with either Shelly or Karen and agree to appoint the property to one of them if she will agree to transfer a significant amount of the property to George.

(c)   He should release the power and claim the reversion immediately as Paula's heir.

(d)   He should adopt George and let the property pass to him under the terms of the trust.

(e)   There is no clear way to ensure that the trust assets will ever benefit George.

24.   Decedent was a long-time employee of General Motors. At his death, he was survived by three children and his ex-wife. His pension plan and life insurance through his employer designated the ex-wife as beneficiary. He failed to change this designation after the divorce and the property settlement incident to the divorce did not mention the pension plan or life insurance. His will also named his ex-wife as primary beneficiary, and provided that in the event she predeceased him, all his property should go to his children. He also failed to make any changes in his will after the divorce. In a UPC state, who is likely to inherit from Decedent?

    (a)   The ex-wife will take the pension plan proceeds, the life insurance and the probate estate.

    (b)   The children will take the pension plan proceeds, the life insurance and the probate estate.

    (c)   The ex-wife will take the pension plan proceeds and the life insurance and the children will take the probate estate.

    (d)   The ex-wife will take the pension plan proceeds and the children with take the life insurance and the probate estate.

    (e)   The ex-wife and the children will split everything.

25.   A trust includes the following clause: "No beneficiary of this trust shall have the power to assign his interest in the trust to anyone, including creditors, and no creditor of a beneficiary of this trust shall have to power to compel a distribution from the trust on behalf of the beneficiary." Which of the following is generally true about the effectiveness of this clause?

    (a)   The clause will not be enforced as it is against public policy.

    (b)   The clause will not be enforced against the creditors of the Grantor.

    (c)   The clause will not be enforced against pre-existing creditors of any of the trust beneficiaries.

    (d)   Both B and C.

    (e)   All of the above

EXAM 7

Wills, Trusts, and Estates

Exam Seven

1. Settlor creates a trust in which "the trustees may pay to Andy so much of the income or principal as the trustees deem Andy capable of investing." Settlor has created

    (a) A spendthrift trust.

    (b) A mere successive-interest trust.

    (c) A support trust.

    (d) A discretionary trust.

    (e) A postponement-of-enjoyment trust.

2. The evidence at trial demonstrates that Testator told her lawyer to destroy her will and codicil. The lawyer suggested, however, that Testator keep the will and codicil as models in case she decided to draft a new will. The lawyer wrote 'null and void' on the back of the will and the back of the codicil and Testator signed underneath these notations. Testator died shortly thereafter leaving a large estate. In a harmless error jurisdiction, are the will and codicil revoked?

    (a) No. The attempts at revocation by physical act fail because the acts of cancellation do not touch the words of the will.

    (b) No. The attempts to revoke by subsequent writing fail because not all of the material portions of the purported revoking instruments are in the hand of the testator.

    (c) Yes. The will and codicil are revoked by physical act.

    (d) Yes. The will and codicil are revoked by subsequent instrument.

    (e) A and B.

3. Testator executes a will leaving a large legacy to his son Paul. Subsequently, Testator executes a codicil which states in full "I hereby revoke the gift to Paul in my earlier will." The evidence shows that shortly before the revocation, a friend told Testator that Paul had died. In fact, Paul survived the testator. Under traditional common law doctrine, should the court give effect to the revocation of the gift to Paul??

    (a) No. The court should apply the doctrine of dependent relative revocation to save the gift to Paul.

    (b) No. The court should impose a constructive trust for the benefit of Paul, provided that both the testator and the friend were mistaken about Paul having died.

    (c) No. The court should apply the anti-lapse statute to save the gift to Paul.

    (d) A and B.

    (e) Yes, even though this would likely frustrate the intent of the testator.

4. Which of the following is true of the doctrine of republication by codicil?

    (a) The doctrine applies only where updating the will carries out the testator's intent.

    (b) The doctrine only works in conjunction with the doctrine of acts of independent significance.

    (c) The doctrine applies only to a prior validly executed will.

    (d) A and C.

    (e) A, B and C.

5. Which of the following is an important rationale of the drafters of the modern Uniform Probate Code elective share?

    (a) The spouses in a marriage owe each other a duty of support during their lifetimes, which duty continues, to some extent, after death.

    (b) The illusory transfer test rationale.

    (c) Committed partners are entitled to share in the fruits of the economic union regardless of whether the partners formally married.

    (d) All of the above.

    (e) A and C.

6.   A trust-like gift that is not intended to benefit the transferee and does not have any specific beneficiary who can enforce the trust as a gift, but has a specific non-charitable purpose is a

     (a)   Precatory trust.

     (b)   Resulting trust.

     (c)   Constructive trust.

     (d)   Honorary trust.

     (e)   None of the above.

7.   A quantity or type (but not a specific item) of property to be satisfied out of a specific asset if available, otherwise from general assets of the estate is

     (a)   A residuary gift.

     (b)   A general gift.

     (c)   A specific gift.

     (d)   A demonstrative gift.

     (e)   None of the above.

8.   A court finds that Francis has equitably adopted Carlos. Which of the following statements generally is not true in most American jurisdictions that recognize the doctrine of equitable adoption?

     (a)   If Francis dies intestate, Carlos will inherit from Francis as would a biological and legal child of Francis.

     (b)   If Carlos dies intestate, Francis will inherit from Carlos as would a biological and legal parent of Carlos.

     (c)   If Francis predeceases Carlos, Carlos will inherit through Francis as would a biological and legal child of Francis.

     (d)   B & C.

     (e)   None of the above.

9. When Tom executed his will he had three living siblings - Peter, Paul, and Mary, and a niece Louise, who was Mary's daughter. Tom's will made certain specific bequests to Louise and devised the residuary of his estate to Peter and Paul. The will further provided that "I do not want any of my property to pass to Mary either under this will or by intestacy." At Tom's death, he is survived only by Mary and Mary's daughter Louise. Peter and Paul died without issue before Tom. Who takes Tom's residuary estate at common law?

    (a) Peter's estate will take 1/2 and Paul's estate will take 1/2..

    (b) The state.

    (c) Mary.

    (d) Mary will take 1/3, Peter's estate will take 1/3, and Paul's estate will take 1/3.

    (e) Louise.

10. June and Bill purportedly were married in Year 1. Bill, however, was already married to May at the time of his marriage ceremony to June. June, therefore, was never legally married to Bill. Bill died intestate in Year 10 survived only by May and June. The court finds that May and Bill were never divorced and that June had no knowledge of Bill's earlier marriage to May. If the jurisdiction accepts the putative spouse doctrine, the court most likely will:

    (a) Award Bill's entire intestate estate to June.

    (b) Award Bill's entire intestate estate to May.

    (c) Award at least some of Bill's intestate estate to June.

    (d) Award at least some of Bill's intestate estate to May.

    (e) None of the above.

11. Testator's will provides: I leave Blackacre in trust to A for life, then to B. At common law, if B fails to survive A, who will get Blackacre at A's death?

    (a) A's issue.

    (b) A's estate

    (c) B's issue

    (d) B's estate

    (e) Testator's estate

12.   Evan created a POD account at Second State Bank, naming his niece Nancy as the POD beneficiary. Shortly before his death, Evan wrote a codicil to his will that stated: I have $100,000 on deposit in a POD account at Second State Bank. I will that money to be split equally between my niece Nancy and my nephew Norman. Assuming that Evan died in a UPC state:

  (a)   Nancy and Norman will split the $100,000.

  (b)   Nancy will take the entire $100,000 because codicils can only pass tangible personal property.

  (c)   Nancy will take the entire $100,000 because you cannot revoke or amend a POD account by will.

  (d)   The $100,000 will pass outside of probate, thereby avoiding federal estate taxes.

  (e)   Both (C) and (D).

13.   Tony's will left his entire estate to his friends, Sam and John. John failed to survive Tony but left a daughter, Debra. Tony's closest living relative at his death was his sister Sara. How should Tony's estate be distributed under the UPC?

  (a)   Sam should take the entire estate because he is the only surviving residuary taker.

  (b)   Sam should take half the estate and Debra should take the other half of the estate as a substitute taker for John.

  (c)   Sam should take half the estate and John's estate should take the other half.

  (d)   Sam should take half the estate and Sara should take the other half.

  (e)   Sam should take the entire estate because the residuary gift qualifies as a class gift.

14.   Joan's will made the following gifts: "I leave my home to Sally. I leave $100,000 to Josh. I leave my 100 shares of Rockwell stock, currently valued at $100 per share, to Pat. I leave the rest of my property to Gwen."

At Joan's death, she owned a home worth $500,000, but subject to a mortgage of $300,000, $350,000 in cash, and the 100 shares of Rockwell stock, which was trading at $50 a share. She had no debts, other than the mortgage. Under the UPC, how should Joan's estate be distributed?

   (a)   Sally should get the home free and clear since it was a specific devise and Josh should get the rest of the cash. Pat should get the Rockwell stock.

   (b)   Sally should get the home subject to the mortgage. Josh should get $100,000 in cash. Pat should get 100 shares of Rockwell stock, and Gwen should get the rest.

   (c)   Sally should get the home free and clear under the doctrine of exoneration. Josh and Pat should split the rest since they both got specific bequests.

   (d)   Sally should get the home subject to the mortgage. The executor should purchase another 100 shares of Rockwell stock so that 200 shares at $50 can be distributed to Pat. Josh should get $100,000 and Gwen should get the rest.

   (e)   If the will directs the executor to pay off the mortgage, then the gifts to Josh and Pat will abate equally since they are both specific bequests.

15.   In 2006, Frank gave his mother a car worth $25,000. He has consulted you about whether he needs to file a gift tax return. You tell him:

   (a)   Since the gift was to his mother, it is not taxable.
   (b)   Since he is obligated to support his mother, the car is not really a gift.
   (c)   Since the car's value is under $1.0 million, he has not made a taxable gift and does not need to file a gift tax return.
   (d)   He should file a gift tax return reporting a taxable gift of $25,000.
   (e)   He should file a gift tax return reporting a taxable gift of $13,000.

16.   Rich Testator created a testamentary trust in his will and willed the old family home in downtown Ames to the trust. The City of Ames was named as the trustee of the trust and was directed by the trust to maintain the home as public housing for the homeless men of the city. Hannah Homeless heard about the trust and consults a public interest law firm to see if she can sue the City to demand equal housing for homeless women. You have been asked to write a research memorandum identifying the key issues raised by her potential challenge. The most complex and challenging issue you have uncovered is:

   (a)   Whether Hannah has standing to sue the city.

   (b)   Whether a city that enforces a private trust is a "state actor."

   (c)   Whether or not cy pres can be applied to a trust of this sort.

   (d)   Whether or not Rich Testator can be characterized as a "state actor."

   (e)   Whether the trust violates the rule against perpetuities since, under its terms, it can last forever.

17.   Assume you are in a state that follows the majority rule that a check written by a decedent will not be honored by the bank if it is presented by the payee after the decedent's death. Doris, on her deathbed, calls you for estate planning advice. She says she wants to give to each of her 15 nephews and nieces a present gift in the amount of the current annual exclusion. She has a savings account with approximately $200,000 in it that she could access easily to do this. Which of the following do you advise her:

   (a)   She should transfer $180,000 from the savings account to her checking account and write a check to each of the 15 nieces and nephews in the amount of the annual exclusion and mail it to them with instructions to cash them as soon as possible.

   (b)   She should execute an irrevocable declaration of trust, declaring herself as trustee of the savings account for the immediate benefit of the 15 nieces and nephews.

   (c)   She should draft a codicil to her will making these gifts.

   (d)   She should open a joint bank account with all the nieces and nephews and deposit enough money in it to make the desired gifts.

18. Fred died intestate at the age of 90, survived only by his lineal descendants. The state's intestacy statute provides that a decedent's intestate share first goes to the spouse, and if none, "the estate shall pass to the decedent's lineal descendants per stirpes." Fred was survived by daughter Barbara, aged 65, and her two sons, Saul and Sam. He was also survived by a granddaughter, Betsy, the daughter of a deceased son, Steve, and by two great-grandsons, Jeff and Jim, sons of a deceased daughter of Steve. Fred's son Evan, predeceased him, never having had any children.

Under the intestacy statute described above, Fred's estate should be distributed as follows:

  (a)   One-fourth to each of the surviving four descendants, Barbara, Betsy, Jeff and Jim.

  (b)   One-third to Barbara, one-third to Betsy, one-sixth to Jeff, and one-sixth to Jim.

  (c)   One third to Barbara and two-ninths each to Betsy, Jeff, and Jim.

  (d)   One-third to Barbara, one-third to Evan's estate, and one-third to be split evenly between Betsy, Jeff, and Jim.

  (e)   One half to Barbara, one fourth to Betsy, one-eighth to Jeff, and one-eighth to Jim.

19. Larry's will creates a trust in the residuary clause with the following instruction to the trustee: "pay the income to my daughter Dorothy for life, then to her surviving children for their respective lives, and at the death of her last surviving child, the estate shall be divided into as many shares as there are then living grandchildren of Dorothy and deceased grandchildren of Dorothy who have left surviving decedents and the shares shall be distributed per stirpes to all entitled to take." Larry was survived by his daughter and her two children, Ames and Allen, aged 40 and 42. He was also survived by a grandson, George, the only son of Larry's son, Mitch. It was Larry's intent to disinherit George by leaving him nothing. Neither Ames nor Allen had any children or grandchildren at that time, but 5 years later, Allen fathered a child, Cindy. At Dorothy's death, she was survived by Ames and Allen and Cindy and George. Applying general principles of common law, what should happen to the trust property at Dorothy's death?

(a) The property should continue to be held in trust and the income should be paid to Ames and Allen.

(b) The property should continue to be held in trust and the income should be paid to Ames and Allen for their lives and then the entire estate will vest in Cindy.

(c) The trust should terminate due to a violation of the Rule against Perpetuities and the trust assets should be delivered to Ames and Allen as the two intestate heirs of Larry.

(d) The trust should terminate due to a violation of the Rule against Perpetuities and the trust assets should revert to Larry's estate.

(e) No matter what happens to the property, George will not inherit anything.

20.   Thomas executed an irrevocable trust that provided as follows: "All income to my wife, and at her death, the corpus is to be divided among all my children who reach age 25." At the time, Thomas was 50 years old, married to Abigail, aged 48, and they had three children, Arthur (age 18), Deborah (age 15), and Carolyn (age 10). Thomas died at age 70 survived by Abigail and his three children. Abigail dies five years later, survived by only Arthur and Carolyn. Deborah left a spouse, Howard, but no lineal descendants. The residuary clause in Thomas's will left all his property to the Second Methodist Church. At common law, which of the following is the likeliest distribution of the trust corpus at Abigail's death?

     (a)   To Arthur and Carolyn equally

     (b)   To Arthur and Carolyn and Deborah's estate equally.

     (c)   To the Second Methodist Church.

     (d)   To the estate of Thomas to be distributed as intestate property.

     (e)   To Abigail's estate.

21.   Testator's will leaves everything equally to his daughter from a prior marriage and to his stepson, who is the son of his current wife. He leaves nothing to his current spouse. The will is witnessed by the stepson and daughter. Under state law a will must be witnessed and signed by two competent and disinterested witnesses.

The state probate code provides:
> A beneficial devise or legacy to a subscribing witness shall be void unless there are two other subscribing witnesses to the will who are not similarly benefited thereunder; however, the beneficiary is entitled to receive so much of the devise or legacy given to him by the will as does not exceed the value of the share of the testator's estate to which he would be entitled were the will not established.

At testator's death he is survived by his spouse and by his stepson and daughter. The state's intestacy statute provides for half of the estate to go to the surviving wife and the other half to his issue, if any, from a prior marriage. Testator's property should be distributed:

(a)   The will is invalid and all the property should be distributed to Testator's intestate heirs, half to spouse and half to daughter.

(b)   The will is valid and the estate is distributed to the spouse because the statute prevents both daughter and stepson from taking any of the estate.

(c)   The will is valid and the estate is distributed as follows: 75% to daughter and 25% to spouse.

(d)   The will is valid and the estate should be distributed half to daughter and half to spouse.

(e)   The will is valid and the entire estate should be distributed to the daughter.

22.   Probate law has a long history of protecting spouses against disinheritance. Elective share statutes are one form of protection. In which of the following situations are the spouses least protected:

    (a)   Spouses have lived all their married lives in a community property state which has no elective share statute.

    (b)   Spouses have recently moved to a community property from a common law property state and have agreed, in a valid contract, that all of their property, both presently-owned and to be acquired in the future, is community property. The community property state has no elective share statute.

    (c)   Spouses have recently moved to a community property state from a common law property state. The community property state has an elective share that applies to separate property, which is based on the UPC

    (d)   Spouses have been married for at least 20 years and live in a common law state with an elective share statute that provides as follows: "surviving spouses can elect against the will of a deceased spouse and claim up to one-third of all property owned by the deceased spouse at the time of death."

    (e)   Spouses have been married for at least 20 years and reside in a UPC state.

23.   Toni Testator, who has dabbled in oil painting, lives in a UPC state that does not recognize holographic wills. She has never married and has no lineal descendants. She has many family heirlooms that she wants to leave to her nieces and nephews or their issue. But every time they visit her, she changes her mind about who should get what. After consulting with an attorney, she adds a codicil to her will that says: "At my death a memorandum signed and dated by me will be in the right hand desk drawer in my study. My property should be distributed in accord with directions in that memorandum." The codicil was dated May 2, 2005. At her death, in June of 2006, her executor searched the desk and found an envelope exactly where the will said it would be. It was marked "testamentary memorandum," dated June 1, 2006 and signed by Toni. The memorandum provided as follows:

China to Nan
Artwork on walls to Bill
Artwork in studio to John
Stock in left desk drawer to Steve
Jewelry in bedroom to Barbara.
CD collection to Jean
Wine in wine cellar to Pat

The most likely distribution of the property described in the memorandum is:

(a)   All of the property will go to her residuary taker because the memorandum cannot be probated as a holographic will.

(b)   All of the property will go to the named individuals in the memorandum under the doctrine of incorporation by reference.

(c)   All of the property will go to the named individuals in the memorandum under the doctrine of Acts of Significant Independence.

(d)   All but one of the beneficiaries named in the memorandum will be entitled to the gifts identified.

(e)   All but two of the beneficiaries named in the memorandum will be entitled to the gifts identified.

24. Clark's will leaves several small legacies to his children, Sam and Sally, and then contains a single residuary clause that states: "I leave the rest of my estate as follows — 25% to my sister, if she survives me; 50% to my wife, if she survives me; and 25% to the University of Pennsylvania. If my sister fails to survive, her interest shall pass to my wife."

Both Clark's sister and his wife predecease him. He is survived by his two children, Sam and Sally, who are also the children of Clark's deceased wife and who claim they are entitled to 75% of the residuary estate. The University of Pennsylvania claims it is entitled to 100% of the residuary estate. The children are likely to win their claim if:

   (a)   Clark died domiciled in a community property state.

   (b)   Clark died domiciled in a state that follows the "no residue of a residue" rule.

   (c)   Clark died domiciled in a state that has repealed the "no residue of a residue" rule.

   (d)   Clark died domiciled in a state that has an anti-lapse statute that is limited to lapsed gifts to a testator's descendants.

   (e)   Clark died domiciled in a state that presumes a testator intended his property to pass by will rather than by intestacy.

25. Vicki executed her will in year #1. Two years later, she executed a second will (will #2), specifically revoking will #1, but she never destroyed will #1. A year before her death, Vicki was adjudicated incompetent and her daughter was appointed as guardian under state law. Shortly before her death, she asked her daughter to bring her both wills. The daughter did and Vicki tore them both up. Vicki's estate should be distributed:

   (a)   To the beneficiaries named in will #2 because she had no capacity to revoke.

   (b)   To the beneficiaries in will #2 because tearing up both wills at the same time is not the way to revoke will #2.

   (c)   To her intestate heirs because both wills were validly revoked by physical act.

   (d)   To her intestate heirs provided they can prove that she was in a lucid moment at the time she tore up the wills.

EXAM 8

1. Omar attempts to create a trust by orally declaring that he holds his farm for the benefit of Zachary. Has Omar created a valid trust?

    (a)   No, because a trust may not be created orally.

    (b)   No, because one must use the word "trust" in order to create a trust orally.

    (c)   No, because a trust for land must be in writing.

    (d)   No, because there is no assurance that the farm will produce profits; thus, there is not sufficient trust property for the creation of a trust.

    (e)   Yes, because this trust has a settlor with the intent to create a trust, trust property, a beneficiary, and a trustee.

2. Settlor transfers property "to Xavier in trust, to pay the income to Adam for life, to be used for Adam's support." Settlor has created

    (a)   A spendthrift trust.

    (b)   A mere successive-interest trust.

    (c)   A support trust.

    (d)   A and C.

    (e)   None of the above.

3. Which of the following donor-imposed conditions attached to a donative transfer is a court least likely to enforce?

    (a)   Testator devises "To my son Daniel, provided that he is divorced from his Catholic wife Mary at the time of my death."

    (b)   Testator devises "To my son Daniel, provided that he divorces his Catholic wife Mary within 7 years of my death."

    (c)   Testator devises "To my son Daniel, provided that he is married to a Jewish woman at the time of my death."

    (d)   Testator devises "To my son Daniel, provided that he marries a Jewish woman within 7 years of my death."

    (e)   Donor offers Daniel an inter vivos gift provided that Daniel divorces his Catholic wife Mary.

4. Anna's will devised in part "To my daughter May I leave $1,000,000 in trust. May is to use whatever income from the trust is needed to care for my dog Fido for Fido's life or for 21 years after my death, whichever is less." Which of the following is true?

(a)   Anna's will establishes a valid private trust.

(b)   Anna's will establishes a valid honorary trust.

(c)   Anna's will establishes a valid charitable trust.

(d)   **A & B.**

(e)   B & C.

5. Testator's will provides: I leave Blackacre in trust to A for life, then to B. B fails to survive A. Under the UPC, who is entitled to Blackacre at A's death?

(a)   A's issue, but only if A is Testator's son.

(b)   B's issue, but only if B is Testator's son.

(c)   B's issue.

(d)   B's estate.

(e)   Testator's estate

6. Testator's will provides: I leave Blackacre in trust to A for life, then to B. B fails to survive A. Under the UPC, who is entitled to Blackacre at A's death if B has no surviving descendants?

(a)   A's estate.

(b)   B's estate

(c)   T's estate.

(d)   T's residuary taker.

(e)   T's residuary taker if he survives A

7.   Ivan Intestate died in a UPC jurisdiction in 2005, survived by the following family members: (1) grandson Eric, the son of Ivan's deceased daughter Eva; (2) grandsons Jim and John, sons of Ivan's deceased daughter Joan; (3) step-son Karl, the son of Ivan's now deceased second wife, Willa; (4) his first wife, Wanda, who was the mother of Eva and Joan. Under the UPC who will inherit Ivan's estate?

   (a)   Eric, Jim and John each take one-third of Ivan's probate estate.

   (b)   Eric takes one-half of Ivan's probate estate and Jim and John each take one-fourth.

   (c)   Karl, Eric, Jim and John share equally, each taking one-fourth of the estate

   (d)   Karl takes the share of the estate that would have passed to Willa and the rest of the estate is split between Eric, Jim, and John per stirpes.

   (e)   The estates of Eva and Joan each take one half of the estate.

8.   Tom Testator executed a will in 1995 leaving all of his property to "my best friend Dan." Dan died in 1999. Tom died in 2005 never having revoked or changed his 1995 will. Dan was survived by his wife, Susan, who was also his primary beneficiary under his will, and his father, Fred. Tom was survived by his father Joe and his step-mother, Alice, and his half brother, Ted (i.e., the son of Joe and step-mom). Who is entitled to Tom's estate?

   (a)   Tom's estate should go to Dan's estate to be distributed according to Dan's last will and testament.

   (b)   Tom's estate should go to his father Joe.

   (c)   Tom's estate should be divided between his father Joe and his step-mother, Alice.

   (d)   Tom's estate should be distributed half to his father, Joe, and half to his half brother, Ted.

   (e)   Tom's estate should go to Fred, who is Dan's only heir.

9.   Alice died on July 2, 2005, survived by her mother, Agnes, and two sisters, Sara and Susan. No other family members survived. Sara, who was closer to Alice than her mother and Susan were, says she saw a will 6 months before Alice's death naming Sara as the primary beneficiary. The will was in Alice's desk in her bedroom. The will cannot be found after Alice's death, but the lawyer who drafted the will has a copy. Under general principles of law:

    (a)   The lost will can be admitted to probate, but Sara will have a tough time overcoming the presumption of revocation.

    (b)   If Sara cannot take under the will, she will nonetheless take her one-fourth intestate share of Alice's estate.

    (c)   Sara can inherit the entire estate provided both Agnes and Susan agree to renounce their intestate share.

    (d)   All of the above.

    (e)   Only A and C above.

10.   Martha and Moe, who had been living together for a year, opened a joint savings account in a state bank in 2001. They signed a signature card that identified the account as a joint tenancy and on which they marked a box that said "Amounts on deposit are payable to Martha or Moe." All deposits in the account were made by Martha. In 2002 Moe withdrew $1,000 from the account to open a joint checking account on which either one of them could write checks for household expenses. That signature card also said "payable to Martha or Moe." Martha died in early 2005. Moe claimed he was entitled to the $50,000 balance in the savings account as of Martha's death, but Martha's estate objected. In the absence of any controlling judicial precedent, Martha's estate:

    (a)   Has no valid claim to the funds because joint savings accounts are conclusively presumed to belong to the survivor.

    (b)   Should argue that the signature card is ambiguous so that extrinsic evidence of intent to create a power of attorney arrangement can be admitted.

    (c)   Should argue that the funds belong to Martha since she made all of the deposits.

    (d)   Should argue that Moe cannot take because, even if Martha intended to make a gift to Moe, the gift was never delivered during Martha's lifetime.

    (e)   Should argue that the joint savings account is a testamentary instrument and invalid for lack of testamentary formalities.

11.   Dexter's will, executed in 1999, leaves everything to his sister, Sandra. In 2001, Dexter married Terry. After they were married, Dexter took out a life insurance policy in the amount of $200,000 and named Terry as the sole beneficiary. Dexter died in 2005, never having revoked or amended the 1999 will. His estate consisted of various real estate holdings and valued at $2.0 million, plus approximately $50,000 in cash reserves and $50,000 in other personal property. Dexter had no other assets and Terry owns very few assets of her own. Under the UPC:

(a)   Terry should claim a spousal elective share.

(b)   Terry should claim her intestate share since the will is revoked upon marriage.

(c)   Terry should claim as an omitted spouse because the will was executed before their marriage.

(d)   Terry should claim as an omitted spouse and, in the alternative, she should claim her elective share.

(e)   Sandra will take the entire estate since the will was never revoked.

12.   Tom created an irrevocable trust in 1990 to pay income to his son, Sam, for life, then to distribute assets to his granddaughter, Gloria. He named First National Bank as trustee. All interests in the trust were subject to a spendthrift clause. It is now 2005, and the value of the trust has dwindled to a mere $100,000. Sam and Gloria have asked whether they can terminate the trust. Tom is still alive. What do you tell them?

(a)   The trust cannot be terminated because it contains a spendthrift clause

(b)   If they can persuade Tom to terminate the trust, the trust can be terminated.

(c)   If they can persuade First National Bank to terminate the trust, the trust can be terminated.

(d)   If they can persuade Tom and the First National Bank to terminate the trust, the trust can be terminated.

(e)   The trust can be terminated only because it has dwindled in value.

13.   Ella had two sons, Jamail and Devon. In 1995, she gave Devon $10,000 to help him purchase a home. At the time she told Jamail that she would even things up with him by leaving him an extra $10,000 in her will. Shortly after that, Devon wrote Ella a letter, thanking her for the "advance on his inheritance." In 2005, Ella died intestate, with net assets worth $50,000. She was survived by both Jamail and Devon, her closest living relatives. How should her estate be distributed?

   (a)   Devon and Jamail should split the $50,000 equally, with each taking $25,000 because the UPC has repealed the common law doctrine of advancements.

   (b)   Devon should pay back the $10,000 to Ella's estate and then each son should get $30,000.

   (c)   Devon should get $20,000 from the estate and Jamail should get $30,000 because Ella told Jamail that is what would happen.

   (d)   Devon should get $20,000 from the estate and Jamail should get $30,000 because Devon's letter provides the necessary written evidence of Ella's intent.

   (e)   The only way to even up the gifts is for Devon to renounce $10,000 of his inheritance.

14.   Jane has never made a taxable gift. In the year 2006, the maximum amount she can give to any one person without having to pay any tax is:

   (a) $3,000
   (b) $12,000
   (c) $1.0 million
   (d) $1,012,000.

15. Damon, a widower, plans to leave his entire estate to his son Sam. His tax attorney estimates that an estate tax of approximately $200,000 will be payable on the estate and advises Damon to take out a life insurance policy to cover the tax bill so that none of the assets will need to be liquidated to pay the tax. The best way for Damon to do this is:

    (a) Damon should take out the policy and name Sam as the beneficiary.

    (b) Sam should take out the policy and name Damon's estate as the beneficiary.

    (c) Damon should take out the policy, naming Sam as the beneficiary, and then gift the policy to Sam.

    (d) Sam should take out the policy on Damon, naming Sam as the beneficiary.

16. Testator had written a will in 1974 leaving her property equally to her two sons. In 2006, the day before she went into the hospital for surgery to remove a malignant brain tumor, she signed a new will leaving her entire estate to her best friend, William. Testator did not survive the surgery. The sons contested the new will and William defended. Evidence showed that Testator and William had been close for the last five years and that Testator had suffered a number of bouts of hysteria. She was particularly concerned that little green men were coming to take her away. William and the two sons often worked together to calm her down from these fits. The best argument for the sons to make in order to set aside the will in favor of William is:

    (a) Testator suffered from an insane delusion.

    (b) William unduly influenced Testator.

    (c) Testator was not of sound mind.

    (d) Children are the presumed natural objects of a parent's bounty.

17.   Florence and David have been married for over 20 years and have no children. When Florence's sister Sally (a widow) is hospitalized with cancer, Florence and David take in Sally's daughter Delores, who is 12 years old. Sally ultimately succumbs to the cancer and dies one year later. Delores continues to live with Florence and David until she goes to college. When she is 21, Delores wins $1.0 million in a contest. One year later she dies in an automobile accident, leaving an estate of over $1.0 million. She has no will and is survived by Florence and David and Florence's brother Willy. The most likely distribution of her estate is as follows:

   (a)   Florence and David will inherit under the doctrine of common law adoption.

   (b)   Florence and David will inherit under the doctrine of equitable adoption.

   (c)   Florence and David and Willy will share the estate equally as the closest surviving relatives.

   (d)   Florence and Willy will share the estate equally as the closest surviving relatives.

   (e)   No one will inherit. The estate will escheat to the state.

18.   Doug dies intestate survived by his daughter Peggy, her two children, Adam and Annie. He is also survived by another grandchild, Bonnie, the daughter of a deceased son. Doug's estate is worth approximately $2.0 million, net of debts and administrative costs. Peggy would like to take about $200,000 and disclaim the rest so that her children can share in the estate. Under the UPC:

   (a)   Peggy cannot disclaim only part of the estate. To be effective, the disclaimer will have to apply to her entire interest.

   (b)   If Peggy disclaims as planned, she will take $200,000, Adam and Annie will take $400,000 each and Bonnie will take $1.0 million.

   (c)   If Peggy disclaims as planned, she will take $200,000, and Adam and Annie and Bonnie will each take $600,000.

   (d)   Peggy cannot disclaim an intestate share. If she takes $200,000 and gives $800,000 to her children, she will be viewed as making a gift to them.

19.   Gary gives Blackacre to his son Stuart, subject to the following condition: "If the Chicago Cubs win the World Series, Stuarts ownership of Blackacre shall cease and Blackacre shall vest in the University of Chicago. The University of Chicago:

(a)   Will never become the owner of Blackacre because the divesting event violates the rule against perpetuities.

(b)   Will never become the owner of Blackacre because the Cubs will never win the World Series.

(c)   Will become the owner of Blackacre if the Cubs ever win the World Series because of the charitable exception to the rule against perpetuities.

(d)   Will become the owner of Blackacre only if the Cubs win the World Series during Stuart's lifetime.

20.   Testator's will devises Blackacre "to my son for life, then to his widow for life and then to my son's then living children. The residuary clause leaves "all the rest and residue of my estate to my son, Norm. " Testator is survived by son Norm, who is 35 years old, and by Norm's wife, Nora. They have one child, Susan, aged 4. At common law:

(a)   Susan has a vested remainder in Blackacre subject to open.

(b)   Susan has a contingent remainder in Blackacre which will vest if she survives Nora.

(c)   Norm owns both a life estate and a remainder interest in Blackacre.

(d)   At Nora's death, Susan and her then living siblings will take Blackacre in fee.

(e)   The gift to Norm's widow is void.

21.   Assume the same devise as in the prior question. One year later, Norm and Nora have another child, Carrie. Five years later, Norm dies, survived by Nora and Susan and Carrie. Under the UPC:

(a)   The gift to Nora is valid.

(b)   The gift to the children is void.

(c)   The gift to the children may be valid, but we won't know until Nora's death.

(d)   Both A and B.

(e)   Both A and C.

22.   Testator's will leaves everything equally to his daughter from a prior marriage and to his stepson, who is the son of his current wife. He leaves nothing to his current spouse. The will is witnessed by the stepson and daughter. At Testator's death, he is survived by his spouse, his daughter, and his stepson. Under the UPC, the most likely distribution of the estate is:

      (a)   100% to his surviving spouse via intestacy.

      (b)   An intestate share for the spouse and an intestate share for the daughter.

      (c)   Half to daughter and half to the spouse.

      (d)   75% to daughter and 25% to the spouse.

      (e)   Half to the daughter and half to the stepson.

23.   Herman and Wanda, Texas residents, have been married for 20 years. Herman is President of a successful company and Wanda is a poet, who does not like to be bothered with financial decisions. Herman maintains all of the couple's investments. All real property is in his name and all bank accounts, stock brokerage accounts, and similar investments are listed in his name as well. Wanda has a small checking account in her name, in which she deposits royalty checks for the poetry she publishes. At Wanda's death, her will was probated. It had one dispositive provision which left everything to her sister, Sally. Sally is claiming half of the real estate, bank accounts, brokerage accounts, and other property held in Herman's name alone. Herman contests claiming that the property in his name is owned by him and Sally has no claim to it. Herman's strongest argument for this position is:

      (a)   Record title to property is conclusive as to ownership.

      (b)   Herman and Wanda had a tacit understanding that his earnings were his and her earnings were hers.

      (c)   Under Texas law, a husband is the sole intestate heir of community property.

      (d)   Herman brought a substantial amount of property into the marriage and invested it in the real estate and other properties, all of which have been maintained in his name alone. His salary has paid for their current living expenses.

24. Grandfather's will left most of his estate in trust for the benefit of "my son Walter for his life and then as he appoints by will among his children." The residuary clause left the rest of his estate to his niece, Laura. At Walter's death 15 years later, he was survived by two children, Ann and Amy. His son, Dan, had died five years earlier, survived by his spouse, who was the primary beneficiary under his will, and two children. No one could find a will at Walter's death. The probate code of the state contains a typical anti-lapse statute, but has no provisions dealing with powers of appointment. The most likely distribution of the assets in Grandfather's trust is:

    (a)   To Ann and Amy.

    (b)   To Ann and Amy and Dan's estate.

    (c)   To Ann and Amy and Dan's two children.

    (d)   To Laura.

    (e)   To Grandfather's estate.

25. Elaine and Jess have been domestic partners for over 2 years, but they live in a state that doesn't recognize their relationship. Elaine has consulted you for legal advice. Title to their home is in her name alone and she wants to execute a deed transferring title to herself and Jess as joint tenants. She is reluctant to make this commitment public and so prefers not to record the deed. In fact, she has asked you to draft the deed for her to execute and then wants you to hold it in your files until she tells you to record it. If you follow her directions and Elaine dies before the deed is recorded:

    (a)   The transfer of title will be effective, but not against BFPs who have no actual notice of the transfer.

    (b)   The transfer of title will be effective, but not against anyone other than Elaine and her estate unless and until it is recorded.

    (c)   The transfer of title will be sufficiently effective to avoid probate of the property when Elaine dies.

    (d)   The deed will not transfer title effectively.

    (e)   Both A and C.

ANSWER KEY
EXAM 1

1. The best answer is (b). Under the doctrine of incorporation by reference as it existed at common law, a document that has not been executed with the formalities for the execution of a will can be given testamentary effect under a will provided that (1) the document was in existence at the execution of the will, (2) the will manifests the testator's intention to incorporate the document into the will, and (3) the will sufficiently identifies the document to be incorporated. Technically, the document that is being incorporated by reference does not become a part of the will. In the hypothetical, if we treat the handwritten portion of the single sheet of paper as a separate document from the typed portion, the handwritten portion would seem to be a valid holographic will. Since T referred to "this will" as incorporating the typed material, there is a good argument that T thought of the typed material as separate from the will and it should be treated as separate from the holographic will. A holographic will may incorporate by reference a document that is typed. The holographic will sufficiently expresses an intention to incorporate the typed matter, and sufficiently identifies the document to be incorporated ("the typed matter above"). Finally, the typed matter seems to have been in existence at execution of the holographic will. Therefore, a strong argument exists that the doctrine of incorporation by reference may be used to give effect to devises 1 though 9.

    Answer (a) is not correct.   The doctrine of integration provides that a document that is present at the execution of the will and that T intends to be a part of the will is a part of the will. The doctrine of integration cannot be used to validate devises 1 through 9, however, because if those devises are considered a part of the purported executed will, the entire will fails (and devises 1 through 9 necessarily fail as well). If the typed matter is a part of the will, then will is not a valid holographic will because the will contains material provisions that are not in T's handwriting. Moreover, the will cannot be a valid non-holographic will because it has not been witnessed.

    Answer (c) is not correct. When applied, the doctrine of republication by codicil re-executes an earlier will and brings the date of execution of the earlier will up to the date of execution of the codicil. The doctrine of republication by codicil is properly applied only to a validly executed prior will and only if doing so will carry out the intent of the testator. A court may not properly apply the doctrine on the facts of this hypothetical, therefore, because the typed matter is not a validly executed prior will. (It is unsigned and unwitnessed.)

Additional reference: See William M. McGovern, Jr. and Sheldon F. Kurtz, Wills, Trusts and Estates § 6.2 (3d ed. 2004).

2.   **The best answer is (c).** In general, the law of a decedent's domicile at his death provides the law governing the intestate passing of his personal property. In general, the law of the situs of real property provides the law governing the intestate passing of that real property at the death of the owner. California law, therefore, will govern the passing of D's intestate personal property, even though most of that personal property is physically located in Nevada. Georgia law will govern the intestate passing of D's real property because that real property is located in Georgia. A court may respect a testator's or settlor's direction that the law of a given state shall govern, respectively, a will or a trust. A court may refuse to give effect to such a designation if such application of law would defeat a public policy (such as the policy supporting provision of an elective share to a surviving spouse) of the forum state or, in some cases, the state with the most significant relationship to the matter. In this hypothetical, however, D died intestate.

Additional reference: See William M. McGovern, Jr. and Sheldon F. Kurtz, Wills, Trusts and Estates § 1.2 (3d ed. 2004).

3.   **The best answer is (d).** Both answer (a) and answer (b) are correct. The comment to UPC § 2-102 states that empirical studies "have shown that testators in smaller estates (which intestate estates overwhelmingly tend to be) tend to devise their entire estates to their surviving spouses, even when the couple has children. " The comment further states that "[t]he theory of this section is discussed in Waggoner, "The Multiple-Marriage Society and Spousal Rights Under the Revised Uniform Probate Code," 76 Iowa L. Rev. 223, 229-35 (1991)." Professor Waggoner' s law review article itself at p. 232 explains: "The 1990 UPC is predicated on the notion that decedents . . . see the surviving spouses as occupying somewhat of a dual role, not only as their primary beneficiaries, but also as conduits through which to benefit their children.   If [the intestate decedent] died prematurely, at a time when their children were still minors, [the surviving spouse] would be better equipped than their children to use [decedent]'s property for the benefit of their children as well as for herself. If [the decedent] was older at death, when their children were middle-aged working adults, [the surviving spouse] would probably be older and have greater economic needs than their children. In this latter case, the conduit theory assumes that [the decedent]'s children will eventually inherit any unconsumed portion of his property from [the surviving spouse] upon her death."

• Additional reference: Lawrence W. Waggoner, "The Multiple-Marriage Society and Spousal Rights Under the Revised Uniform Probate Code," 76 Iowa L. Rev. 223, 229-35 (1991).

4.   **The best answer is (d).** A pour-over will is a will that devises property to the trustee (as trustee) of an inter vivos trust to be distributed in accordance with the terms of the inter vivos trust. Today, legislation (in most states a version of the Uniform Testamentary Additions to Trusts Act ("UTATA")) validates pour-over wills in each state. Prior to statutory validation, however, the issue arose of whether a pour-over will violated the wills act in that it sought to dispose of property at death by means of a document that had not been executed with the formalities for execution of a will (the trust instrument). Both the doctrine of incorporation by reference and the doctrine of acts of independent significance could be used to overcome this objection and validate a pour-over will. Under the doctrine of incorporation by reference as it existed at common law, a document that has not been executed with the formalities for the execution of a will can be given effect as part of the will provided that (1) the document was in existence at the execution of the will, (2) the will manifests the testator's intention to incorporate the document into the will, and (3) the will sufficiently identifies the document to be incorporated. A problem arose with the incorporation by reference approach to validating a pour-over will, however, if the trust instrument was not in existence at execution of the will or was amended after execution of the will. In such a case, the incorporation by reference doctrine was unavailable since the document to be incorporated was not in existence at execution of the will. The acts of independent significance doctrine provides that the identification of the person who shall receive a devise or the property covered by a devise (or both) can be determined by an act or event outside the will provided that the act or event has a significance apart from passing property under the will. For example, the taker of a devise "to my oldest sister alive at my death" will be determined by events — the continuation or expiration of the testator's sisters' lives — that has a significance apart from passing property under the will. The execution of an inter vivos trust instrument can have a significance apart from passing property under the will: The trust instrument's independent significance is that it governs the management of property in the inter vivos trust. A problem arose with the acts of independent significance approach to validating a pour-over will, however, if the trust was not funded during the life of the testator (and, therefore, the trust instrument was not governing the management of any property). Under the modern version of UTATA, a pour-over devise will not be invalid merely because the trust instrument was executed or modified after execution of the will or because the trust was not funded during the testator's life.

Additional reference: See William M. McGovern, Jr. and Sheldon
F. Kurtz, Wills, Trusts and Estates § 6.2 (3d ed. 2004).

5.   The best answer is (e). This gift is presumed not to be a class gift, but it
will be treated as a class gift if there is sufficient proof that the donor
intended the consequences of a class gift. In general, a class gift is a gift
to be divided among a group described such that membership in the class
can fluctuate based on lifetime events. For example, a gift of a future
interest in an inter vivos trust "to my children alive at my death" is
presumed to be a class gift since membership in the class can change if the
donor has additional children or if existing children die. A gift that
specifies the takers by name or number is presumptively not a class gift,
even if the members of the group of takers form a natural class, since
membership in the group of takers cannot fluctuate. Thus, a gift to "my
children Kevin, Brian, and Danny" is presumptively not a class gift.
Similarly, the gift in the hypothetical to "my three children" is
presumptively not a class gift. Courts have been known to disregard these
rules, however, and treat a gift as a class gift even when the takers have
been specified by name or number, if so treating the gift as a class gift
would carry out the intent of the donor. For example, assume that a court
finds that the donor of a general testamentary gift to "my children Kevin,
Brian, and Danny" would want the surviving members of the group to take
the portion of any member whose gift lapsed. (Assume further that no
anti-lapse statute applies in this case so that the common law rules for
lapse apply.) If the gift to Danny lapses and this is not a class gift,
Danny's gift will pass to the testator's residuary beneficiary. At common
law however, members of a class absorbed any lapsed gift to a fellow class
member. If the gift is a class gift, therefore, Kevin and Brian will absorb
Danny's lapsed gift. Thus, the court can better carry out the donor's intent
if it treats the gift to "my children Kevin, Brian, and Danny" as a class
gift, even though such a gift, which specifies the takers by name,
presumptively is not a class gift.

Additional reference: See William M. McGovern, Jr. and Sheldon
F. Kurtz, Wills, Trusts and Estates § 8.3 (3d ed. 2004).

6.   The best answer is (a). Ademption by extinction is the nullification of a
bequest because the item devised is not found in the testator's estate at his
death. Ademption by extinction applies only to specific gifts. There are
two approaches to ademption. Under the identity theory of ademption, a
gift of a specific item is adeemed if it cannot be found in the testator's
estate at his death. In general, under the identity theory, whether or not
the testator intended to adeem the gift, in theory, is not relevant. Under
the intent theory of ademption, a gift of a specific item that cannot be

found in the testator's estate at his death is adeemed only if the testator intended for the gift to be adeemed. UPC § 2-606 adopts an intent theory of ademption.

The question asks you to assume an identity theory jurisdiction. In the hypothetical, the testator devised "My house to my sister Susan" at a time when he owned the house at 1307 W. James St. That house cannot be found in the testator's estate at his death because the testator sold that house and bought a new house — the house at 11 Shawnee Lane — a year before his death. One might conclude, therefore, that the gift to Susan is adeemed and Jeff takes the house at 11 Shawnee Lane as the residuary devisee. **But answer (b) is incorrect.** Susan takes the house because a court will apply a "time of death construction" to the devise. When the language "my house" is applied to the testator's circumstances at his death, the language refers to the house at 11 Shawnee Lane. That house is found in the testator's estate at his death, and so the gift to Susan is not adeemed. Had the testator instead devised "My house at 1307 W. James St. to my sister Susan," a court would not be able to apply a time of death construction to prevent ademption of the gift to Susan. In that case, answer (b) would be correct. The gift to Susan of the house at 1307 W. James St. would be adeemed because not found in the testator's estate at his death, and Jeff would take the house at 11 Shawnee Lane as the residuary devisee.

Many have argued that the identity theory of ademption too often undermines the most likely intent of the testator. The "time of death construction" is just one of several techniques and exceptions that courts apply to avoid what many consider to be the unfortunately harsh consequences of the identity theory of ademption. Others include "reclassifying" an arguably specific devise as general (since ademption applies only to specific devises), finding that the property devised is in the estate in a changed form (for example, securities acquired in a merger in exchange for devised securities might be held to be the devised securities in a changed form), and allowing the devisee of property later involuntarily transferred out of the estate (for example, by a conservator) to take the proceeds resulting from the transfer.

- Additional reference: See William M. McGovern, Jr. and Sheldon F. Kurtz, Wills, Trusts and Estates § 8.1 (3d ed. 2004).

7.   **The best answer is (c).** The court should probate the first will but impose a constructive trust on Marc for the benefit of Fred even though Marc was wholly innocent of the fraud committed by Jake. A constructive trust is really not a trust at all. Rather, a constructive trust is a remedy imposed in

order to prevent unjust enrichment, particularly in cases of fraud, duress, or undue influence. **Answer (a) is not the best answer.** Even though Marc is innocent of any fraud, he still would be unjustly enriched if allowed to keep the property devised under T's first will because, absent Jake's fraud, T would have executed a new will revoking Marc's gift and devising his estate to Fred.

Neither answer (b) nor answer (d) is the best answer. Since T never executed the second will revoking the first will, the court should not find that T died intestate. **Answer (e) is not correct.** T never executed the second will. Therefore, it cannot be probated.

   • Additional reference: See William M. McGovern, Jr. and Sheldon
     F. Kurtz, Wills, Trusts and Estates § 6.1 (3d ed. 2004).

8.   **The best answer is (b).** Under a traditional purging statute, an interested witness to a will (a witness who otherwise would take a devise under the will) loses (is purged of) his gift and, thereby, (so the theory goes) becomes disinterested. The will, therefore, will not fail for lack of sufficient disinterested witnesses due to the circumstance that one or more witnesses also is a beneficiary under the terms of the will. Modern purging statutes also have the effect of preventing the will from failing for lack of sufficient disinterested witnesses due to the circumstance that one or more witnesses also is a beneficiary under the terms of the will. **Answer (a), therefore, is not the best answer** whether we are in a jurisdiction with a traditional purging statute or a jurisdiction with a modern purging statute.

Under a modern purging statute, the interested witness does not necessarily lose his entire gift, and does not necessarily lose any portion of his gift. Rather, the interested witness loses that portion of his gift that is in excess of what he would have taken from the testator's estate had the will he witnessed as an interested witness not been executed. Applying this approach of the modern purging statute to the facts of the hypothetical, however, BW should be purged of his entire gift in Will #2. The problem tells us that BW is unrelated to T. We know, therefore, that BW was not an heir and would not have taken any portion of T's intestate estate had T died intestate. When BW acted as a witness to Will# 1, therefore, all of the $170,000 devise of Google stock was "excess" and BW was entitled to take nothing under will #1. (BW would take zero under intestacy. A gift worth $170,000 to BW under Will #1 would increase his take by $170,000. All of this $170,000 is excess, therefore, over what BW would have taken had Will #1 not been executed.) Given that BW was entitled to take nothing under will #1, all of the $70,000 gift of real property to BW in Will#2, to which BW also was a witness, is excess. The purging statute purges BW of this excess, and he takes nothing under Will#2.

Note that UPC § 2-505(b) does away with the purging of gifts to witnesses: "The signing of a will by an interested witness does not invalidate the will or any provision of it."

> Additional reference: See William M. McGovern, Jr. and Sheldon F. Kurtz, Wills, Trusts and Estates § 4.3 (3d ed. 2004).

9.   **The best answer is (d).** Answer (d) states the standard for the harmless error principle (such as that of UPC § 2-503). Under the harmless error principle, a document that has not been executed with the formalities prescribed for execution of a will may nonetheless be probated as a will if the court finds that there is clear and convincing evidence that the testator intended the document to be his will. Thus, an unattested holographic will can be probated in a harmless error jurisdiction even if the jurisdiction does not otherwise recognize holographic wills. **Answer (a) is not correct.** It states the predominant standard in jurisdictions that recognize holographic wills for what material must be in the handwriting of the testator for a holographic will to be valid. The question states, however, that Nirvana does not recognize holographic wills. **Answer (c) is not correct.** It states the standard for substantial compliance with wills formalities. Even in a substantial compliance jurisdiction, however, T's attempt at a will should not be probated as an attested will. T has made no attempt to obtain witnesses for his will. He has not substantially complied with the witnessing requirement.

10.   **The best answer is (d).** Under the doctrine of administrative deviation, a court may modify the administrative terms of a trust, such as a restriction on the trustee's investment power, if, due to circumstances the settlor did not foresee, the administrative direction threatens the primary purposes of the trust. This is in theory an intent promoting doctrine. The thinking is that the settlor would not want a direction of secondary importance (here, the settlor's direction that the trustee may not sell the buildings) to threaten the primary purpose of the trust — which must be to benefit the beneficiaries. **For this reason, answer (c) is not the best answer.** It should be noted that the court may not modify the administrative terms of the trust merely because to do so would likely produce a better return for the beneficiaries. Rather, the administrative direction must seriously threaten the purposes of the trust for the court to apply the doctrine of administrative deviation. **Answer (a) is not the best answer** because generally the trustee has a duty of impartiality between the life tenant and the remainderman. The trustee should petition for administrative

deviation, therefore, if the decline in value of the buildings threatens to seriously erode the remainderman's interest in the trust.

- Additional reference: See William M. McGovern, Jr. and Sheldon F. Kurtz, Wills, Trusts and Estates § 9.6 (3d ed. 2004).

11.   **The best answer is (a).**   A testator may revoke a will by performing a sufficient physical act on the will with the intent to revoke it. The performance of the physical act and the intent to revoke must coincide in time. Marking the words of the will in such a way as to indicate an intent to revoke the will, such as by placing an "X" on each page of the will, is a sufficient act. This is called cancellation. In most jurisdictions, the mark of cancellation must touch the words of the will. Other sufficient physical acts include burning the will, tearing the will, and obliterating the will. In general, the burning, tearing, and obliterating need not touch the words of the will. The physical act may be performed by someone other than the T if done at T's direction and in T's presence. That person performing the physical act at T's direction need not be an attorney.   **(Answer (d), therefore, is incorrect.)**

The will in the hypothetical is not revoked, however, because Mark marked a copy of the will. In most jurisdictions, a physical act performed on a copy of the will is to no effect even if T performs the act with the intent to revoke the will. In contrast, a sufficient physical act performed on a duplicate of the will is effective if performed with the intent to revoke the will. A duplicate is created when the testator executes two identical documents with the formalities needed for execution of a will. Both documents are an original. Both documents are a duplicate. A copy is a photocopy of an executed will.

- Additional reference: See William M. McGovern, Jr. and Sheldon F. Kurtz, Wills, Trusts and Estates § 5.2 (3d ed. 2004).

12-14:

General comments on questions 12-14: There are a few universal rules for applying an intestacy statute: A first rule to keep in mind is that only persons who survive a property owner are eligible to take a portion of the property owner's intestate estate. A descendant of the intestate property owner who predeceases the intestate property owner might, however, have a share of the intestate property assigned to him, which share then would have to pass by representation to his own descendants. A second rule to keep in mind is that for a descendant of the intestate property owner to be eligible to take an intestate share or, if he has predeceased the intestate property owner, to have such a share assigned to him (and then pass by representation) the descendant must not have any living ancestor who is a descendant of the intestate property owner. Thus, if the intestate's grandson has a living parent who is the child of the intestate, the grandson will not take any intestate property or have any intestate property assigned to him. A third rule to keep in mind is that if a descendant of the intestate property owner predeceased the intestate property owner and (a) has no living ancestor who is a descendant of the intestate property owner and (b) himself left issue who survive the intestate property owner, those issue will take a portion of the intestate property owner's intestate property by representation. The portion that those issue take by representation will be determined by the specifics of the intestacy scheme. At this point, it becomes necessary to know if the scheme is classic per stirpes, modern per stirpes, or per capita at each generation.

Given the fact pattern, we first should address the issue raised by the near simultaneous death of Scott and Zelda. Under the Revised Uniform Simultaneous Death Act, one must survive a property owner by at least 120 hours in order to take from that property owner by intestacy. Otherwise we treat the survivor as having predeceased the property owner. Zelda survived Scott, but by only 72 hours. Therefore, under the Revised Uniform Simultaneous Death Act, we treat Zelda as having predeceased Scott for the purposes of distributing Scott's intestate property. Zelda takes nothing. And Victor and William do not take any of Scott's property through Zelda. Moreover, stepchildren generally are not takers under intestacy law. (There is a fairly complicated exception under California law, which we will ignore for the purposes of this question.) Therefore, Victor and William will take nothing in their own right and **Answer (a) is not correct** in any of the questions 12 through 14.

Additional reference: See William M. McGovern, Jr. and Sheldon F. Kurtz, Wills, Trusts and Estates § 2.2 (3d ed. 2004).

12.   **The best answer is (c).**   Under the classic per stirpes approach, (1) we begin dividing the intestate property into shares at the generation level immediately below the intestate decedent. (2) We assign a share to (a) any living descendant in that generation and (b) any predeceased descendant in that generation who left issue who survived the intestate property owner. (3)(a) Any share assigned to a living descendant of the intestate property owner goes to that living descendant of the intestate property owner. (3)(b) Any share assigned to a predeceased descendant of the intestate property owner who left issue that survived the intestate property owner passes by representation to the descendants of the predeceased descendant. (4) In dividing property among those descendants of the predeceased descendant, we essentially repeat steps 1 - 3 above.

We apply the above rules to the fact pattern as follows:

(1) We begin dividing the intestate property into shares at the generation level that contains Scott's children — A, B, and C.

(2) A, B, and C all predeceased Scott but left issue who survived Scott. Therefore, A, B, and C each is assigned a 1/3 share of Scott's intestate estate.

(3) A's share will pass by representation to A's descendants, B's share will pass by representation to B's descendants, and C's share will pass by representation to C's descendants.

(4)

-As to A's 1/3 share: (1) We begin dividing at the generation level immediately below A. (2) A's two children E and F failed to survive the intestate property owner. E left issue who did survive the intestate property owner. F did not leave any issue. Therefore, E is assigned all of A's 1/3 share. (3) E's share (1/3 of the intestate estate) then passes equally to L and M who each take $\frac{1}{2}$ of the 1/3 or 1/6 of the intestate estate.

-As to B's 1/3 share: (1) We begin dividing at the generation level immediately below B. (2) G predeceased the intestate property owner and left no issue, so we treat him as though he never existed: No share is assigned to G. H and I survive and are each assigned $\frac{1}{2}$ of B's share. (3) H and I will take $\frac{1}{2}$ of B's 1/3, which computes to 1/6 of the intestate estate. Notice that N and 0 take nothing because both have an ancestor alive who is a descendant of the intestate property owner. N has her ancestor H, and 0 has his ancestor I.

-As to C's 1/3 share: (1) We begin dividing at the generation level immediately below C. (2) J is alive, and K is dead but left a descendant who survived the intestate property owner. Therefore, J and K are each assigned $\frac{1}{2}$ of C's 1/3 (which = 1/6). (3) J, who is alive takes his 1/6. K's 1/6 passes by representation to his daughter R. Thus, J and R each take 1/6 of the intestate estate. Notice that P and Q take nothing because each has a living ancestor who is a descendant of the intestate property owner. P and Q have their parent J alive.

13.   **The best answer is (b).** The modern per stirpes approach has one major difference from the classic per stirpes approach: Rather than begin dividing the intestate property into shares at the generation level immediately below the intestate decedent, we begin dividing the intestate property into shares at the first generation level below the intestate decedent where we find a living descendant. Otherwise, the modern per stirpes approach is the same as the classic per stirpes approach. Under the modern per stirpes approach, therefore (1) we begin dividing the intestate property into shares at the first generation level below the intestate decedent where we find a living descendant. (2) We assign a share to (a)

any living descendant in that generation and (b) any predeceased descendant in that generation who left issue who survived the intestate property owner. (3)(a) Any share assigned to a living descendant of the intestate property owner goes to that living descendant of the intestate property owner. (3)(b) Any share assigned to a predeceased descendant of the intestate property owner who left issue that survived the intestate property owner passes by representation to the descendants of the predeceased descendant. (4) In dividing property among those descendants of the predeceased descendant, we essentially repeat steps 1 - 3 above.

We apply the above rules to the fact pattern as follows:
(1) Scott's children – A, B, and C have all predeceased Scott. Therefore, we begin dividing the intestate property into shares at the generation level that contains Scott's grandchildren – the first generation of Scott's descendants where we find someone alive.
(2) E, H, I, J, and K are either living (H, I, and J) or have predeceased Scott but left issue who survived Scott (E and K). Therefore, E, H, I, J, and K each is assigned a 1/5 share of Scott's intestate estate.
(3) Since H, I, and J each is alive each takes a 1/5 share. The 1/5 share assigned to E will pass by representation to his descendants. The 1/5 share assigned to K will pass by representation to his descendant.
(4)
-As to E's 1/5 share: We divide the 1/5 of Scott's intestate property equally among E's children - L and M.- both of whom survived the intestate property owner. L takes 1/10, and M takes 1/10.
-As to K's 1/5 share: The share passes to K's only descendant - R - who survived the intestate property owner.
Notice again that we treat people who predecease the intestate property owner and leave no descendants who survive the property as though they never existed. We simply ignore them for the purposes of the intestacy calculation. F and G are examples of such a person. Notice again also that N, O, P, and Q all take nothing even though they survived the intestate property owner because each has a living ancestor who is a descendant of the intestate property owner.

14.   **The best answer is (d).** The per capita at each generation approach has one major difference from the modern per stirpes approach: Property that is assigned for calculation purposes to an individual who has predeceased the intestate property owner but left issue who survive the intestate property owner is not necessarily distributed to the descendants of the predeceasing individual. Rather, the property is gathered back and brought down to the next generation, where the assignment of shares begins anew. (This should become clearer with an illustration.) Under the per capita at each generation approach, therefore (1) we begin dividing the intestate

property into shares at the first generation level below the intestate decedent where we find a living descendant. (2) We assign a share to (a) any living descendant in that generation and (b) any predeceased descendant in that generation who left issue who survived the intestate property owner. (3)(a) Any share assigned to a living descendant of the intestate property owner goes to that living descendant of the intestate property owner. (3)(b) Any share assigned to a predeceased descendant of the intestate property owner who left issue that survived the intestate property owner is gathered back up and becomes available for assignment in the next generation according to the same steps 1-3.

We apply the above rules to the fact pattern as follows:
(1) Scott's children – A, B, and C have all predeceased Scott. Therefore, we begin dividing the intestate property into shares at the generation level that contains Scott's grandchildren – the first generation of Scott's descendants where we find someone alive.
(2) E, H, I, J, and K are either living (H, I, and J) or have predeceased Scott but left issue who survived Scott (E and K). Therefore, E, H, I, J, and K each is assigned a 1/5 share of Scott's intestate estate.
(3) Since H, I, and J each is alive each takes a 1/5 share. The 1/5 share assigned to E and the 1/5 share assigned to K (a total of 2/5 of the intestate estate) is gathered back and brought down to the next generation where assignment of shares starts anew using the same rules as above.
(4) As to this final 2/5: In the generation below the E-through-K generation, we find three people – L, M, and R – who are alive and who do not have a living ancestor who is also a descendant of the intestate property owner. Each is assigned a 1/3 share of the 2/5 of the intestate estate that was gathered back and brought down for assignment in this generation. (If there existed in this generation any person who had predeceased the intestate property owner but left issue who survived the intestate property owner, and who did not have a living ancestor who is also a descendant of the intestate property owner, we would have assigned them a pro rata share of the 2/5 of the intestate estate that was gathered back and brought down for assignment in this generation. There are no such persons in this generation.) 1/3 of 2/5 = 2/15. L, M, and R each takes 2/15. Notice again also that N, O, P, and Q all take nothing even though they survived the intestate property owner because each has a living ancestor who is a descendant of the intestate property owner.

If we have done the per-capita-at-each-generation calculation correctly, then persons who take a share of the intestate estate will take the same proportion of the estate as others in the same generation as themselves who take a portion of the estate. That is to say – persons who are equally related to the intestate decedent and who take a share of the intestate estate, take the same proportion of the estate. In our example, Scott's grandchildren who take a portion of the estate all take 1/5 of the estate.

Scott's great-grandchildren who take a portion of the estate all take 2/15 of the estate.

15.   **The best answer is (c).** When Erica predeceases Doug, her devise lapses. The anti-lapse statute does not apply to the devise to Erica because Erica is not among Doug's issue and, therefore, she does not fit within the relationships the statute sets out between the testator and the devisee in order for the anti-lapse statute to apply. The devise to Erica (and to State U) is a residuary devise. (A residuary devise is a devise of what is left over after all of the specific, general, and demonstrative gifts are paid. In the hypothetical, there are no specific, general, or demonstrative devises.) At common law, there was no residue of a residue. This meant that, a residuary devise that lapsed passed by intestacy. The hypothetical provides, however, that the jurisdiction has abolished the no-residue-of-a-residue rule. The effect is that a lapsed residuary gift will pass to and be divided among the remaining residuary devisees, if any. State U is the only other residuary devisee. State U, therefore, takes the 90% of the residuary devised to Erica as well as the 10% of the residuary devised to it.

    •   Additional reference: See William M. McGovern, Jr. and Sheldon F. Kurtz, Wills, Trusts and Estates § 8.3 (3d ed. 2004).

16.   **The best answer is (a).** In general, one may disclaim an inheritance to avoid having one's creditors seize the property. Under the "relation-back" doctrine, the theory is that disclaimer relates back to the time of the decedent's death. Thus, the theory goes, the property passes directly from the decedent to the person or persons who take as a consequence of the disclaimer. For the purposes of creditor's rights, it is as though the person disclaiming predeceased the decedent. There is one creditor who can reach the disclaimed property and that is the federal government, provided a valid tax lien is in effect. See Drye v. United States, 528 U.S. 49 (1999)(holding disclaimer does not defeat federal tax liens). But as a general matter, all other creditor claims will be defeated. An heir or devisee also may disclaim to avoid adverse estate and gift tax consequences. A disclaimer allows the heir or devisee to, in effect, give the property to another without incurring gift tax liability or, at the subsequent death of the person disclaiming, estate tax liability for the estate of the person disclaiming. **Answers (b), (c), and (d) are not correct.** In general, one may not disclaim to avoid ineligibility for public assistance. One who qualifies for public assistance or seeks to qualify for public assistance may still disclaim. The state, however, will impute the property to the person disclaiming for the purposes of determining that person's eligibility for public assistance.

- Additional reference: See William M. McGovern, Jr. and Sheldon F. Kurtz, Wills, Trusts and Estates § 2.8 (3d ed. 2004).

17. **The best answer is (a).** The traditional approach to delegation is reflected in the non-delegation doctrine: Under this doctrine, the trustee must not delegate duties that the trustee reasonably can be expected to perform himself. As a general rule, this approach forbids the trustee from delegating discretionary duties. Discretionary duties are those that require the exercise of judgment. The investment function certainly is a discretionary duty. The Uniform Prudent Investor Act abrogates the non-delegation doctrine. Under the modern rule (also as reflected in the Restatement (Third) of Trusts), the trustee may delegate investment decisions. In fact, under the modern approach, the trustee has a duty to delegate investment decisions under some circumstances. The trustee must exercise care in the selection of the agent to whom he is delegating, must instruct the agent with respect to the trust's investment objectives, and must monitor the agent's actions. **Answers (b) and (c) are not correct.** The traditional approach to evaluating the trustee's investment decisions looked at each investment in isolation from others. Moreover, the law forbids the trustee from investing in "speculative" investments even if an individual investment that was "speculative" in isolation reduced the risk of the investment portfolio when evaluated in the context of the entire portfolio. In contrast, the modern approach evaluates the investment portfolio as a whole rather than evaluating each investment in isolation. Relatedly, the Uniform Prudent Investor Act also abandons the view that the trustee must avoid "speculative" investments. A "speculative" investment may be entirely proper when viewed in the context of the entire portfolio.

- Additional reference: See William M. McGovern, Jr. and Sheldon F. Kurtz, Wills, Trusts and Estates §§ 12.7 and 12.8 (3d ed. 2004).

18. **The best answer is (b).** A provision in a will that purports to devise property to a devisee who shall hold the property as trustee, but which fails to specify the beneficiary of the trust or important terms of the trust is a semi-secret trust. In most American jurisdictions, a semi-secret trust fails (because not in compliance with the requirements for the execution of a will) and a resulting trust arises by operation of law channeling the property back to the testator's estate to pass to the testator's residuary devisees or (as in the case of a residuary clause that sets out the semi-secret trust) to the decedent's intestate heirs. In some jurisdictions, in the case of a semi-secret trust, the court will impose a constructive trust in favor of the intended (but not named in the will) beneficiaries.

- Additional reference: See William M. McGovern, Jr. and Sheldon F. Kurtz, Wills, Trusts and Estates § 6.1 (3d ed. 2004).

19.   **The best answer is (a).** A reversion is the interest that is created in the transferor (or, perhaps more precisely, retained by the transferor) when he transfers an estate that is less than the estate that he had at the time of the transfer. A reversion can only be created in the transferor. A reversion can never be created in a transferee. (A transferee, however, might come to own a reversion that previously arose in the transferor.) **Answers (b), (c), and (d) are not correct.** Vested remainders, contingent remainders, and executory interests are future interests that can only be created in a transferee.

20.   **The best answer is (a).** At the time of the original grant Ben was given a vested remainder subject to divestment. The condition that could have divested Ben was Ben's death without issue surviving him. Issue did in fact survive him (i.e., Seth) and so he is not divested. He is, however, dead, and so we have to figure out where his vested interest went. It went to Ben's estate. Thus, answer (a) is correct.

Answer (b) is not the best answer. There is no language giving Seth anything. Seth might inherit from Ben's estate, but there is nothing in the stated facts that tells you that is the case. Therefore, option A is preferable since answer (b) might not be true. You might think that Seth was an intended beneficiary of this gift because the gift to Ben was conditioned on his being survived by issue. Could there perhaps be an implied gift to Seth in the event Ben is survived by issue – or more correctly an implied gift to Ben's issue? The implied gift argument is certainly worth making on behalf of Seth if Ben's estate is going to someone other than Seth. Common law courts, however, are more likely to opt in favor of the preference for construing language to create vested remainders, in which case answer (a) remains the better answer.

Answer (c) is incorrect because there is no longer any divesting event. Carol had an executory interest at the time of the original transfer from Ollie, but now she has nothing because the condition precedent to her ability to take will never happen. We know that the minute Ben dies survived by issue. **Answer (d) is incorrect** because Seth was given nothing by the original grant. Thus, he cannot have a contingent remainder. **Answer (e) is incorrect** because Carol does not and never did have a contingent remainder. She had an executory interest which is extinguished at Ben's death.

21.   **The best answer is (a).** This is a gift of a future interest, but the gift is not in trust. UPC 2-707 creates an implied condition of survival only when the future interest is in trust. If UPC 2-707 had applied, then both answers (b) and (c) would have been true. But since there is no implied condition of survival, **answers (b) and (c) are incorrect.** As a result, **answer (e) is also incorrect.** The remainder interest in Ben is vested and it stays vested since Ben died survived by issue. Thus, **answer (d) is incorrect** because the gift did not fail and there is nothing to fall into the residuary.

22.   **Answer (c) is the best answer. Answer (d) is not the best answer** because it is not clear from these facts that Linda did enough to constitute an intentional and felonious killing. She does provide him with the means of ending his life and with full knowledge that he is likely to use the pills for this purpose, but her state of mind may fall short of the "intent" requirement for intentional and felonious killing. In fact, Ben may not win at all on his argument since this looks like a mercy killing and the law is currently unsettled on the level of culpability for someone like Linda. But, if Ben is to succeed, he will need one of the four arguments outlined. So the point is to pick the best one. **Answer (c) is the best answer** because, even if Linda is not criminally liable, Ben can argue that what she did was "wrong." This characterization could trigger the equitable principle that a person should not benefit from his or her own wrongdoing. **Answer (a) is not correct** because Ben doesn't own any interest in Brent's estate. There is nothing in the eyes of the law that is "rightfully" his. **Answer (b) is plausible, but it is not the best answer** because the facts do not provide enough information to conclude that Brent (solely because of his terminal illness) lacked testamentary capacity. Testamentary capacity is a low level of competence and presumably if he had the wherewithal to understand his fate, ask Linda for her help, and administer to himself a lethal dose, he was sufficiently conscious of his surroundings and of who his relatives and friends were to meet the level of capacity required to execute a will.

23.   **The best answer is (e),** none of the above. No one is under an affirmative obligation to offer the will for probate unless requested to do so by an interested person. See UPC 2-516. Thus, **answer (a) is incorrect.** Failure to probate does not create a transfer for gift tax purposes. The property simply passes by intestacy to the heirs. Since Mary has no part in directing who those heirs are, she is not making a transfer. Thus, **answer (b) is incorrect. Answer (c) is also incorrect** because, absent a request by an interested party, there is no responsibility to probate. The estate can be administered without a will. **Answer (d) is incorrect.** This answer may appear to be correct because UPC 1-201 includes creditors as "interested persons." But that section also says that the meaning of "interested person" may vary depending on the circumstances. Case law generally

holds that a person is not interested for purposes of forcing probate of the will unless he or she has an interest that might be lost for failure to probate the will. Arthur's estate is liable to his creditors whether the will is probated or not. Administration of the estate can occur without probate of the will. That is, intestate estates are often administered and, in cases where there are creditors, ought to be administered because that will normally provide a shorter period of limitations to creditors. If the estate is not administered, then the distributees of the deceased (in this case the intestate heirs) take the property subject to creditors claims. See UPC 3-901.

24. **The best answer is (c).** Under UPC §2-102, the spouse receives the entire estate only if all of Harold's surviving descendants (Kate, Kim and Ronald) are also descendants of Elizabeth. Since Ronald is not a descendant of Elizabeth, she does not qualify under 2-101(1) as the sole taker. Thus, **answer (d) is wrong.** Under subparagraph (2) of UPC 2-101, she takes the first $200,000 only if Harold has no surviving descendants. Since he clearly has surviving descendants, **answer (a) is wrong.** Under subparagraph (3) of UPC 2-101, she takes the first $150,000 only if all of Harold's descendants are also her descendants (which they are not) and so **answer (b) is wrong. Answer (c) is correct** because even though Ronald is not her descendant, the surviving spouse is always entitled to the first $100,000. Since answer (c) is correct, **answer (e) is incorrect.**

25. **The best answer is (e).** Obviously if he has a valid will that doesn't give anything to Ned, Ned can't take anything under the will. The only way Ned can take is by intestacy and if the will is valid, then Thomas does not die intestate. The facts tell you that the will is valid so you must assume that it is valid to answer the question. Thus **option (a) will work.** Under the UPC, **option (b) will work as well.** UPC § 2-101(b) specifically authorizes a "negative will" such as this one. If Ned survives Thomas, the effect of this negative will is to treat Ned as though he disclaimed his share of the estate. Since both options (a) and (b) and will work, **(e) is the best answer.** Option (c) could work although it does give Ned $1. That hardly seems like enough to prevent Ned from contesting the will. However, **answer (c) cannot be the best answer** because both (a) and (b) will work. Option (d) might work as well but Thomas would have to put all his future property holdings into joint tenancy as well. That might be hard to do. For example, if Thomas died before collecting his last paycheck, that claim would be a debt owed to him and his estate and not a joint tenancy piece of property. Since option (d) is not foolproof, **answer (d) is not the best answer.** After comparing all the options, answers (a) and (b) are better answers than (c) and (d). And since (a) and (b) are equally effective, that makes (e) the best option.

Wills, Trusts, and Estates
Answer Key and Explanations
Exam Two

1.   **The best answer is (b).** For a testator to revoke a will, he must (1) have the intent to revoke the will and (2) while he has that intent to revoke, he must either execute a subsequent will revoking the earlier will or perform a sufficient physical act upon the will he wishes to revoke. The doctrine of dependent relative revocation (DRR) works to negate the first element (T's intent to revoke) in certain cases where the court concludes that such negation actually would promote T's intent. The doctrine of DRR provides that where T purports to revoke a will while laboring under a mistake of fact or law, the court will disregard the revocation if T would have preferred that result had he known the truth about the mistake he was making. For example, as set out in the hypothetical, if T purports to revoke a will while mistakenly believing that by doing so he will revive an earlier will, the court will disregard the revocation (by concluding that T did not really have the intent to revoke) if the court concludes that T would not have revoked the later will had he known that the earlier will would not be revived by his revoking the later will.

There are three general approaches to the issue of revival: (1) when a will that revoked an earlier will is itself revoked, the earlier will automatically is revived; (2) when a will that revoked an earlier will is itself revoked, the earlier will is not revived unless the testator re-executes the earlier will with the formalities necessary for the execution of a will; and (3) when a will that revoked an earlier will is itself revoked, the earlier will is revived if the testator intended for the earlier will to be revived when he revoked the later will. The UPC adopts the third approach and employs a series of presumptions intended to lead the court to the correct conclusion regarding the testator's intent in more cases than not.

Given that the legatees under Will #2 are arguing that the court should apply the doctrine of DRR, and the court agrees, T must have been mistaken in his belief that revoking Will #2 would revive Will #1. **Answer (a) is not correct.** If the jurisdiction applied the rule that when a will that revoked an earlier will is itself revoked, the earlier will automatically is revived, then Will #1 would have been revived when T revoked Will #2. **Answer (c) is not correct.** If the jurisdiction applied the rule that when a will that revoked an earlier will is itself revoked, the earlier will is revived if the testator intended for the earlier will to be revived when he revoked the later will, then Will #1 would have been revived when T revoked Will #2 because (as the facts expressly state) T intended for Will #1 to be revived. **Answer (b) is correct.** Therefore, this jurisdiction must apply the remaining approach to revival – when a will that revoked an earlier will is itself revoked, the earlier will is not revived unless the testator re-executes the earlier will with the formalities necessary for the execution of a will.

- Additional reference: See William M. McGovern, Jr. and Sheldon F. Kurtz, Wills, Trusts and Estates § 5.3 (3d ed. 2004).

2.   **The best answer is (d).** Ademption by extinction is the nullification of a bequest because the item devised is not found in the testator's estate at his death. Ademption by extinction applies only to specific gifts. There are two approaches to ademption. Under the identity theory of ademption, a gift of a specific item is adeemed if it cannot be found in the testator's estate at his death. In general, under the identity theory, whether or not the testator intended to adeem the gift, in theory, is not relevant. Under the intent theory of ademption, a gift of a specific item that cannot be found in the testator's estate at his death is adeemed only if the testator intended for the gift to be adeemed. UPC § 2-606 adopts an intent theory of ademption.

The question asks you to assume a jurisdiction that has adopted UPC § 2-606. Under the intent theory of ademption adopted by § 2-606, in theory, the gift to Susan will be adeemed if T intended to adeem the gift when he sold the house at 1307 W. James St. And the gift to Susan will not be adeemed if T did not intend to adeem the gift when he sold the house at 1307 W. James St. To help courts arrive more times than not at the correct finding with respect to T's intent, the UPC adopts a presumption against ademption when "replacement" property for the specifically devised property is found in T's estate at his death. And the UPC adopts a presumption in favor of ademption when no replacement property for the specifically devised property is found in T's estate at T's death. *See* UPC § 2-606(a)(6) and comment (as amended in 1997). Replacement property is property that is a "mere change in form" from the specifically devised property. Ask yourself whether the property in question serves the same function as the specifically devised property. If so, it likely is replacement property. In the hypothetical, the house at 11 Shawnee Lane serves the same function as the specifically devised house at 1307 W. James St. It would seem to be a "mere change in form" from the specifically devised house. Thus, it likely is replacement property. Under § 2-606(a)(5), a devisee of a specific gift is entitled to "any real property or tangible personal property owned by the testator acquired as a replacement for specifically devised real property or tangible personal property." Susan presumptively is entitled, therefore, to the house at 11 Shawnee Lane.

Answer (b) is not the best answer. UPC § 2-606(a)(6) adopts a mild presumption in favor of ademption when the specific property devised is not found in T's estate at T's death and also there is no replacement property for the specifically devised property found in T's estate at T's death. If there were no replacement property in the hypothetical, then there would be a mild presumption in favor of ademption and Susan presumptively would be entitled to nothing. But the house at 11 Shawnee Lane is replacement property for the house at 1307 W. James St. UPC § 2-606(a)(6), therefore, is not applicable.

Answer (c) is not the best answer. UPC § 2-606(a)(6) provides that where there is no replacement property, and certain other provisions [UPC § 2-606(a)(1) through (a)(4)] are not applicable, and where the claimant has overcome the mild presumption in favor of ademption arising because there is no replacement property, a specific devisee is entitled to "a pecuniary devise equal to the value as of its date of disposition of other specifically devised property disposed of during the testator's lifetime." If there were no replacement property in the hypothetical, therefore, Susan might be entitled to the value of the house at 1307 W. James St. at the time it was sold. But the house at 11 Shawnee Lane is replacement property for the house at 1307 W. James St. UPC § 2-606(a)(6), therefore, is not applicable.

3.   **The best answer is (c).** Abatement is the reduction of a testamentary gift in order to satisfy an estate obligation of a higher priority. For example, testamentary gifts may be subject to abatement so that the estate can satisfy obligations to creditors. If there is not enough property in the estate to pay all of the creditors and satisfy all of the testamentary gifts, some or all of the testamentary gifts will be subject to abatement. In general, the order in which testamentary gifts abate is determined by the classification of the gifts. A common order of abatement is – first, residuary gifts abate; second, if necessary, general gifts abate; third, if necessary, specific gifts abate. Within a class, generally gifts abate pro-rata. Gifts to certain devisees, however, might be given a preferred order of abatement. For example, a general gift to a relative might abate only after all general gifts to non-relatives have fully abated, or a gift to a spouse might abate last regardless of the class of gift.

The gift of "$100,000 to A, to be paid from the sale of my home, or from other sources if the sale is insufficient" is a demonstrative gift. A demonstrative gift is a gift of a type or quantity of property (here - $100,000) to be paid out of a specified asset in the estate (here – the testator's home) if that specified asset is available and sufficient to satisfy the gift, and to be paid out of general assets of the estate if that specified asset is not available and sufficient to satisfy the gift. Demonstrative gifts abate with specific gifts to the extent that the specified asset identified in the gift is available to satisfy the gift, and they abate with general gifts for amounts beyond that. In the hypothetical, the specified asset identified in the gift – the home – is available and sufficient to satisfy the gift. The home sold for $500,000. These proceeds are more than sufficient to pay the $100,000 gift. Therefore, if A's gift is subject to abatement, it will abate with the specific gifts. See generally UPC § 3-902.

- Additional reference: See William M. McGovern, Jr. and Sheldon F. Kurtz, Wills, Trusts and Estates § 8.2 (3d ed. 2004).

4. **The best answer is (e)** because each of the types of property listed would be included within the UPC's augmented estate. Property passing from the decedent to one other than the surviving spouse by a payable-on-death account would be included under UPC § 2-205(1)(iii). Property passing from the decedent to the surviving spouse by means of an inter vivos revocable trust would be included under UPC § 2-206(3). Certain inter vivos transfers from the surviving spouse within two years of the decedent's death would be included under UPC § 2-207(a)(2). And the decedent's property passing by intestacy would be included under UPC § 2-204.

5. **The best answer is (c).** When applied, the doctrine of republication by codicil brings the date of execution of the will up to the date of execution of the codicil. Thus, if the doctrine is applied on the facts of the hypothetical, the date of the will (executed in Year 1) will, in effect, become Year 3. The doctrine of republication by codicil should be applied only to a validly executed will and only if doing so will carry out the intent of the testator. The court should apply the doctrine on the facts of this hypothetical, therefore, only if it believes that T would not have wanted child C to take a portion of his estate as a pretermitted heir. This is so because the effect of applying the doctrine in this case would be to destroy child C's status as a pretermitted heir under the statute of this jurisdiction.

A pretermitted heir statute is intended to protect a child from unintentional disinheritance. When the statute applies, typically, the pretermitted child receives the share of his parent's estate that he would have received had his parent died intestate. It should be noted, however, that there are many variations across jurisdictions on how to determine what portion of the estate the pretermitted child will receive. Most pretermitted heir statutes apply only to a child of the testator born after execution of the will. (Other pretermitted heir statutes protect any child of the testator from unintentional disinheritance regardless of when the child was born.) The theory behind such a statute is that the testator who has a child after execution of the will but does not then revise the will to provide for the child probably overlooked the fact that his extant will did not provide for his child born after execution of the will. The statute, in essence, fixes this mistake for the testator by providing the pretermitted child with a share of the estate.

If the court does not apply the doctrine of republication by codicil on the facts of the hypothetical, child C will qualify for protection from unintentional disinheritance under the jurisdiction's pretermitted heir statute: The will was executed in Year 1, and the child was born a year later. If the court does apply the doctrine of republication by codicil, however, the date of the will is brought up to Year 3. In effect, child C would then have been born a year before the date of the will's execution. He will not qualify for protection, therefore, under the jurisdiction's pretermitted heir statute since the statute applies only to children born after execution of the will. Thus, the court should apply the doctrine of republication by codicil in this case only if T would have wanted to disinherit C.

6.   **The best answer is (e).** To create a trust, a settlor must have the intention to create a trust, he must place property in the trust, he must name a beneficiary, and the trust must have a trustee. One person may serve as the settlor, the trustee, and the beneficiary. **Therefore, answer (c) is incorrect.** Where the settlor is also the trustee, there need not be delivery of the property from the settlor to the trust. **Therefore, answer (d) is incorrect.** To be valid, however, the trust must have at least one beneficiary who is not also the sole trustee. The justification for this rule is that the trustee must owe duties to someone other than himself so that there is some beneficiary who can insist that the trustee perform his duties as trustee. **Answers (a) and (b) are incorrect** because the trust is not valid.

7.   **The best answer is (d).** Ultimately, this is a question of T's intent. If the court concludes that T intended for his will to be effective only if he did not return from this trip to the jungle, then the court should not probate the will. But, it is likely that T spoke of his trip to the jungle only because this event prompted him to consider his mortality and that prompted him to execute a will. If there is no evidence that T would want his estate to be distributed as set forth in his will only if he died in the jungle, but would want his estate to be distributed in a different manner if he returned from the jungle, then the court should ignore the conditional language in order

to give effect to T's true testamentary intent. The seminal case of *Eaton v. Brown*, 193 U.S. 411 (1904), is in accord with this reasoning.

8.   **The best answer is (a).** First, the power is an inter vivos power of appointment. The donor of the power did not specify when the holder of the power could exercise it. Since the holder's authority with respect to a power is presumptively unlimited, the holder can exercise it at any time unless the donor says otherwise when he creates the power. Therefore, Daniel can exercise this power at any time. An inter vivos power is one that can be exercised during the life of the holder of the power. It might also be exercisable by the donee's last will, but so long as it is exercisable during the life of the donee as well, it is an inter vivos power. A testamentary power is one that is exercisable only by the donee's last will. The fact that a power is created by a testator's will is irrelevant to its classification. Since Daniel can exercise the power during his lifetime (as the donee of the power did not limit when Daniel could exercise the power), the power is an inter vivos power. Even though Daniel can exercise the power by his will, the power is not testamentary since it is not a power that can be exercised only by will. Moreover, the fact that Testator created this power in his will does not make this a testamentary power. Since this is not a testamentary power, **answers (b) and (c) are not correct.**

Second, the power is a general power of appointment. A general power of appointment is one that includes within the class of permissible appointees at least one of the following: the donee, the donee's creditors, the donee's estate, or the creditors of the donee's estate. In contrast, a special power of appointment does not include within the class of permissible appointees the donee, the donee's creditors, the donee's estate, or the creditors of the donee's estate. In the hypothetical, Testator gave Daniel the power to appoint "to such person or persons as Donee shall appoint." Daniel may appoint to himself, his creditors, his estate or the creditor's of his estate. Therefore, Daniel holds a general power of appointment. Since this is not a special power, **answer (d) is not correct.**

 • Additional reference: See William M. McGovern, Jr. and Sheldon F. Kurtz, Wills, Trusts and Estates § 10.4 (3d ed. 2004).

9.   **The best answer is (c).** An heir is free to disclaim her inheritance (as is a devisee). Generally, today the law treats one who disclaims her inheritance (whether an heir or a devisee) as having predeceased the decedent (at least for purposes of distributing the disclaimed property). But this approach gives rise to issues of potential unfairness under both a modern per stirpes intestacy approach and a per capita at each generation intestacy approach.

The UPC has modified its approach to calculation of the intestate share in cases of disclaimer to address these issues of potential unfairness. To see both the problem of potential unfairness and the UPC solution to the problem, it is helpful to begin by doing the intestacy calculation as though the disclaimant had not disclaimed.

Under the per capita at each generation approach, (1) we begin dividing the intestate property into shares at the first generation level below the intestate decedent where we find a living descendant (2) We assign a share to (a) any living descendant in that generation and (b) any predeceased descendant in that generation who left issue who survived the intestate property owner. (3)(a) Any share assigned to a living descendant of the intestate property owner goes to that living descendant of the intestate property owner. (3)(b) Any share assigned to a predeceased descendant of the intestate property owner who left issue that survived the intestate property owner is gathered back up and becomes available for assignment in the next generation according to the same steps 1-3. We apply the above rules to the fact pattern in the question as follows: B is alive and is in the first generation below the intestate decedent. We begin dividing the intestate property, therefore, at that first generation below the intestate decedent. We assign 1/2 the property to B (who is alive) and 1/2 the property to A (who has predeceased the intestate decedent but left issue who survive the intestate decedent). B takes her ½. A's ½ is gathered back up and carried to the next generation. At that generation, A's three children are alive and will split his ½.. Thus, E, F, and G each will take 1/6 of the intestate estate. C is alive in that generation as well, but he is not eligible to take because he has a living ancestor (B) who is also a descendant of the intestate decedent. In sum, absent B's disclaiming, B will take ½ of the property, and E, F, and G each will take 1/6 of the property.

If B disclaims and we treat her as having predeceased the intestate decedent, the calculation would change as follows: No one remains alive at the generation level immediately below the intestate decedent. In the next generation, E, F, G, and C all survive. We begin dividing the intestate property, therefore, at the generation level that contains E, F, G, and C. Each takes 1/4 of the intestate property.

The issue of unfairness is now apparent. By disclaiming, B has cost her branch of the family 1/4 of the intestate estate. (If B does not disclaim, she takes ½ of the intestate estate; if B does disclaim, her child takes only 1/4 of the intestate estate.) The issue of unfairness sometimes runs the other way in that the disclaimant's act of disclaiming increases the portion of the estate passing to his branch of the family. (To see an example of this, assume that A had survived the intestate decedent but disclaimed, and B did not survive the intestate decedent. The result of A's disclaimer would be to increase the portion of the intestate estate passing to his side of the family from ½ to 3/4.)

UPC § 2-1106(3)(A) remedies this issue of unfairness by providing:

> "If the disclaimant is an individual, the disclaimed interest passes as if the disclaimant had died immediately before the time of distribution. However, if, by law or under the instrument, the descendants of the disclaimant would share in the disclaimed interest by any method of representation had the disclaimant died before the time of distribution, the disclaimed interest passes only to the descendants of the disclaimant who survive the time of distribution."

Thus, under UPC § 2-1106(3)(A), only the disclaimed property is affected by the disclaimer. (This is made clear by the first sentence of UPC § 2-1106(3)(A).) Moreover, where the disclaimed property would have passed by representation to the disclaimant's descendants had the disclaimant actually predeceased the intestate decedent, that disclaimed property passes only to the descendants of the disclaimant. A helpful way to apply this provision is to calculate the intestate distribution as though the disclaimant had not disclaimed, and then pass the disclaimant's portion of the intestate estate (that is, the disclaimed property) to his descendants by representation.

Applying this provision to the hypothetical, had B not disclaimed, she would have taken ½ of the intestate estate (see the calculation above). Only the property B would have taken but for the disclaimer is affected by the disclaimer. B's disclaimed property passes to her child C. Thus, C takes ½ of the intestate property and E, F, and G split the other half of the intestate property. Notice that under UPC § 2-1106(3)(A), B's disclaimer does not affect the amount of property which passes to her branch of the family (or to A's branch of the family).

- Additional reference: See William M. McGovern, Jr. and Sheldon F. Kurtz, Wills, Trusts and Estates § 2.8 (3d ed. 2004).

10.   **The best answer is (c).** Under the Revised Uniform Simultaneous Death Act, one must survive a property owner by at least 120 hours (five days) in order to take from that property owner by intestacy or by will (unless the

will provides a different rule). Otherwise, we treat the survivor (who survives the decedent by less than five days) as having predeceased the property owner. Carol failed to survive Mike by five days. We treat her, therefore, as having predeceased Mike for the purposes of interpreting Mike's will and distributing his estate. Mike's will expressly provides that if Carol fails to survive him, Greg, Peter, and Bobby take his estate.

11.   **The best answer is (c).** Section 502(a) of the Uniform Trust Code, in accordance with the traditional rule, provides that "[a] spendthrift provision is valid only if it restrains both voluntary and involuntary transfer of a beneficiary's interest." If a beneficiary's interest is subject to a valid spendthrift provision, the beneficiary may not assign his interest in the trust, and his creditors may not attach his interest prior to the beneficiary receiving the distribution from the trust. (Certain "exception creditors," such as a child owed child support by the beneficiary, might be able to attach the beneficiary's interest despite an otherwise valid spendthrift provision.)

- Additional reference: See William M. McGovern, Jr. and Sheldon F. Kurtz, Wills, Trusts and Estates § 13.1 (3d ed. 2004).

12.   **The best answer is (c).** That the transaction was fair and reasonable is not alone a defense to self-dealing. Self-dealing in the context of a trust occurs when the trustee buys property from the trust in his personal capacity or sells property to the trust in his personal capacity. In a case of self-dealing, the court will apply the "no-further-inquiry" rule. Under the no-further-inquiry rule, the court only asks whether the trustee engaged in self dealing: The court does not inquire into the fairness or reasonableness of the transaction. If the court finds that the trustee has engaged in self-dealing, the court may set aside the transaction and order the trustee to disgorge any profits regardless of whether the transaction was fair to the beneficiaries at the time of the transaction. There are, however, three defenses to self-dealing. Those defenses are set out in answers (a), (b), and (d). The first defense is that the settlor authorized the self-dealing, and the transaction was fair and reasonable. The second defense is that the beneficiaries consented to the self-dealing after full disclosure, and the transaction was fair and reasonable. The third defense is that the court approved the transaction before hand. **Answers (a), (b), and (d), therefore, are not correct.**

13.   **The best answer is (a).** Under the doctrine of incorporation by reference as it existed at common law, a document that has not been executed with the formalities for the execution of a will can be given testamentary effect under a will provided that (1) the document was in existence at the

execution of the will, (2) the will manifests the testator's intention to incorporate the document into the will, and (3) the will sufficiently identifies the document to be incorporated. Technically, the document that is being incorporated by reference does not become a part of the will. The memorandum entry with respect to Ginny did not exist at the execution of the will. The common law doctrine of incorporation by reference alone, therefore, will not validate the devise to Ginny. In conjunction with the doctrine of republication by codicil, however, the devise to Ginny should be given effect. When applied, the doctrine of republication by codicil re-executes an earlier will and brings the date of execution of the earlier will up to the date of execution of the codicil. The doctrine of republication by codicil is properly applied only to a validly executed prior will and only if doing so will carry out the intent of the testator. Applying the doctrine in this case would carry out the intent of the testator – that Ginny take the home on Dilido Island. If the date of the will is brought up to the date of the codicil (Year 9), the memorandum entry in favor of Ginny (made in Year 5) was in existence at the execution of the will. Since the will sufficiently identifies the document to be incorporated by reference ("a memorandum that I will title "Distribution of My Real and Personal Property"") and sufficiently manifests an intention to incorporate that document into the will ("Certain of my real and personal property shall be distributed to such person or persons as I will designate in a memorandum that I will title "Distribution of My Real and Personal Property""), the prerequisites for application of the doctrine of incorporation by reference are satisfied. **Answer (d) is not correct.** Given the effect of the doctrine of republication by codicil, it is not controlling that the memorandum entry in favor of Ginny was not in existence in Year 1 when the will originally was executed.

Answers (b) and (c) are not correct. Under the common law doctrine of incorporation by reference, the document to be incorporated need not be signed by the testator. Moreover, the common law doctrine of incorporation by reference is not limited to devises of personal property. It is not correct, therefore, to say that the doctrine does not apply to devises of real property. UPC § 2-510 is in accord with the common law doctrine of incorporation by reference. ("A writing in existence when a will is executed may be incorporated by reference if the language of the will manifests this intent and describes the writing sufficiently to permit its identification.") The UPC also has a second incorporation by reference provision: UPC § 2-513 allows for incorporation by reference of a document that was not in existence at the execution of the will. UPC § 2-513 requires, however, that the testator must have signed the document to be incorporated by reference. Moreover, UPC § 2-513 applies only to devises of tangible personal property. On the facts of the hypothetical, however, UPC § 2-513 is not needed since the devise to Ginny can be given effect under the common law doctrine of incorporation by reference in conjunction with the republication by codicil doctrine.

- Additional reference: See William M. McGovern, Jr. and Sheldon F. Kurtz, Wills, Trusts and Estates § 6.2 (3d ed. 2004).

14.   **The best answer is (e).** A constructive trust is really not a trust at all in the sense of contemplating an on-going fiduciary relationship between the "constructive trustee" and the beneficiary. Rather, a constructive trust is a remedy a court imposes in order to prevent unjust enrichment, particularly in cases of fraud, duress, or undue influence. Commonly, the court orders as a constructive trust remedy that the holder of certain property transfer the property to another. **Answer (a) is not correct.** Where the donor transfers property and expresses his "desire," "hope," or "wish" (or uses similar precatory language) that the transferee use the property to benefit a third party, the court will have to decide if the donor intended to impose a legal obligation on the transferee to hold the property in trust (in which case a true trust arises), or whether the donor merely intended to impose at most a moral obligation on the transferee. In the latter case, the donor has created a mere "precatory trust." Despite the name, this is no trust at all, as it is not a fiduciary relationship with respect to the property. **Answer (c) is not correct.** An honorary trust is a trust-like gift that is not intended to benefit the transferee and does not have any specific beneficiary who can enforce the trust as a gift, but has a specific non-charitable purpose. The honorary trust lacks the "for the benefit of another" element of a trust. **Answer (d) is not the best answer.** When a trust fails or terminates of its own terms and the settlor has not directed what is then to happen to the property (or the settlor's direction cannot be carried out) a resulting trust arises by operation of law channeling the property back to the settlor (or the settlor's estate). A resulting trust does not involve the on-going management of property or a fiduciary relationship with respect to property.

- Additional reference: See William M. McGovern, Jr. and Sheldon F. Kurtz, Wills, Trusts and Estates §§ 6.1, 6.4 (3d ed. 2004).

15.   **The best answer is (e).** The testator's "then surviving issue" have a contingent remainder. A remainder is contingent if it is subject to a condition precedent or if it is given to takers who are not ascertained at the time of its creation. The remainder in the problem is contingent either because (with respect to issue alive at the testator's death) it is subject to a condition precedent of survival or because (with respect to unborn issue at the time of the testator's death) it is given to unascertained persons. In

sum, it is contingent because we cannot presently ascertain who will qualify as "then surviving issue" until the death of the last of Kevin, Brian and Danny to die. The testator's estate retains a reversion. The reversion will become possessory if no issue of the testator survive Kevin, Brian, and Danny. The reversion will be divested (all reversions are vested) if issue of the testator survive Kevin, Brian, and Danny.

16.   **The best answer is (c).** As a general rule joint tenancy real assets cannot be reached by creditors after death because the deceased joint tenant's property interest ceases at his death. See UPC §6-102. A creditor can always reach whatever interest the debtor owns in the property before death. Thus, before death, Bob's creditors could have pressed their claims and caused a partition of the joint tenancy (because Bob himself had the right to partition as a joint tenant). In that case the creditor would have been able to reach 50% of the joint tenancy property to satisfy the claim. However, after death, Bob owns nothing. His estate owns nothing. So there is nothing for a creditor to attach. Thus **answer (a) is incorrect. Answer (b) is incorrect** because these are creditors of Bob, not of Ellen. Thus they have no right to pursue her property to pay off Bob's debt. In a community property state, creditors might be able to reach community assets for payment of a community debt, but this fact situation does not occur in a community property state. In some states, a spouse could be held liable for a deceased spouse's debts provided the debt was for certain expenditures such as living expenses or necessaries. But this loan was made for Bob to pay off a gambling debt, a debt that was his own, not his wife's. Nor did Bob engage in a fraudulent transfer as to Klare since the property was already in joint tenancy when Klare made the loan. **Thus answer (d) is incorrect**.

> [Note: Rules vary from state to state regarding a creditor's right to reach assets in a joint bank account after the death of a joint tenant. In most states, joint bank accounts are viewed differently from true joint tenancies because the depositor usually has the right to withdraw the funds up until the moment of death. Thus, they more closely resemble revocable transfers, which creditors can usually reach. The general rule under the UPC is that the funds of the depositor are presumed to belong to the depositor even after they are deposited in a joint bank account. So, Klare might have been able to reach funds in a joint bank account had Bob created the account with his own funds.]

17.   **The best answer is (b).** A lawyer does have an affirmative obligation to acquire relevant facts about a client's family and assets before giving estate planning advice, but it is unlikely that a court would expect a lawyer

to do an independent investigation of a client's claims about family status. If Larry Lawyer asked Ted about his family and Ted declined to mention his wife, then Larry should be justified in relying on Ted's representations. **Answer (a) is not correct** because a spouse can waive a right to an elective share under UPC 2-213. The waiver may not be effective if it fails to comply with the provisions of 2-213. Nonetheless, a spouse CAN waive the right. **Answer (c) would be correct in some states** (e.g., Texas, Nebraska), **but those states are in the minority**. The growing trend is to allow claims of malpractice by disappointed beneficiaries despite the lack of privity between them and the lawyer who drafted the will. **Answer (d) is incorrect** because it is not against public policy to leave property to a paramour. Ever since *Marvin v. Marvin* was handed down by the California Supreme Court in 1976, holding that contracts between paramours could be enforced and were not against public policy, so long as they were not contracts providing for payment of sexual services, almost every other state has upheld the *Marvin* principle. While wills are not contracts, provisions in wills have sometimes been struck down on the basis of public policy. Nonetheless the *Marvin* principle that contractual transfers to paramours are not against public policy should extend to testamentary transfers such as the one in this problem. **Answer (e) is incorrect.** Wills are revocable and thus ambulatory. This will did not take effect until Ted's death in 2006. At any time before that, the harm to Pam could have been remedied, e.g., by Ted's divorcing Flo, by Flo's death, or by having Flo execute a valid waiver of her right. Thus, the harm did not occur until 2006 and that is when the statute of limitations should begin running.

18.   **The best answer is (a).** UPC 2-102 gives everything to the surviving spouse provided all the descendants of the decedent are also the descendants of the surviving spouse. The question is whether or not Ronald, who was adopted by Elizabeth, is a descendant of Elizabeth. UPC 1-201 defines descendant with reference to the parent and child relationship, which is defined at 2-114. UPC §2-114(b) provides that an adopted child is a child for purposes of intestate succession. Thus, Ronald is Elizabeth's child and Elizabeth meets the requirement of being the parent of all of Harold's children. She will inherit the entire estate no matter what its size.

19.   **The best answer is (c).** An attorney in fact has the power to disclaim under the UPC provision and under similar provisions in most states. Thus **answers (a) and (b) are incorrect**. Testator's estate will be subject to an estate tax because it exceeds the exemption equivalent, which is $2.0 million in 2006. Disclaimers do not avoid estate taxes. Rather they avoid gift taxes. If Evelyn accepted the bequest and then gave it to Evan the

property would be the subject of two transfers, one at death which is subject to the estate tax (and perhaps the generation skipping tax) and a second one which is a gift from Evelyn to Evan and is subject to the gift tax. The disclaimer creates a single transfer from Testator to Evan and thus avoids the gift tax. **Answer (d) is incorrect** because the disclaimer does not avoid estate taxes. **Answer (e) is incorrect** because Evelyn's creditors cannot attach disclaimed property for debts that may occur in the future.

20.   **The best answer is (d).** So long as Bill and the executor agree that the property should not be destroyed, no one has standing to enforce the request. Thus answer **(a) is correct. But answer (a) is not the best answer because answer (b) is also true**. There are a handful of reported cases in which testators have ordered their executors to destroy a certain piece of property. The majority rule is that destruction of a house is against public policy so long as the house is in good condition and there is no reason to destroy it other than the whim of the testator. Arguments are sometimes made that since the testator could have destroyed the house during his lifetime he ought to have that right at death. But courts hold that right ends at death. The harm to the beneficiaries and the neighbors is more important as a matter of policy than the carrying out of the direction to destroy. This is true even though American law recognizes a strong policy in freedom of testation. **Thus answer (c) is incorrect** because the public policy interest in maintaining valuable property for the benefit of the living is likely to trump the policy in favor of freedom of testation where the direction to destroy was included merely to satisfy a whim of the testator.

21.   **The best answer is (d).** A videotape is not a writing and a holographic will must be in writing to be effective as a will. Thus **answer (a) is wrong**. A nuncupative will is an oral will, but nuncupative wills statutes require that the will be made in the last sickness of the decedent. Here, Frank died two years later. In addition, nuncupative wills require witnesses and here there were none. Thus **answer (b) is wrong. Answer (c) is also wrong**. The harmless error statutes only apply to wills in writing and this is not a will in writing.

22.   **The best answer is (b).** The statute is clear. The divorce revokes the gift and distributes it as though Lon were dead. In that event, Ted takes. If she really wanted Lon to take despite the divorce, she'd have to include that language in a testamentary instrument. Remaining friends is not sufficient to overcome the statute. Thus, **answer (a) is incorrect**. While the UPC revokes gifts to the relatives of the ex-spouse, this state's statute is silent as to that matter. Thus only Lon's gift is revoked and **answer (c) is incorrect. Answer (d) is also incorrect** because the statute is sufficient to

provide a "constructive" death. The property is to be distributed as though Lon had predeceased and the will provides that in that case, the property goes to Ted.

23.   **The best answer is (e), none of the above. Option (a) won't work** because the body is not property that can be willed to anyone. **Option (b) won't work** because a power of attorney is revoked upon the death of the principal, Van. **Option (c) won't work** for the same reason. A durable power of attorney can survive the principal's disability, but it still is revoked upon Van's death. **Option (d) won't work** because living wills are merely directives to physicians to restrain from resuscitation where appropriate. They have nothing to do with burial arrangements or cremation.

24.   **The best answer is (e).** Because the question asks which statements are "not true" – i.e., which are false – the best approach in answering this question is to mark each option true or false and then determine the answer on the basis of the options marked false. **Both answer (c) and answer (d) are false.** The facts in this problem are based on the facts in *Reed v. Campbell*, a Texas case in which the nonmarital child claimed a share in the estate but under state law was prevented from inheriting because nonmarital children could only inherit from their fathers if their parents subsequently married. See 476 U.S. 852 (1986). The statute was struck down on the basis of equal protection thereby allowing the child of Prince Ricker to proceed with her claim. By analogy, Clarissa should inherit in this fact situation as a child of Prince. Thus answer (c) is false. Answer (d) is also false because Zoe does have a basis for claiming part of the estate. She can claim as a putative spouse. Whether she will get a distribution or not depends on the state law regarding putative spouses and their inheritance rights, but she at least has a basis for a claim. **Since both (c) and (d) are false, answer (e) is the best answer. Answer (a) is wrong** because it is true that Minnie will be considered the only legal spouse of Prince. **Answer (b) is wrong** because it is true that Clarissa will be considered a nonmarital child since her parents' marriage is not legal.

25.   **The best answer is (b).** The rule applied to omitted spouses is based on the assumption that most testators favor their spouses in their testamentary plans. In the absence of a rule that revokes a will upon marriage, a premarital will remains valid and can prevent the surviving spouse from getting anything. The omitted spouse statute creates the same result with respect to a spouse as a rule that revokes a premarital will upon marriage. A surviving spouse who married the testator after the will was executed will be entitled to a spousal intestate share under either rule. In turn, the spousal intestate share, which can amount to 100%, is crafted to reflect the distribution scheme that most

testators favor. Thus, the omitted spouse statute is justified on grounds that it is most likely to carry out testator's intent. The purpose of the elective share statute, by contrast, is to protect a spouse who has been disinherited by the testator. The limit to one-third of the estate may not seem fair in cases of a long-term marriage. That is why the UPC has adopted a sliding scale, under which the share available to the electing spouse increases in amount with the age of the marriage. Some states, however, still embrace the old dower-driven elective share which typically gives the surviving spouse a one-third interest. **Answer (a) is incorrect** because, even though the one-third elective share can be traced to dower, that is not a sufficient explanation for why the two provisions are different. **Answer (c) is incorrect** because frequency of use should have nothing to do with the size of the spousal share in the two statutes. **Answer (d) is incorrect** because the difference does matter to a surviving spouse who does not qualify as an omitted spouse as that spouse can only claim an elective share. **Answer (e) is incorrect** because even if the elective share comes off the top on a par with other creditors, that does not explain why an omitted spouse can take the entire estate that is available after creditors' claims are satisfied.

Wills, Trusts, and Estates
Answer Key and Explanations
Exam Three

1.   **The best answer is (c).** The elective share percentage is employed to implement the marital-sharing theory that grounds the UPC's elective share. The marital-sharing theory holds that the surviving spouse is entitled to end up with one-half of the marital property accumulated during the marriage. Partly for reasons of administrative convenience, however, the UPC rejects an approach that would trace assets to determine which are marital and which are not. Rather, the UPC uses an approximation scheme. The elective share percentage is a critical component of that scheme as is the augmented estate concept. The elective share percentages set out in UPC § 2-202 help to approximate the amount of property that the spouses own that is marital property for a marriage of any given length. More precisely, the elective share percentage when multiplied by the value of the augmented estate is meant to yield a value equal to one-half of the combined marital property owned by either spouse (as the surviving spouse is entitled to only one-half of the total marital property owned by the spouses). We need to double the elective share percentage, therefore, to determine how much of the augmented estate is approximated to be marital property. Thus, if the elective share percentage for a marriage of ten-year duration is 30%, we know that the drafter's assumed that in a marriage of ten-year duration 60% of the augmented estate property is marital property.

     - Additional reference: Lawrence W. Waggoner, "The Multiple-Marriage Society and Spousal Rights Under the Revised Uniform Probate Code," 76 Iowa L. Rev. 223, n. 79 (1991).

2.   **The best answer is (a).** To create a trust, a settlor need not use the word "trust" or "trustee." But he must manifest an intent that one person hold the property for the benefit of another. The testator in the hypothetical has not stated clearly an intention that Susan hold the property in trust for the benefit of Jeff. Rather, the testator has used words of desire but not words of direction. The testator has created a "precatory trust." Despite the name, this is no trust at all. Susan may have a moral obligation to use the profits from the ranch to benefit brother Jeff, but she does not have a legally enforceable obligation to do so. Susan owns the ranch outright.

     - Additional reference: See William M. McGovern, Jr. and Sheldon F. Kurtz, Wills, Trusts and Estates § 4.6 (3d ed. 2004).

3.   **The best answer is (d).** The UPC's harmless error principle (UPC § 2-503) provides that a document may be probated as T's will if there is clear

and convincing evidence that T intended the document to be his will. The UPC, however, does not dispense with the formalities for execution of a will. Rather, the UPC maintains formalities for execution of the will as a safe harbor for those who comply, yet adopts the harmless error principle so that a document might still be probated as a will even if the testator failed to comply with the specified formalities, provided that the court is convinced by clear and convincing evidence that the testator intended the document to be his will. Thus, **answer (a) is not the best answer.**

4.   **The best answer is (b).** The Claflin doctrine (named after the leading case of Claflin v. Claflin, 149 Mass 19, 20 N.E. 545 (1889)), which is followed in most American jurisdictions, provides that the beneficiaries of a trust may modify or terminate the trust provided that all of the beneficiaries consent to the modification or termination of the trust (and are capable of doing so), and such modification or termination of the trust will not defeat a material purpose of the settlor. The question asks you to assume that all of the beneficiaries have consented to early termination of the trust. The issue, therefore, is which of these trusts has a material purpose of the settlor that would be defeated by early termination of the trust. In general, a spendthrift trust, a discretionary trust, a support trust, and a postponement-of-enjoyment trust all are considered to have a material purpose of the settlor that would be defeated by early termination. A mere successive interest trust (also known as a bypass trust) generally is thought not to have a material purpose of the settlor that would be defeated by early termination.

Trust 1 is a support trust: The amount of income that is paid to A is measured by A's need for support. Trust 2 is a postponement-of-enjoyment trust: The settlor likely postponed Son's access to the principal until age 35 because the settlor felt that Son should have a certain level of maturity before he enjoyed the freedom to control this property. Trust 5 is a spendthrift trust: A's interest is not assignable and is not attachable by his creditors. The settlor's purpose in setting up a spendthrift trust generally is thought to be to protect the beneficiary from his own ineptitude at financial management. Trusts 1, 2, and 5 each has a material purpose that would be defeated by the beneficiaries' early termination of the trust. Each is not destructible, therefore, under the Claflin doctrine.

Trust 3 is a mere successive interest trust. Trust 4 also is a mere successive interest trust. Trust 4 is not a support trust regardless of the language "to be used for A's support" because, under the terms of the trust, A receives all of the income, not just an amount of the income measured by his need for support. Mere successive interest trusts are destructible under the Claflin doctrine. Trust 6 is a spendthrift trust.

Ordinarily, a spendthrift trust is not destructible under the Claflin doctrine. In this case, however, the settlor wishes to terminate the trust, but did not retain the power to terminate the trust. If the settlor and the beneficiaries agree to terminate the trust, they can do so even if the trust is otherwise a material purpose trust. This makes sense since the material purpose we are concerned with protecting is that of the settlor. If the settlor wishes to defeat what was once his material purpose, we need not be concerned with protecting his intent by preventing early termination of the trust.

- Additional reference: See William M. McGovern, Jr. and Sheldon F. Kurtz, Wills, Trusts and Estates § 9.6 (3d ed. 2004).

5.　**The best answer is (c).** Steven most likely holds a power that he can exercise at any time and that he can exercise to benefit himself. Therefore, a court likely will enforce his contract to exercise the power in the future in favor of Harriet's children even if the contract also benefits Steven. When the holder of a power that is not presently exercisable (for example, a testamentary power) contracts to exercise the power, a court will not enforce the contract. The best reasoning supporting this approach is that the donor of the power intended for the holder of the power to be able to change his mind about who to benefit by exercise of the power up until the time that the power becomes exercisable. For example, the donor of a testamentary power (a power that is exercisable only by the will of the holder of the power) intended for the holder of the power to be able to change his mind about who to benefit by exercise of the power up until the time of the holder's death. To enforce a contract in which the holder of a testamentary power has agreed to exercise the power in a certain manner, therefore, would defeat the intent of the donor of the power. If Steven held a power that was not presently exercisable, therefore, a court would not enforce the contract. In the hypothetical, however, Steven holds an inter vivos power of appointment, which usually is presently exercisable. For this reason, **answer (a) is not the best answer.**

In cases in which a general power is not presently exercisable (usually because it is a testamentary power), some courts will enforce a contract to release the power, even though they would not enforce a contract to exercise the power. When the holder of a power contracts to release the power, he agrees not to exercise the power and to allow the appointive property to pass to the takers in default. The power in the hypothetical, however, is an inter vivos power and is most likely presently exercisable. **Answer (b), therefore, is not the best answer.**

Moreover, a holder of a special power commits "fraud on the power" when he exercises the power to benefit someone who is not an object of the power. When the holder of the power contracts to exercise the power, he presumably receives consideration for agreeing to exercise the power in a certain way. Thus, the holder benefits himself by contracting to exercise the power. If the power is a special power, by definition, the holder may not benefit himself, his creditors, his estate, or the creditors of his estate. Therefore, when the holder of a special power contracts to exercise the power, he commits a "fraud on the power." In the hypothetical, however, Steven holds a general power of appointment. By definition, Steven is an object of the power. It is not an obstacle to enforcement of the contract, therefore, that Steven benefits when he contracts to exercise the power. For this reason, **answer (d) is not the best answer.**

- Additional reference: See William M. McGovern, Jr. and Sheldon F. Kurtz, Wills, Trusts and Estates § 10.4 (3d ed. 2004).

6.   **The best answer is (d).** Benny is not entitled to anything under T's will. **Answer (c) is not the best answer.** T's crossing out of the $50,000 gift is a sufficient partial revocation by physical act (the physical act is cancellation) such that the gift is revoked, provided that T had the intent to revoke the gift when he performed the physical act. The question asks that you assume that this jurisdiction does not apply the doctrine of dependent relative revocation. Therefore, that doctrine is not available to undo the partial revocation pursuant to the legal fiction that T did not have the intent to revoke when he performed the act of cancellation on the will. The $50,000 gift, therefore, should be held to be revoked. **Answer (b) is not the best answer.** The handwritten notation –"$60,000" – would not be a valid holographic codicil to the typed will even though T signed and dated the notation. A typed attested will can have a holographic codicil. But a holographic will (and a codicil is a species of will) is not valid unless, at a minimum, the material provisions of the will are in T's handwriting. (In a minority of jurisdictions that recognize holographic wills, the entire will must be in T's handwriting for the will to be valid as a holographic will.) At a minimum, the names of the beneficiaries and the property they are to receive under the will are material provisions. The name of "Benny" is typed in the document in question. Therefore, the material provisions of the attempted holographic codicil are not all in T's handwriting, and the purported codicil is not valid. The net result is that Benny is devised $0 under the will.

- Additional reference: See William M. McGovern, Jr. and Sheldon F. Kurtz, Wills, Trusts and Estates § 4.4 (3d ed. 2004).

7.   **The best answer is (b).** Benny is entitled to $60,000. To be clear, the handwritten notation –"$60,000" – would not be valid as a duly executed

holographic codicil to the typed will even though T signed and dated the notation. A typed attested will can have a holographic codicil. But a holographic will (and a codicil is a species of will) is not valid in a strict compliance jurisdiction unless, at a minimum, the material provisions of the will are in T's handwriting. (In a minority of jurisdictions that recognize holographic wills, the entire will must be in T's handwriting for the will to be valid as a holographic will.) At a minimum, the names of the beneficiaries and the property they are to receive under the will are material provisions. The name of "Benny" is typed in the document in question. Therefore, the material provisions of the attempted holographic codicil are not all in T's handwriting, and the purported codicil is not valid as a duly executed holographic will.

Under the harmless error principle (*see* UPC § 2-503), however, a document that has not been executed with the formalities prescribed in a jurisdiction for execution of a will may nonetheless be probated as a will if the court finds that there is clear and convincing evidence that the testator intended the document to be his will. The hypothetical arguably presents clear and convincing evidence that T intended by crossing out the "$50,000" figure and writing in its place "$60,000" for Benny to receive $60,000 under his will. Thus, in short, Benny is entitled to $60,000 under the will because there is clear and convincing evidence that T intended for Benny to take $60,000 at his death pursuant to the document which he intended to be his will.

Because the harmless error principle is available in this jurisdiction to give effect to T's intent, the doctrine of dependent relative revocation (which can be used to give effect to T's second preference when he has made a mistake of fact or law which precludes a court from recognizing his first preference) is not relevant on the facts of the hypothetical.

- Additional reference: See William M. McGovern, Jr. and Sheldon F. Kurtz, Wills, Trusts and Estates § 4.4 (3d ed. 2004).

8.   **The best answer is (c).** First, Bennie will not receive the $60,000 gift that

T attempted to leave him under the purported codicil. **Answer (b), therefore, is not the best answer.** The handwritten notation –"$60,000" – would not be a valid holographic codicil to the typed will even though T signed and dated the notation. A typed attested will can have a holographic codicil. But a holographic will (and a codicil is a species of will) is not valid unless, at a minimum, the material provisions of the will are in T's handwriting. (In a minority of jurisdictions that recognize holographic wills, the entire will must be in T's handwriting for the will to be valid as a holographic will.) At a minimum, the names of the beneficiaries and the property they are to receive under the will are material provisions. The name of "Benny" is typed in the document in question. Therefore, the material provisions of the attempted holographic codicil are not all in T's handwriting, and the purported codicil is not valid.

Second, the $50,000 gift to Bennie will be revoked, and Bennie will get nothing, unless the revocation can be "undone" pursuant to the doctrine of dependent relative revocation. T's crossing out of the $50,000 gift is a sufficient partial revocation by physical act (the physical act is cancellation) such that the gift is revoked, provided that T had the intent to revoke the gift when he performed the physical act. The doctrine of dependent relative revocation (DRR), however, may negate T's intent to revoke.

For a testator to revoke a will, he must (1) have the intent to revoke the will and (2) while he has that intent to revoke, he must either execute a subsequent will revoking the earlier will or perform a sufficient physical act upon the will he wishes to revoke. The doctrine of dependent relative revocation works to negate the first element (T's intent to revoke) in certain cases where the court concludes that such negation actually would promote T's intent. The doctrine of DRR provides that where T purports to revoke a will while laboring under a mistake of fact or law, the court will disregard the revocation if T would have preferred that result had he known the truth about the mistake he was making. For example, as set out in the hypothetical, if T purports to revoke a will while mistakenly believing that he simultaneously is executing a new will (or, as in this case, a codicil), the court will disregard the revocation (by concluding that T did not really have the intent to revoke) if the court concludes that T would not have revoked the earlier will had he known that the subsequent will he was attempting to execute would not be valid.

On the facts of the hypothetical, DRR should be applied to undo the revocation of the $50,000 gift to Bennie. It seems clear that T's intent to revoke the $50,000 gift to Bennie was premised on his mistaken belief that his notation "$60,000" would be effective to devise Bennie an even larger gift. If DRR is not applied, Bennie will receive nothing. As T wanted to leave Bennie $60,000 but failed to properly execute the codicil, T certainly would prefer that Bennie receive $50,000 rather than nothing. Therefore, the court should conclude that T's intent to revoke the $50,000 was premised on a mistake of law (believing that the new codicil would be effective) and under the doctrine of DRR should be negated. Without the intent to revoke, the physical act (the cancellation) is of no effect. Bennie, therefore, should receive $50,000.

- Additional reference: See William M. McGovern, Jr. and Sheldon F. Kurtz, Wills, Trusts and Estates § 5.3 (3d ed. 2004).

9.   **The best answer is (c).** As a preliminary matter, whenever dealing with

the issue of potential advancements, the first issue to address is whether there is sufficient evidence that the intestate property owner intended for a lifetime gift to be an advancement of an heir's intestate share. The question, however, asks that you assume that the lifetime gifts listed qualify as advancements. The only issue then is to calculate how the advancements affect the intestate shares of the heirs (that is, to calculate the "hotchpot").

In calculating how one or more advancements affects the intestate distribution: (1) add the value of the advancements (generally, calculate the value of each advancement as of the time the donee came to enjoy the advancement) to the value of the net intestate estate; (2) calculate an intestate distribution as though the intestate estate were valued at that figure arrived at in Step 1; and (3) subtract each heir's advancement from the amount they otherwise would take under step 2 to arrive at that heir's intestate share. Applying these rules to the facts of the hypothetical: First, we add the $150,000 (home), $100,000 (boat), and $25,000 (car) advancements to the $800,000 net probate estate. We get a total figure of $1,075,000. We divide this figure by five (the number of children who, putting advancements aside, would split the intestate estate equally - each taking 1/5) and arrive at a preliminary intestate share of $215,000 each. Because E and F did not receive an advancement during D's lifetime, E and F will each take $215,000. To calculate the final intestate share of each of the other children, we must subtract that child's advancement from this figure. Doing that, we arrive at $65,000 for A ($215,000 - $150,000); $115,000 for B ($215,000 - $100,000); and $190,000 for C ($215,000 - $25,000).

Notice that if you have done the calculation correctly, the total value of the intestate shares should add up to the value of the actual net intestate estate. Note also that if an heir's advancement is larger than his preliminary intestate share, he does not have to repay the estate for any amount of the advancement, but he gets no portion of the intestate estate. In that case, we ignore that heir (and his advancement) when re-calculating the hotchpot.

- Additional reference: See William M. McGovern, Jr. and Sheldon F. Kurtz, Wills, Trusts and Estates § 2.6 (3d ed. 2004).

10.   **The best answer is (b).** The question gives a definition of fraud in the inducement. In contrast, fraud in the execution exists where a person intentionally makes a misrepresentation concerning the content or character of a document that is intended to and does in fact cause the testator to believe that the document is that which the testator wishes to be his will. **Answer (a), therefore, is not correct.**

11.   **The best answer is (b).** The law of the marital domicile at the time that personal property is acquired determines the characterization of that property as separate or marital (community). While some experts have advised married couples domiciled outside of Alaska to create Alaskan trusts of personal property in order to have the trust property classified as community, the general rule is that the marital domicile will determine the character of personal property acquired during marriage. Thus answer (b) is clearly the best answer. **Answer (a) is not correct.** In general, the law of the situs of real property controls choice of law questions concerning that real property. **Answer (c) is not correct.** In general, the law of the decedent's domicile at death provides the choice of law rules with respect to the survivor's right, if any, to an elective share.

   - Additional reference: See William M. McGovern, Jr. and Sheldon F. Kurtz, Wills, Trusts and Estates § 3.8 (3d ed. 2004).

12.   **The best answer is (c).** A provision in a will that purports to devise property to a devisee who shall hold the property as trustee, but which fails to specify the beneficiary of the trust is a semi-secret trust. **Answer (a) is not correct.** An honorary trust is a trust-like gift that is not intended to benefit the transferee and does not have any specific beneficiary who can enforce the trust as a gift, but has a specific non-charitable purpose. **Answer (b) is not correct.** A secret trust exists when a will purports to make an absolute gift, but there is an undisclosed agreement between T and the legatee that the latter will hold the property in trust for another. This differs from a semi-secret trust in that, in the case of a secret trust, the face of the will does not reveal that the testator/settlor intended to make a gift in trust. **Answer (d) is not correct.** To create a trust, a settlor must manifest an intent that one person hold the property for the benefit of another. Where the donor transfers property and expresses his "desire," "hope," or "wish" (or uses similar precatory language) that the transferee use the property to benefit a third party, the court will have to decide if the donor intended to impose a legal obligation on the transferee to hold the property in trust (in which case a true trust arises), or whether the donor merely intended to impose at most a moral obligation on the transferee. In the latter case, the donor has created a mere "precatory trust." Despite the name, this is no trust at all. **Answer (e) is not correct.** When a trust fails

or terminates of its own terms and the settlor has not directed what is then to happen to the property (or the settlor's direction cannot be carried out) a resulting trust arises by operation of law channeling the property back to the settlor (or the settlor's estate).

- Additional reference: See William M. McGovern, Jr. and Sheldon F. Kurtz, Wills, Trusts and Estates § 6.1 (3d ed. 2004).

13. **The best answer is (c).** A person's heirs are those who would take that person's property in intestacy if the person died intestate. In general, we determine a person's heirs at that person's death. Thus, ordinarily we would determine the testator's heirs at the testator's death. **But, answer (b) is not the best answer.** That is because the question involves a rule of construction, not a rule of law. What did Testator mean when he said "to Elizabeth for life and then to my heirs?" The will speaks at Testator's death. If Elizabeth is his only heir, then the devise is to Elizabeth for life, then to Elizabeth. This result appears incongruous. See Restatement (Second) of Property: Donative Transfers § 29.1 through § 29.5. The general rule is that a gift over to Testator's heirs is to be construed as a gift to the heirs of Testator determined as of Testator's death. But evidence of a contrary intent, will change this result. The issue is whether or not the incongruous result of devising to the same person a life estate and a vested remainder is sufficient evidence of a contrary intent. The Restatement (Second), cited above adopts the position that the incongruity is sufficient evidence. The rationale is that the testator likely did not intend for Elizabeth to be both the life tenant and a taker of the remainder. Most states follow the Restatement principle and thus would determine Testator's heirs as of Elizabeth's death in order to avoid the incongruity, provided Elizabeth is also an heir. Some states adopt the Restatement position only if Elizabeth is the only heir and some adopt it if Elizabeth is merely one of the heirs. In this latter circumstance, a few states will construe the language to mean "Testator's heirs, other than Elizabeth, determined at his death". But since that option was not offered in this question, that position is irrelevant to the answer. **Answer (a) is not the best answer,** but it is the result under most modern statutes dealing with this issue. See UPC Section 2-711. It is also the preferred result in the Restatement (Third) Property: Wills and Other Donative Transfers §16.1 (gift over to T's heirs means heirs of T at time of distribution rather than at T's death). Support for the rule stated in the Restatement (Third), however, comes primarily from statutory provisions rather than from case law.

14. **The best answer is (d).** See UPC §3-312. All of Jerry's assets pass outside of probate except for the $20,000 of stock and personal items.

Since most of the property passes outside of probate, she will not need to initiate a formal administration to clear up title to most of the property. **Thus, answer (a) is incorrect**. While Samantha may be able to claim ownership of the personal items solely because of possession, she will need to take some action to transfer title of the Rockwell stock from Jerry to her. **Thus, answer (c) is incorrect**. She cannot use the affidavit process because the value of the estate, even after accounting for debts, exceeds $5,000. See UPC §3-1201. **Thus, answer (b) is incorrect**. In some states this process is available for estates somewhat larger than $5,000. In Connecticut, for example, it is available for estates up to $20,000 in value, provided no real estate is involved. But as a general rule, the availability of an affidavit process in lieu of administration would not require that there be no minor children. As a result answer (b) is still incorrect. And **answer (e) is incorrect** because once she acquires title to the stock as a universal successor, she can sell it and use the proceeds to pay of the debt on the residence.

15.   **The best answer is (a)**. There is no sufficient evidence to prove whether Larry survived Jane and so the statute says that his property will be distributed as if he did survive her. For Jane (or Jane's estate) to take as beneficiary under the policy she would have to survive Larry because beneficiaries must survive in order to take. **Thus, answer (b) is incorrect**. Mildred can only inherit through Jane, but Jane did not survive long enough. Thus, **answer (c) is incorrect**. Since Jane did not survive, the contingent beneficiary provision kicks in and gives the insurance proceeds to Esther. If Larry had not named a contingent beneficiary, the proceeds would have gone to his estate (option (d)). But **answer (d) is incorrect** because he did name a contingent beneficiary.

16.   **The best answer is (a)**. The trust creates a contingent interest in Lawrence's heirs. The only contingency is that Dorothy die without any surviving issue. That contingency occurs at Dorothy's death and vests the heirs or their distributees at that time. Lawrence's heir, i.e., the person who would have inherited as his intestate heir if had died intestate, is his brother Benjamin. This would be true under the UPC intestacy scheme and the scheme of states generally. Some states provide for stepchildren to inherit, but typically not before siblings and their issue. Heirs are determined as of the moment of death and as of the Lawrence's death, his only heir was Benjamin. Benjamin's contingent interest was not destroyed by his death. Instead, it passed under his will to his wife, Millie. Thus, at Dorothy's death, Millie becomes vested and takes the full trust corpus. Note that a different result would occur under the UPC. Under UPC §2-711, the trust assets would go to Luke. But **answer (d) is incorrect**

because the question assumes that there is no applicable statute like §2-711.

17.   **The best answer is (d)**. UPC §2-711 provides that a gift over to heirs such as the remainder in Lawrence's trust should be distributed to "those persons, including the state, and in such shares as would succeed to the designated individual's intestate estate under the intestate succession law of the designated individual's domicile if the designated individual died when the disposition is to take effect in possession or enjoyment." The gift in the trust was to "my heirs" and so Lawrence is the designated individual. The persons who would take as his heirs if he had died at the time the trust ended (i.e., at Dorothy's death) are the children of his deceased brother Benjamin. Luke is the only child and so he is the person who will take the remainder interest.

18.   **The best answer is (e)**. UPC §2-804 revokes all testamentary gifts to an ex-spouse and to the ex-spouse's relatives. Thus the will cannot give property to either Willa or Stella. The property passes as if the spouse and all her relatives disclaimed. That leaves no one to take the property so the property escheats to the state. UPC §2-804 applies to any revocable gift in favor of an ex-spouse. Life insurance beneficiaries can be changed by the owner. Thus 2-804 applies to life insurance and so the gift of the life insurance proceeds to Willa is revoked as well. Since none of her relatives can take either, the life insurance proceeds go to the estate and escheat to the state along with the rest of the probate estate.

19.   **The best answer is (d)**, all of the above. The problem is that the description of the property is not very specific. Had Truman said "I give Annie the Ansel Adams photograph located in my desk drawer," there would be no problem. But the word "contents" is not very specific. While the will speaks as of death, we have to look at the time it was executed as well to see if we can determine what Truman intended. The facts state that we don't know when Truman purchased the photograph, so certainly if the challengers can prove that it was purchased after the execution of the will, they can argue that he did not intend to give Annie the photograph. **Thus answer (c) is certainly a viable argument**. And if the photograph was purchased after the will was executed and placed in the desk drawer at that time, the act of placing it there is akin to amending the will. Yet, there are no testamentary formalities (e.g., witnesses) to that action. **Thus, answer (b) is also a good argument**. Finally, we allow changes that occur after the execution of a will to affect its meaning, but we generally require that those changes constitute acts of independent significance. The act of storing a valuable photograph in a drawer may be significant but it doesn't stand on its own – so it isn't *independently* significant. In fact, most

people do not store valuable photographs in their desk drawers. If Truman had a photography gallery and was constantly changing what was hanging there, one might argue that hanging an Ansel Adams photograph on the wall of the gallery was an act of independent significance. In any event, the argument outlined in **answer (a) is certainly viable in this case. Thus (d) is the best answer**.

20.   **The best answer is (c)**. Trustees generally do not have standing to contest a will and it would certainly make no sense for a trustee named under the will to contest the will that names him (or her). If the trustee did not like the terms of the trust in the will, the trustee could resign and a successor trustee would be named. As a rule, trustees do not have a sufficient enough interest in the estate to allow them to challenge the will. **Answer (a) is clearly wrong** since adopted children are heirs and heirs can challenge. **Answer (b) is incorrect** because any beneficiary in an earlier will, contingent or otherwise, can argue that harm will result if the current will revoking that earlier will is admitted to probate. **Answer (d) is incorrect**. This person is not the wife of the testator because the first wife is still the legal spouse. But there are doctrines she can use to claim a portion of the estate. The most likely option is to claim that she is a putative spouse – i.e., that she had a good faith belief that they were married. Putative spouses are sometimes given an intestate share. Thus, a putative spouse should have standing to contest a will that cut her out completely.

21.   **The best answer is (e),** the state of M. When Will predeceases Betsy, the gift to him lapses. His estate cannot take. **Thus, answer (a) is incorrect**. The antilapse statute, §2-603 UPC, would save the gift for Will's son, Darwin, if Will had been related to Betsy as required by the statute. He would have to be a grandparent or descendant of a grandparent of Betsy or, alternatively, a stepchild of Betsy. He isn't, and **so answer (b) is wrong**. As a result, Betsy died intestate. Her closest relative is Colin, a grandchild of Betsy's mother's great aunt, Sarah. Sarah and Colin are descended not from Betsy's grandparents, but from her great-grandparents, who would have been the parents of great aunt Sarah. The UPC intestacy statutes stop at descendants of grandparents. More remote relatives, such as Colin, are not heirs. UPC §2-103. **Thus, answer (c) is wrong**. The property escheats and goes to the state of M.

22.   **The best answer is (d)**. The conveyance is irrevocable and so the interests are fixed upon delivery of the deed. Ellen has a vested life estate and a contingent remainder should she survive Harvey. If she does in fact survive him, she is certain to get the property. **Answer (a) is wrong** because Harvey can unilaterally sever the joint tenancy thereby destroying

the survivorship right. A unilateral severance can occur without Ellen's knowledge (e.g., Harvey transfers his interest in the property to his brother). It will convert the title into a tenancy in common. **Answer (b) is wrong** because the tenancy in common gives her only a 50% interest in the property and although the will leaves her the other 50% interest, a will can be revoked or amended at any time. The tenancy by the entirety is a better option than the first two options because there is no possible unilateral severance. Still, the tenancy will be revoked upon divorce since it is only available for married couples. Upon divorce the tenancy would convert to a tenancy in common. **Thus, answer (c) is not the best answer. Answer (e) is wrong** because the trust is revocable by Harvey. Thus it offers no protection.

23.   **The best answer is (a).** While there is no doubt that Decedent is the genetic father according to these facts, the amendment of the Probate Code as late as 2005 means that the legislature must have had cases of conception after death in mind when they drafted this language. By 2005, at least three states had reported cases involving the question of whether or not a child conceived after death could be an intestate heir. Several states have adopted statutes providing for inheritance in such cases provided there was written consent before death on the part of the Decedent. Several states, however, have rejected the possibility by amending their probate codes to provide that such children, conceived after death, will not inherit unless they are named in a will. The statute of State G, modeled on a Georgia statute, presents two problems: (1) It requires that the child be conceived before death, which was not the case, and (2) It requires that the child be born within ten months of the decedent's death, which is not likely to occur since impregnation did not occur until six months after death.

Some courts have been willing to construe language that appears to limit afterborn heirs to those conceived before the father's death liberally so as to include afterborns conceived after death. A liberal construction is in keeping with legislative intent to include afterborn heirs generally and is possible in cases in which the legislation was enacted long ago before legislators knew anything about new reproductive technologies. But in this case, with an enactment date of 2005, this afterborn child would have a very difficult time asking a probate court to construe the statute in a way that totally ignores its plain meaning.

Could the afterborn child attack the statute on constitutional grounds? Yes, the child could make an argument that the statute violates equal protection by invidiously discriminating against afterborn children who are conceived after death as compared with those conceived before death. But the state could defend based on its interest in seeing that estates are settled timely and that title to property is determined soon enough to ensure stability. If conception can occur at any time, then estates would have to be held open for lengthy periods of time to ensure that all children conceived post-death could receive an intestate share. Similar arguments were made in cases like *Trimble v. Gordon*, 430 U.S. 762 (1977), which challenged probate statutes that disinherited a father's children if born out of wedlock. The *Trimble* Court recognized the state interest in timeliness and stability, but held that the statute in that case was overbroad because it excluded nonmarital children from inheriting from their fathers even when paternity had been established during the father's lifetime. In similar fashion, a court could apply *Trimble* and hold that the G statute is overbroad in excluding too many after-conceived children. The lines could be redrawn to include a time limit that would sufficiently protect the after-conceived child and the interests of the state. If the statute were struck down on these grounds, then the child could make a claim, but would nonetheless still have to prove that he or she was a child of Decedent. The definition of parent and child, usually contained in the family law statutes, is not included in the facts of this problem. If the woman was inseminated after the death of decedent, it is possible under certain versions of the UPA that the sperm donor will not be considered a parent. He probably will not be considered a parent in any state unless there was some evidence of intent to become a parent. In any event, the question asks what the **Probate Court** is likely to do. The Probate Court is likely to follow the plain meaning of the statute and rule that the afterborn child is not an heir. In many states, the jurisdiction of the Probate Court is limited and so that court would not have jurisdiction to hear a constitutional challenge to the statute. As a result of all of these considerations, the Probate Court is likely to distribute the full estate to Decedent's mother as his intestate heir.

Answer (b) is incorrect because the UPC intestacy statute recognizes the surviving parent as heir to the exclusion of siblings. **Answer (c) is incorrect** because the child is excluded by the plain meaning of the statute. **Answer (d) is not the best answer** because the child is excluded by the plain meaning of the statute. **Answer (d) is the second best option** in this fact situation and could turn out to be the right outcome if the statute's constitutionality is successfully challenged and if the child can establish the required parent-child relationship, which should be possible with evidence of the father's intent. But answer (d) is not the best answer because the question asks what the Probate Court is likely to do. **Answer (e) is incorrect** because even if the mother became the child's guardian for purposes of holding the child's property, the child is still excluded from taking under the plain meaning of the statute.

24.   **The best answer is (c).** These facts present a classic purchase money resulting trust hypothetical. Gene provided the money for the purchase and the land was supposed to be his, but record legal title is vested in Frank. A resulting trust acknowledges Frank's legal title, but declares that the beneficial interest is vested in Gene. If all Frank owns is legal title and no beneficial interest, the property should not be part of his probate estate and Rose has no claim to it. **Answer (a) is wrong** because record title is only prima facie evidence of ownership. The facts indicate that Gene can rebut Frank's ownership by proving that he (Gene) provided the funds to purchase the property. **Answer (b) is incorrect** because a constructive trust is an equitable remedy to be used in cases in which a person in Frank's shoes has defrauded Gene or done something wrong. The constructive trust prevents the wrongdoer (or others) from benefiting from the wrong. But here Frank has done nothing wrong. Courts sometimes confuse constructive trust theories and resulting trust theories. Both produce the same end result and give the property to the person who ought to have beneficial ownership. But since you are asked to pick the best answer, the "resulting trust" solution is more accurate than "constructive trust."

        Answer (d) is wrong because even though courts often presume gifts in cases such as this where the monetary transfer occurs between family members, there appears to be enough evidence to rebut that presumption here and thus it is unlikely that Rose will win. **Answer (e) is also wrong**. While it would help Gene quite a bit if the deed indicated that Frank was acting on behalf of Gene, that is not the only theory under which Gene can win.

25.   **The best answer is (d)**, all of the above. The will that is offered for probate is the amended will which includes the revised Article V. The Testator never signed that will. Instead he signed the original will. The same argument is available for the two witness requirement. The witnesses signed the original will, not the amended will. The doctrine of integration requires that all pages of the will be together when the will is signed, but here, the last page, the amended Article V, was not integrated with the original will, which is the only will that was ever signed. Since all of these arguments are possible under this fact situation, none of them standing alone would be the best answer. **Answer (e) is incorrect because at least one of the arguments is available**.

1.   **The best answer is (e).** We cannot know who takes T's property unless we know T's intent. UPC 2-509 provides that if Will #2 in this problem is revoked by physical act (which it isn't), then Will #1 may be revived, but only if there is evidence that T intended to revive Will #1. Note that the presumption is against revival, so the burden of proof will be on the persons claiming under Will #1. . But in this case Will #2 is revoked by Will #3 and the rule in such cases is that Will #1 remains revoked unless it is clear from the terms of Will #3 that Will #1 was to be revived. Again, the presumption is that Will #1 is revoked and that there is no revival. Rebutting the presumption is more difficult when the revocation of Will #2 occurs by execution of a subsequent will, here, Will #3. That is because evidence of T's intent appears to be limited to the terms of Will #3. In this case, the terms of Will #3 say nothing explicit about T's intent to revive Will #1, but one could argue that it is fair to infer from the terms of Will #3 (no dispositions of property, only a revocation of Will #2 and no mention of Will #1) plus some other facts (e.g., Will #1 was never explicitly revoked and is still in the possession of the Testator) that T's intent was for Will #1 to take effect. If proponents of Will #1 lose on this argument, then the primary rule of "once revoked, always revoked" will apply and the property will pass via intestacy. Thus, **answer (e) is a better answer than answers (a) or (c),** because both options are possible solutions. **Answer (b) is clearly incorrect** because Will #3 is effective to revoke Will #2.

   - Additional reference: See William M. McGovern, Jr. and Sheldon F. Kurtz, Wills, Trusts and Estates § 5.3 (3d ed. 2004).

2.   **The best answer is (b).** When the holder of a power of appointment fails to exercise the power, the property passes to the takers in default, provided that the donor of the power named takers in default. Where the holder of a power of appointment fails to exercise the power and the donor of the power of appointment failed to name takers in default, the rules for passing of the appointive property are as follows: Where the power is a general power, the appointive property passes back to the donor or the donor's estate. Where the power is a special power, a court may imply takers in default if the class of permissible appointees is a defined limited class. In such a case, the appointive property will be divided equally among the implied takers in default. The class of permissible appointees is a defined limited class if the class is not very large and it is easy to identify the permissible appointees and divide the property among them. An example where this would not be the case is where the special power

could be exercised in favor of anyone except the donee, the donee's creditors, the donee's estate, and the creditors of the donee's estate. Where the power is a special power, the appointive property passes back to the donor or the donor's estate if the class of permissible appointees is not a defined limited class.

In the hypothetical, Harold died intestate. He failed, therefore, to exercise the testamentary power that he held. Gary, the donor of the power of appointment, failed to name takers in default. The power is a special power: The class of permissible appointees does not include the donee, the donee's creditors, the donee's estate, or the creditors of the donee's estate. The class of permissible appointees consists of three identified individuals - Oscar, Oprah, and Andrew. This is an example of a defined, limited class of permissible appointees. A court, therefore, is likely to imply that Oscar, Oprah, and Andrew are the takers in default. The appointive property will pass, therefore, to Oscar, Oprah, and Andrew in equal shares. **Answer (e) is not the best answer** because the class of permissible appointees for this special power of appointment is a defined limited class. Were the class of permissible appointees for this special power of appointment not a defined limited class, the appointive property would pass back to Gary or Gary's estate and answer (e) would be the best answer.

Answer (a) is incorrect. Property subject to a special power of appointment that the holder of the power does not exercise does not pass to the estate of the holder. (Where the holder of a general power of appointment makes an ineffective appointment, as opposed to failing to exercise the appointment, the appointive property might pass to the holder or his estate under a doctrine called "capture" if the donee manifested an intent to assume control of the appointive property for all purposes. The issue is whether the holder would prefer that, given an ineffective exercise, the property pass to her estate or would prefer that the property pass to the takers in default or back to the donor.) Indeed, since Harold held a special power of appointment, by definition, he could not exercise the power in favor of his estate. Thus, answer (a) would not make sense at all.

Answer (c) is not correct. An appointee is one in whose favor a power has been exercised. In the hypothetical, Harold did not exercise the power. Therefore, there were no appointees and no class of appointees. Rather, there was a class of permissible appointees.

- Additional reference: See William M. McGovern, Jr. and Sheldon F. Kurtz, Wills, Trusts and Estates § 10.4 (3d ed. 2004).

3.   **The best answer is (e).** This gift will abate in part with the general gifts and in part with the specific gifts. Abatement is the reduction of a testamentary gift in order to satisfy an estate obligation of a higher priority. For example, testamentary gifts may be subject to abatement so that the estate can satisfy obligations to creditors. If there is not enough property in the estate to pay all of the creditors and satisfy all of the testamentary gifts, some or all of the testamentary gifts will be subject to abatement. In general, the order in which testamentary gifts abate is determined by the classification of the gifts. A common order of abatement is – first, residuary gifts abate; second, if necessary, general gifts abate; third, if necessary, specific gifts abate. Within a class, generally gifts abate pro-rata. Gifts to certain devisees, however, might be given a preferred order of abatement. For example, a general gift to a relative might abate only after all general gifts to non-relatives have fully abated, or a gift to a spouse might abate last regardless of the class of gift.

The gift of "$500,000 to A, to be paid from the sale of my home, or from other sources if the sale is insufficient" is a demonstrative gift. A demonstrative gift is a gift of a type or quantity of property (here - $500,000) to be paid out of a specified asset in the estate (here – the testator's home) if that specified asset is available and sufficient to satisfy the gift, and to be paid out of general assets of the estate if that specified asset is not available and sufficient to satisfy the gift. Demonstrative gifts abate with specific gifts to the extent that the specified asset identified in the gift is available to satisfy the gift, and they abate with general gifts for amounts beyond that. See UPC § 3-902.

In the hypothetical, the specified asset identified in the gift – the home – is available but is not sufficient to satisfy the gift. The home sold for only $100,000. These proceeds are not sufficient to pay the $500,000 gift to A. General assets of the estate will be used to pay the $400,000 of the gift in addition to the $100,000 of the gift payable out of the proceeds of the house sale. If the gift to A is subject to abatement, it will abate with the specific gifts to the extent that the specified asset identified in the gift – the house – is available to satisfy the gift, and will abate with general gifts for amounts beyond that. That is – $400,000 of the gift will be treated as a general gift and will abate with the other general gifts; the remaining $100,000 of the gift will be treated as a specific gift and will abate with the other specific gifts. For the purposes of abatement, it might help to conceptualize the $500,000 demonstrative gift as two gifts – a specific gift for the amount that the asset specified in the gift can satisfy, and a general gift for the remaining amount of the gift. Thus, one might conceptualize the gift in the hypothetical as a $100,000 specific gift and a $400,000 general gift. The $100,000 specific gift will abate with the other specific gifts, and the $400,000 general gift will abate with the other general gifts.

- Additional reference: See William M. McGovern, Jr. and Sheldon F. Kurtz, Wills, Trusts and Estates § 8.2 (3d ed. 2004).

4.   **The best answer is (d).** Under the per capita at each generation approach, property that is assigned for calculation purposes to an individual who has predeceased the intestate property owner but left issue who survive the intestate property owner is not necessarily distributed to the descendants of the predeceasing individual. Rather, the property is gathered back and brought down to the next generation, where the assignment of shares begins anew. Under the per capita at each generation approach, (1) we begin dividing the intestate property into shares at the first generation level below the intestate decedent where we find a living descendant. (2) We assign a share to (a) any living descendant in that generation and (b) any predeceased descendant in that generation who left issue who survived the intestate property owner. (3)(a) Any share assigned to a living descendant of the intestate property owner goes to that living descendant of the intestate property owner. (3)(b) Any share assigned to a predeceased descendant of the intestate property owner who left issue that survived the intestate property owner is gathered back up and becomes available for assignment in the next generation according to the same steps 1-3.

A necessary result of this per-capita-at-each-generation calculation is that persons who take a share of the intestate estate will take the same proportion of the estate as others in the same generation as themselves who take a portion of the estate. That is to say – persons who are equally related to the intestate decedent and who take a share of the intestate estate, take the same proportion of the estate.

5.   **The best answer is (e).** Section 503 of the Uniform Trust Code provides that an otherwise valid "spendthrift provision is unenforceable against . . . a beneficiary's child, spouse, or former spouse who has a judgment or court order against the beneficiary for support or maintenance." This is in accordance with the rule in many jurisdictions. The Uniform Trust Code does not provide an exception to a valid spendthrift provision for tort judgment creditors. This also would seem to be in accordance with the prevailing rule, although there is not much case law on point.

- Additional reference: See William M. McGovern, Jr. and Sheldon F. Kurtz, Wills, Trusts and Estates § 13.1 (3d ed. 2004).

6.   **The best answer is (d).** Section 505(a)(1) of the Uniform Trust Code provides that "[d]uring the lifetime of the settlor, the property of a revocable trust is subject to claims of the settlor's creditors." This is not the traditional rule, but it is the prevailing rule today. Answers A and B reflect the traditional rule, but do not reflect the Uniform Trust Code position and do not reflect the rule in most American jurisdictions today. **Answers (a), (b), and (e), therefore, are not the best answer.** The creditors of a settlor of a revocable trust can reach the trust assets regardless of whether the trust contains a spendthrift provision. **Answer (c), therefore, is not correct.**

   - Additional reference: See William M. McGovern, Jr. and Sheldon F. Kurtz, Wills, Trusts and Estates § 13.1 (3d ed. 2004).

7.   **The best answer is (c).** The elective share available to a surviving spouse is one of the principal limitations on testamentary freedom. It is designed to provide a portion of the decedent's estate to the surviving spouse even if the decedent intentionally disinherited the surviving spouse. In contrast, both the omitted spouse statute and the anti-lapse statute are default rules that are designed to promote the testator's donative intent and that can be made inapplicable by the testator. The omitted spouse statute provides a share of the decedent's estate to the surviving spouse, in certain circumstances, when the decedent had executed his will prior to his marriage to the surviving spouse and that will fails to contemplate his marriage to the surviving spouse. The theory is that the decedent likely would have wanted to provide for the surviving spouse but overlooked the need to modify his estate plan after his marriage. The anti-lapse statute does not prevent lapse but does change the common law result of lapse. The theory of the anti-lapse statute is that a testator who devises property to a beneficiary who predeceases him and who was within a specified set of relationships with respect to the testator would want the predeceasing beneficiary's issue (in the typical statute) to take her gift rather than having the result of lapse under the common law.

   - Additional reference: See William M. McGovern, Jr. and Sheldon F. Kurtz, Wills, Trusts and Estates §§ 3.6, 3.7 and 8.3 (3d ed. 2004).

8.   **The best answer is (a).** This is a residuary gift. A residuary gift is a gift of whatever remains in the estate after the payment of all specific, general and demonstrative gifts. In this case, T did not make any specific, general, or demonstrative gifts. "All of my estate" is, therefore, what is left over after all of the specific, general, and demonstrative gifts are paid. This is not a general gift. A general gift is a gift of a certain quantity or type of

property, but it does not refer only to, and is not payable only out of property found in the estate at T's death. **Answer (b), therefore, is not correct.** This is not a specific gift. A specific gift is a gift of a particular thing that can be identified as part of the estate. **Answer (c), therefore, is not correct.** This is not a demonstrative gift. A demonstrative gift is a quantity or type (but not a specific item) of property to be satisfied out of a specific asset if available, otherwise from general assets of the estate. **Answer (d), therefore, is not correct.**

9.   **The best answer is (b).** The question gives the accepted definition for a secret trust. **Answer (a) is not correct.** An honorary trust is a trust-like gift that is not intended to benefit the transferee and does not have any specific beneficiary who can enforce the trust as a gift, but has a specific non-charitable purpose. **Answer (c) is not correct.** A provision in a will that purports to devise property to a devisee who shall hold the property as trustee, but which fails to specify the beneficiary of the trust or the important terms of the trust is a semi-secret trust. This differs from a secret trust in that the face of the will reveals that the testator/settlor intended to make a gift in trust. **Answer (d) is not correct.** To create a trust, a settlor must manifest an intent that one person hold the property for the benefit of another. Where the donor transfers property and expresses his "desire," "hope," or "wish" (or uses similar precatory language) that the transferee use the property to benefit a third party, the court will have to decide if the donor intended to impose a legal obligation on the transferee to hold the property in trust (in which case a true trust arises), or whether the donor merely intended to impose at most a moral obligation on the transferee. In the latter case, the donor has created a mere "precatory trust." Despite the name, this is no trust at all. **Answer (e) is not correct.** When a trust fails or terminates of its own terms and the settlor has not directed what is then to happen to the property (or the settlor's direction cannot be carried out) a resulting trust arises by operation of law channeling the property back to the settlor (or the settlor's estate).

- Additional reference: See William M. McGovern, Jr. and Sheldon F. Kurtz, Wills, Trusts and Estates § 6.1 (3d ed. 2004).

10.   **The best answer is (b).** In general, the standard for mental capacity to execute a will is thought to be not as high as the standard for mental capacity to deal with one's property during life, at least insofar as irrevocable inter vivos transfers are concerned. One rationale for this distinction is that the property owner who imprudently manages his property interests during life might consequently lack the resources needed for his own support. Lifetime support is not an issue that arises

out of a decedent having improvidently executed a will. Given that the standard for mental capacity to manage one's property during life is higher than the standard for mental capacity to execute a will, we cannot conclude from the fact that Marc has been adjudicated incompetent to manage his property that Marc lacks the capacity to execute a will. **Answers (a) and (c), therefore, are not correct. Answer (d) is not correct.** The standard for mental capacity to revoke a will is the same as the standard for mental capacity to execute a will.

- Additional reference: See William M. McGovern, Jr. and Sheldon F. Kurtz, Wills, Trusts and Estates § 7.2 (3d ed. 2004).

11.   **The best answer is (a).** A testator might seek to discourage a will contest after his death by including in the will a no-contest clause that provides for forfeiture of an interest under the will if the devisee of that interest challenges the validity of the will or provisions of the will. A jurisdiction's strict enforcement of such no-contest clauses is likely to discourage meritless litigation. For example, a would-be contestant who calculates that he might favorably settle a suit that he knows objectively lacks merit might recalculate that the danger of losing the property that the testator devised to him outweighs the chance of increasing his take through such litigation. But such strict enforcement of no-contest clauses might also discourage litigation that we as a society think should be brought – litigation that challenges the validity of a will that a good argument could be made does not represent the testator's true wishes, perhaps because the will appears likely to have been procured by fraud or undue influence or appears likely to have been executed while the testator lacked capacity. (The stronger the case for invalidity of the will, however, the less likely that the no-contest clause will discourage the litigation regardless of the jurisdictions' strict enforcement of no-contest clauses. If the will contestant is successful in challenging the will, the no-contest clause itself (as part of the invalid will) will be of no effect. The likely success of the litigation (and relatedly, the merits of the contest), therefore, should influence the decision as to whether to bring the contest even in a jurisdiction that strictly enforces no-contest clauses.) The drafters of the UPC sought to balance the interest in discouraging litigation that is without merit, family disharmony arising from such litigation, and the defaming of the deceased testator incident to such litigation on the one hand with an interest in not discouraging litigation that would expose fraud, undue influence, a lack of mental capacity, or other defects in the will, on the other hand, by providing that a court should enforce a no-contest clause only if the suit lacks probable cause. The law is most jurisdictions is in accord. Thus, if the would-be-contestant strongly believes in the merits of his contest, the no-contest clause would not be as

likely to discourage him from bringing the challenge to the will as it would in a jurisdiction that strictly enforced such no-contest clauses.

- Additional reference: See William M. McGovern, Jr. and Sheldon F. Kurtz, Wills, Trusts and Estates § 12.1 (3d ed. 2004).

12.   **The best answer is (a).** At common law, when a specific gift, general gift, or demonstrative gift lapsed, the gift passed to the residuary taker or takers. **Answers (b), (c), and (d), therefore are not correct.** At common law, however, there was no residue of a residue. This meant that, a residuary devise that lapsed passed by intestacy. **Answer (e), therefore, is not correct.**

13.   **The best answer is (a).** Zachary has a remainder that is subject to a condition subsequent and is not subject to a condition precedent. A remainder in an ascertained person that is subject to a condition subsequent and is not subject to a condition precedent is a vested remainder subject to divestment. The Red Cross's interest will divest Zachary's interest if the condition subsequent occurs. Because the Red Cross has a divesting interest it cannot be a remainder. Remainders do not divest previous estates. An interest in a transferee that divests an earlier estate is an executory interest. If the interest divests an interest in another transferee it is a shifting executory interest. (An interest that divests an interest in a transferor is a springing executory interest.) **Answer (b) is not correct.** As noted above, because the Red Cross's interest is a divesting interest it cannot be a remainder. **Answers (c) and (d) are not correct.** For a remainder to be contingent it must be (1) subject to a condition precedent, or (2) created in an un ascertained person. Zachary's remainder does not meet either condition. Moreover, as noted above, the Red Cross does not have a remainder at all. **Answer (e) is not correct.** A springing executory interest divests a preceding estate in the transferor. The Red Cross's interest will divest a preceding estate, if any, in a transferee. The Red Cross's interest, therefore, is a shifting executory interest.

14.   **The best answer is (b)**. UPC 2-702 requires beneficiaries under a life insurance policy (a governing document) to survive by 120 hours in order to be treated as surviving. Since Jane did not survive Larry by 120 hours, she is deemed to have predeceased him. As a result, the contingent beneficiary provision in the life insurance policy kicks in and the proceeds should be paid to Esther.

15.   **The best answer is (d).** Under UPC 2-103, the lineal descendants take by representation. UPC 2-106 defines representation to require dividing the

estate at the first generational level where there are surviving descendants entitled to take. In this fact situation, that is at the grandchild level. The estate is to be divided into as many shares as there descendants alive and able to take (that would be three) and deceased descendants who left descendants who can take as their representatives (that would two additional shares, one for William, who is the parent of Kim and Karl and one for the unnamed grandchild who was the parent of Kathy). Thus the estate should be divided into five shares. Each of the grandchildren takes his or her one-fifth share. That leaves two fifths to be distributed to the great grandchildren. The UPC principle is to distribute equally among descendants at the same generational level. Thus, the great grandchildren should all get an equal share of the 2/5ths that is available to be distributed to their generation. Since there are three of them, they each take one-third of 2/5th, which results in 2/15ths each.

The language in 2-106 provides that the remaining shares are combined (this would be the 2 one-fifth shares for each of the deceased grandchildren) and divided among the surviving descendants at the next level (Kim and Karl and Kathy at the great grandchild level) as if the surviving descendants (e.g., all grandchildren) had all predeceased. What this means is that the balance of the estate (here the 2/5ths share) will be distributed per capita at the great grandchild level because if there were no surviving grandchildren, the statute would call for per capita distribution at the great grandchild level. That is a very indirect way of saying that the remaining part of the estate will be distributed per capita at the next generation, with a share going to each surviving descendant at that generation, who is a descendant of a predeceased descendant. Here, there are no predeceased great grandchildren leaving issue. So we can stop at this generation.

16. **The best answer is (b)**. While many jurisdictions continue to refuse to correct scrivener's errors, this case involves an ambiguity rather than a mistake. **Thus answer (a) is incorrect**. The rule regarding latent ambiguities is that the court will allow extrinsic evidence to help clarify the ambiguity. The clause in Maureen's will contains two latent ambiguities. We don't know the ambiguity concerning the property description until someone points out that she doesn't own 214 Dover Street. **That makes answer (d) incorrect** since it describes this ambiguity as a patent one (i.e, ambiguous on the face of the will). And we don't know that the gift to Annie is uncertain until we know that there are three people who claim to be the intended beneficiary. **Answer (c) cannot be correct** because the testator's intent was clearly stated: the house was to go to one person named Annie, not three. That leaves answer (b) as the best answer and it is in fact what most courts will do.

17.　　**The best answer is (c).** The trust creates a future interest in Susan's then living heirs. Susan's heirs, determined at the time of her death, are her two sons, Thomas and Samuel. For either of them to take, two things must happen: (1) Thomas must die with no surviving issue and (2) the heirs must be then living. #1 did occur, but not #2. Neither of the heirs was then living. Thus the interest fails and the remainder reverts to Susan's estate. Since the gift was in the residuary clause of her will, this reversionary interest passes via intestacy to Susan's heirs – who only had to survive Susan to become heirs. Susan's heirs were Thomas and Samuel so the trust assets must be divided between their estates. **Answer (a) is incorrect** because Thomas cannot inherit to the exclusion of Samuel. **Answer (b) is incorrect** because Samuel cannot inherit to the exclusion of Thomas. **Answer (d) is also incorrect.** Rachel can't take in her own right because she was not literally one of Susan's heirs. Her father, Samuel, was alive at Susan's death and his existence prevented Rachel from being an heir. She may ultimately be the distributee of Samuel's estate, but we don't know that. Samuel may have left a will naming someone else as beneficiary. If so, that is the person who will take from Samuel's estate.

18.　　**The best answer is (b).** While the witnesses can sign after the testator's death, they must sign within a reasonable time. Six months later does not seem reasonable. Both the lawyer and Clara were aware of the fact that the execution of the codicil had not been completed. Clara was sufficiently healthy for a while. There are no facts that suggest it was reasonable for everyone to wait six months to finish the signing ceremony. **Answer (a) is wrong** because the witnesses don't have to witness the signing of the codicil for it to be effective. Witnessing her acknowledgement of her signature is sufficient. **Answer (c) is wrong.** The lawyer witnessed Clara's acknowledgement and there is nothing to prevent him from being a witness. **Answer (d) is wrong** because the witnesses must sign within a reasonable time. **Answer (e) is wrong** because a state with a UPC-style execution statute has decided that the best way to relax formalities is to reduce the formalities required. Such states are not likely to adopt a substantial compliance approach once they have already relaxed the formalities. See *Estate of Peters,* 107 N.J. 263, 526 A.2d 1005 (1987)(holding on similar facts that the doctrine of substantial compliance could not be used to validate the will).

19.　　**The best answer is (d).** While this is a joint will, all that means is that the single document can be probated twice, once at Hank's death and then again at Wilma's death, if she hasn't revoked it. UPC §2-514 deals with contracts concerning succession, in which joint and mutual wills are sometimes used in connection with a contract not to revoke. §2-514 makes it difficult to prove that there was a contract not to revoke unless the terms of the contract are spelled out in the will. Here, we simply have a joint will and not a contract not to revoke. **Thus answer (a), while true, is irrelevant**. The point is that Wilma did not revoke. The will is still available to be probated as her will. This fact situation is no different from a situation in which Hank executes a will leaving everything to Wilma if she survives and if not, to his children, and then Wilma executes a will leaving everything to Hank if he survives, and if not, to her children. Hank dies and his will operates to give everything to Wilma. Then Wilma dies never having revoked her will. It leaves everything she owns to her children. **Answer (b) is wrong** because under the UPC the witnesses do not need to witness the signing of the will if they witness instead the acknowledgement of the signature by the testator. **Answer (c) is wrong** because UPC §2-301 does not give anything to a pretermitted spouse if the premarital will leaves all the property to children of the testator. Since Wilma's will leaves everything to the children, Henry gets nothing under this provision. Henry can claim his elective share, however. Under UPC §2-202, if they were married two years, he can claim 6% of the augmented estate. The children will get the rest. **Answer (e)** is wrong because under the elective share provision, he will take the 6% share rather than nothing.

20.   **The best answer is (d)**. Putting burial instructions in the will is generally a bad idea. Burial often happens before the will is read by the people closest to the decedent. **That makes both answers (a) and (c) unattractive**. And besides, there is no way to legally bind the executor to follow burial instructions. In fact, in this case, the executor might think it better to give the $20,000 of jewelry to the living beneficiaries rather than bury it. **That makes answer (b) impractical**. And restricting payment of burial expenses is not likely to help since they are not likely to exceed $20,000. **Answer (e) is incorrect** because the power of attorney is revoked at her death. That leaves answer (d). A present gift in trust would put the beneficiary on notice that if he carried out her wishes, he would be rewarded. If this person is someone who is not even named in the will, the trade off between burying the jewelry and giving it to beneficiaries does not exist. But the sum must be substantial enough to make it worth the person's time to carry out and it must be substantial enough to resist being bought out by the beneficiaries who would otherwise be entitled to the jewelry.

21.   **The best answer is (e)**. Most states have a slayer rule that will prevent Mary from inheriting from Henry since she is responsible for his death. But before there were slayer statutes, courts formulated an equitable remedy in such cases to prevent a wrongdoer (a slayer) from benefiting from the wrong (here, the killing). Thus, **answer (a) is not the best answer** since, in the absence of a statute, the state is likely to apply the

equitable remedy. **Answer (b) is not the best answer** because, even though ERISA pre-empts state law, there is likely a federal common law rule that would prevent a killer from inheriting in these circumstances. The *Egelhoff* case, decided by the Supreme Court in 2001 (see 532 U.S. 141), held that ERISA pre-empted a state law that revoked upon divorce a life insurance and pension plan benefit in favor of the ex-wife. But the Court stated in dicta that ERISA was not likely to pre-empt the state slayer statute. Cases decided after *Egelhoff* have overwhelmingly held that ERISA does not protect a slayer who is a named beneficiary of the victim's pension plan or related life insurance policy. See, e.g., *Atwater v. Nortel Networks, Inc.*, 388 F. Supp. 2d 610 (M.D.N.C. 2005). **Answer (c) is incorrect** because Mary is only entitled to her half of the community property. She cannot receive Henry's share because of the slayer statute, the equitable doctrine under state law, or because the life insurance is covered by ERISA and federal common law which also adopts an equitable remedy to prevent slayers from benefiting. **Answer (d) is wrong because both (a) and (b) are wrong. Answer (e) is best** because application of the slayer rule would give the assets to the alternative beneficiaries, in this case the children. There is nothing to prevent them from then gifting the assets to their mother.

22. **The best answer is (b)**. See §2-511 UPC. At common law a problem arose if a Testator left property to a trust that was either created after the execution of the will or was modified after the execution of the will. The common law doctrine of incorporation by reference could validate such gifts only if the trust was in existence at the time the will was signed. Answer E looks like it might be correct at common law. But these facts occur in a UPC state. Thus, **answer (e) is incorrect. Answer (a) is incorrect**. The creation of an irrevocable trust funded with $1.0 million should satisfy the "acts of independent significance" doctrine. **Answer (c) is incorrect** because §2-511, which has been adopted in most states, applies to trusts created by persons other than the testator. **Answer (d) is incorrect**. The interests vest 20 years from creation which is within the time period of the Rule Against Perpetuities (lives in being plus 21 years).

23. **The best answer is (e)**. The questions asks for statements that are not true, i.e., that are false. The best way to answer a question like this is to mark each option as true or false. The false options are the correct answers. A survivor can disclaim the joint tenancy property at the death of the first joint tenant. See §2-1107 UPC. The IRS has in the past questioned whether a disclaimer of the property that comes to the survivor as a result of the survivorship right is valid for tax purposes since the disclaimer must occur within 9 months of the creation of the interest in the property. The argument is that the survivorship right and thus all interests that flow from

it are created at the moment the joint tenancy is created. At common law there is no real transfer of anything at the death of the first joint tenant. Instead the surviving joint tenant (or tenants) merely continue to enjoy the same estate as before although now it is enlarged. But current state probate law (as indicated in the UPC) and tax law both recognize the right of the survivor to disclaim the interest that is at least constructively being transferred at death. So, if there's a joint tenancy between A and B, presumptively 50/50, and A dies, then B can disclaim the 50% additional share that is constructively transferred to B at the time of A's death. **Thus, answer (a) is false. But it is not the best answer. Answer (b) is true.** The primary reason to use a joint tenancy arrangement is to avoid probate. The title passes to the survivor outside of probate. **Since the question asked for untrue answers, answer (b) is wrong. Answer (c)** also contains a non-true (false) statement about joint tenancies. Joint tenancies can be unilaterally severed into tenancies in common. The tenants do not all have to agree. **Thus, answer (c) is false, but it is not the best answer. Answer (d) is wrong** because one of the above answers is true and thus does not meet the "not true" requirement of the question. **Answer (e) is best because both (a) and (c) are false** (i.e., not true).

24.   **The best answer is (d).** In 1977 the Supreme Court ruled in *Trimble v. Gordon*, 430 U.S. 762, that a statute that prevented nonmarital children from inheriting from their fathers violated the equal protection clause. One year later, in *Lalli v. Lalli*, 439 U.S. 259 (1978), the Court ruled that a New York statute survived an equal protection challenge when it limited the right of nonmarital children to inherit from their fathers to cases in which paternity had been established during the father's lifetime by a court of competent jurisdiction. *Lalli* would thus seem to bar S's claim. However, *Lalli* can be distinguished because the child in that case, despite having plenty of time to establish paternity, had not done so. S, by contrast has not had a reasonable time in which to establish paternity since the father died before S was born. Even assuming that paternity could be established before birth, the amount of available time to do so was less than 9 months. Cases addressing the constitutionality of limitations on the rights of nonmarital children tend to be very fact sensitive. In cases involving the establishment of paternity for child support payments, the Court has struck down state statutes of limitations in a number of cases, holding that there must be a reasonable amount of time for a child to bring a paternity action. See generally *Clark v. Jeter*, 486 U.S. 108 (1988), striking down a Pennsylvania six year statute and discussing earlier cases that struck down a two year statute (Tennessee) and a one year statute (Texas). While these cases can be distinguished because they involved child support and liability for child support does not generally survive a father's death, they do suggest that each case focusing on a nonmarital

child's treatment under state statute must be analyzed on the basis of the particular facts. Furthermore, it can be argued that for children in S's position, who are given no opportunity to seek a paternity order at any time after their birth, they are completely excluded from the right to inherit, which violates equal protection. Despite the fact that *Lalli* can be cited against S, answer (d) is still the "best" answer.

Answer (a) is wrong because there is no such thing as constructive marriage. Some states recognize common law marriage. But that doctrine only applies to cases in which the couple has agreed to be presently married and is holding themselves out as married. M and F, by contrast, were intending to be married in the future. **Answer (b) is wrong** because no matter how unfair it may be, S will have to establish a legal claim in order to succeed in court. **Answer (c) is wrong** because no one has a fundamental right to inherit. American law allows testators to disinherit their children, even their minor children to whom they owe a duty of support. For that reason, **answer (e) is also wrong**. At common law the duty to support ends at death, absent a contractual obligation on the part of the father. Some states have changed the common law rule by statute. See Gina Mecurio, The Duty to Support Minor Children Does Not Extend to the Estate of a Deceased, but Ends at that Parent's Death, 42 Duq. L. Rev. 905 (2004)(analyzing Pennsylvania law). In addition, intestacy laws include a decedent's children, not because of any obligation of support, but rather because most people who die without a will are presumed to intend that their children inherit.

25.   **The best answer is (c).** It is very difficult to prove abuse of discretion by a trustee, but bad faith, animus toward the beneficiary, and similar improper motives will establish abuse. Here the Trustee is making the decision in order to protect a potential competitor of Tim, which seems a total abuse of discretion since the direction in the trust is to make decisions that are in the best interest of the beneficiaries. (Besides, all trustees have a duty to act in the best interests of the beneficiaries.) If Tim can prove that the Trustee's decision was in fact based on a desire to protect a non-beneficiary of the trust, then the decision will be considered a breach of the duty of loyalty, which in turn is a breach of trust. The remedy for this breach may not be to reverse the decision, but rather to remove the trustee and have a new trustee consider the request. Since Tim is not guaranteed that a different trustee will distribute the requested income, **answer (b) is incorrect. Answer (d) is also incorrect since it includes option (b). Answer (a) is incorrect** because a trustee never has absolute discretion. The discretion must be exercised in good faith.

ANSWER KEY
EXAM 5

1.   **The correct answer is (a).** Sonny takes all because he is related to the decedent in the 6th degree, while both Buddy and Happy are related to the decedent in the 7th degree. In a degree of kinship system, each surviving relative is assigned a degree of kinship with respect to the decedent. The surviving relative with the nearest degree of kinship takes the intestate property. (Note that the degree of kinship system is not a representative system; takers take only in their own right, not as representatives of a predeceasing relative.) If two or more surviving relatives are related to the decedent in the same degree, in most jurisdictions, they will divide the property. In some jurisdictions, however, a parentelic preference is applied so that of those surviving relatives related to the decedent in the same degree, the relative (or relatives) in the lowest parentela takes the property.

To calculate the degree of kinship between the decedent and a surviving relative: (1) find the first ancestor in common between the decedent and the surviving relative; (2) count generations up from the decedent to the common ancestor; and (3) count generations down from the common ancestor to the surviving relative. Adding the number of generations in steps 2 and 3 will give you the degree of kinship. Repeat this process for each surviving relative who might take an intestate share. The surviving relative (or relatives) with the lowest number (the nearest degree of kinship) wins.

Applying these steps to the hypothetical:
Sonny is related to the decedent in the 6th degree. We count 4 generations up from the decedent to the decedent's great-great grandparents (the first common ancestors between the decedent and Sonny). We then count down 2 generations to Sonny. $4 + 2 = 6$.
Buddy is related to the decedent in the 7th degree. We count 3 generations up from the decedent to the decedent's great grandparents (the first common ancestors between the decedent and Buddy). We then count down 4 generations to Buddy. $3 + 4 = 7$.
Happy is related to the decedent in the 7th degree. We count 2 generations up from the decedent to the decedent's grandparents (the first common ancestors between the decedent and Happy). We then count down 5 generations to Happy. $2 + 5 = 7$.

Because Sonny is related to the decedent in the 6th degree, while Buddy and Happy are both related to the decedent in the 7th degree, Sonny take the entire intestate estate.

- Additional reference: See William M. McGovern, Jr. and Sheldon F. Kurtz, Wills, Trusts and Estates § 2.2 (3d ed. 2004).

2. **The correct answer is (c).** Happy takes all because she is a second-line collateral, while Buddy is a third-line collateral, and Sonny is a fourth-line collateral.

The first step to understanding how the parentelic system works is to understand what a "line" (aka a "parentela") is. A line (in relation to any individual) is an ancestor and all of the descendants of that ancestor, excluding any descendants who are included in a lower line. For example, a decedent's first-line relations would be that decedent's parents and any descendants of the parents (excluding the decedent and descendants of the decedent). The decedent's second-line relations would be the decedent's grandparents and any descendants of the grandparents, excluding the first-line relations (decedent's parents and any descendants of the parents) and also excluding the decedent and descendants of the decedent. And so on. Notice that we can figure out which line any particular relative is in by counting generations up from the decedent to the *first* common ancestor between the decedent and that relative. Thus, the first-line relations are descended from the decedent's parents (one generation up), the second-line relations are descended from the decedent's grandparents (two generations up) but not the decedent's parents, the third-line relations are descended from the decedent's great-grandparents (three generations up) but not the decedent's parents or grandparents, and so on. A parentela is conceptually practically the same as a line, except that because we begin numbering parentelas with the decedent and his issue, the number for a parentela is always one less than the number for the corresponding line. Thus, the first line is the second parentela, the second line is the third parentela, the third line is the fourth parentela, and so on. (The decedent and his issue are in the first parentela but not in any line.)

A second important point to understand about the parentelic system is that a living relative in a lower line takes to the exclusion of any relative in a higher line. For example, if a second-line collateral is alive, no collateral from the third-line or any higher line will take any of the intestate estate.

Finally (although it is not relevant to resolution of the hypothetical presented in this question), it is important to know that the parentelic system generally is a representational system. That is, under the parentelic system, a relation of the decedent in the lowest line in which any relation of the decedent is alive may take by representation from a predeceasing ancestor in the same line.

To answer the question, we need to figure out which line each of the claimants is in. The intestate and Happy have as their first common ancestor the intestate's grandparents (two generations up from the intestate). Happy, therefore is a second-line collateral. The intestate and Buddy have as their first common ancestor the intestate's great-grandparents (three generations up from the intestate). Buddy, therefore is a third-line collateral. The intestate and Sonny have as their first common ancestor the intestate's great-great-grandparents (four generations up from the intestate). Sonny, therefore is a fourth-line collateral. Happy takes all because she is a second-line collateral, while Buddy is a third-line collateral, and Sonny is a fourth-line collateral.

- Additional reference: See William M. McGovern, Jr. and Sheldon F. Kurtz, Wills, Trusts and Estates § 2.2 (3d ed. 2004).

3.   **The best answer is (d).** Abatement is the reduction of a testamentary gift in order to satisfy an estate obligation of a higher priority. For example, testamentary gifts may be subject to abatement so that the estate can satisfy obligations to creditors. If there is not enough property in the estate to pay all of the creditors and satisfy all of the testamentary gifts, some or all of the testamentary gifts will be subject to abatement. In general, the order in which testamentary gifts abate is determined by the classification of the gifts. The most common order of abatement is – first, residuary gifts abate; second, if necessary, general gifts abate; third, if necessary, specific gifts abate. Within a class, generally gifts abate pro-rata. Gifts to certain devisees, however, might be given a preferred order of abatement. For example, a general gift to a relative might abate only after all general gifts to non-relatives have fully abated, or a gift to a spouse might abate last regardless of the class of gift.

Testator has given Anthony a specific gift. A specific devise is a gift of a particular item that can be identified as part of the estate. Testator has given Brittany a general gift. A general devise is a gift of a type or quantity of property, and it does not refer to any particular item that can be identified as part of the estate. Testator has given Carlos a residuary gift. A residuary devise is a gift of whatever is left over after all of the general, specific, and demonstrative gifts have been paid. The most likely order of abatement is Carlos's gift (a residuary gift) will abate first, Brittany's gift (a general gift) will abate second, and Anthony's gift (a specific gift) will abate third.

- Additional reference: See William M. McGovern, Jr. and Sheldon F. Kurtz, Wills, Trusts and Estates § 8.2 (3d ed. 2004).

4.   **The best answer is (d).** Section 505(a)(2) of the Uniform Trust Code provides that "[w]ith respect to an irrevocable trust, a creditor or assignee of the settlor may reach the maximum amount that can be distributed to or for the settlor's benefit." This is in accordance with the traditional rule. The rule applies regardless of whether the trust contains a spendthrift provision. **Answer (b), therefore, is not correct.** Moreover, the comment to Section 505(a)(2) of the Uniform Trust Code explains that "[i]f the trustee has discretion to distribute the entire income and principal to the settlor, the effect of this subsection is to place the settlor's creditors in the same position as if the trust had not been created. **Answer (c), therefore, is not correct. Answer (e) is not the best answer.** If more than one person has settled the trust, then each will be treated as the settlor of a portion of the trust in proportion to her contribution. But still, the creditor could reach only as much of the trust as the trustee could distribute to or for the settlor's benefit even if that amount is less than the portion of the trust attributable to the particular settlor's contribution.

- Additional reference: See William M. McGovern, Jr. and Sheldon F. Kurtz, Wills, Trusts and Estates § 13.1 (3d ed. 2004).

5.   **The best answer is (c).** A will substitute is an inter vivos transfer that avoids probate yet has the effect of passing property at the donor's death. Because the transfer is inter vivos, not testamentary, the transfer need not comply with the formalities for the execution of a will. Answer (c), therefore, is not true.

- Additional reference: See William M. McGovern, Jr. and Sheldon F. Kurtz, Wills, Trusts and Estates § 9.1 (3d ed. 2004).

6.   **The best answer is (b).** These are general gifts. A general gift is a gift of a certain quantity or type of property, but it does not refer only to, and is not payable only out of property found in the estate at T's death. A gift of $10,000 is a gift of a certain quantity or type of property (in this case money) and the gift can be paid even if the estate does not contain $10,000 in cash at the death of T. This is not a residuary gift. A residuary gift is a gift of whatever remains in the estate after the payment of specific, general and demonstrative gifts. **Answer (a), therefore, is not correct.** This is not a specific gift. A specific gift is a gift of a particular thing that can be identified as part of the estate. For example, a gift of "the $10,000 I have stashed in my mattress" would be a specific gift. **Answer (c), therefore, is not correct.** This is not a demonstrative gift. A demonstrative gift is a quantity or type (but not a specific item) of property to be satisfied out of a specific asset if available, otherwise from general assets of the estate. **Answer (d), therefore, is not correct.**

7.   **The best answer is (d).** As a general rule, an inter vivos trust of personal property need not be in writing, although a few states have statutes that do require a writing for an inter vivos trust of personal property. Uniform Trust Code § 4.07 requires that an oral trust "may be established only by clear and convincing evidence." **Answers (a) and (c) are not correct.** The statute of wills requires that a will must be in writing and, therefore, that any testamentary trust (a trust created in a will) be in writing. (In the case of a secret trust, however, a court might impose a constructive trust in favor of the settlor/testator's intended trust beneficiaries.) **Answer (b) is not correct.** The statute of frauds requires that a trust of real property be in writing. (Although, again, a court might impose a constructive trust to avoid unjust enrichment of the intended trustee where the property owner transfers land to the intended trustee but the deed does not specify that the transferee is to hold the land in trust.)

- Additional reference: See William M. McGovern, Jr. and Sheldon F. Kurtz, Wills, Trusts and Estates § 4.6 (3d ed. 2004).

8.   **The best answer is (d).** In general, to have standing to challenge a will one must have a direct pecuniary interest in the success of the will contest. That is to say, a successful outcome of the will contest must positively affect how much of the decedent's estate the contestant will take. The rationales for such a rule are first to ensure that one who has standing to challenge a will has an incentive to litigate diligently, and second to limit the number of lawsuits. Mary has standing to challenge the second will because she would take more under the first will if the second will is held invalid. Paul has standing to challenge the second will because he would take 1/3 of the estate by intestacy if the second will is held invalid and the first will also is held invalid, but will take nothing under the second will. Peter does not have standing to challenge the second will because he will take more under it than if it is held invalid and Father's property passes either under the first will or by intestacy.

- Additional reference: See William M. McGovern, Jr. and Sheldon F. Kurtz, Wills, Trusts and Estates § 12.1 (3d ed. 2004).

9.   **The best answer is (c).** Under the traditional cy pres doctrine, a court must find that the purpose of the trust has become impossible or impracticable and that the settlor had a more general charitable intent than the narrow purpose of the trust. If these two prerequisites are met, the court will reform the trust so as to carry out the settlor's original purpose as near as possible. It is not sufficient that the trust has become inefficient. **Answer (b), therefore, is not correct.** Moreover, the requirement that the settlor must have had a more general charitable

purpose means that she had a charitable purpose broader than the specific purpose set out in the trust, not that she wanted to benefit charity generally. The test is whether, given that the original purpose has become impossible or impracticable, the settlor would prefer that the charitable funds be redirected to another charitable purpose or would prefer that the property be removed from charitable channels. This does not mean that the settlor must have had an intent to benefit charity generally. **Answer (a), therefore, is not correct.**

- Additional reference: See William M. McGovern, Jr. and Sheldon F. Kurtz, Wills, Trusts and Estates § 9.7 (3d ed. 2004).

10.   **The best answer is (a).** An anti-lapse statute will specify the necessary relationship between the testator and the predeceased beneficiary that must exist before the statute will apply to redirect a gift. Anti-lapse statutes are somewhat misnamed in that they do not prevent lapse of a gift. The gift to the predeceasing devisee still fails even if the anti-lapse statute applies. **Answer (c), therefore, is not the best answer.** The statute, if applicable, however, will change the common law result of lapse. Rather than fall into the residuary (if the lapsed gift is a specific gift, a general gift, or a demonstrative gift) or pass by intestacy (if the lapsed gift is a residuary gift and the jurisdiction follows the common law no-residue-of-a-residue rule), the lapsed gift will be redirected under the anti-lapse statute to the "substitute takers" specified by the statute. Most anti-lapse statutes specify that the issue of the predeceased beneficiary are the substitute takers. Issue other than children take only by representation. (Issue do not take if they have an ancestor living who is a descendant of the predeceased beneficiary.) In general, anti-lapse statutes do not apply to will substitutes, such as an inter vivos trust. (Indeed, technically, lapse is a concept that relates only to wills.) **Answer (b), therefore, is not correct.** The Uniform Probate Code, however, provides an anti-lapse statute for certain will substitutes and for future interests created in a trust. See Uniform Probate Code §§ 2-706, 2-707.

- Additional reference: See William M. McGovern, Jr. and Sheldon F. Kurtz, Wills, Trusts and Estates § 8.3 (3d ed. 2004).

11.   **The best answer is (e).** In order for a testator to execute a valid will he must have the intent to execute a will and he must comply with the formalities required for the execution of a will. In the hypo, Frank did not have the intent to execute a will. The purported will, therefore, is not a will and **Answer (c) is not the best answer. Answer (d) is not correct** because the intent to execute a will and the execution of the will must

coincide in time. Thus, it is not sufficient that Frank change his mind about leaving his estate to Mary prior to his death.

12. **The best answer is (a).** Testamentary fraud involves an intentional misrepresentation that is intended to deceive the testator and influence the testator's will, and that does in fact deceive the testator and influence the testator's will. Testamentary fraud is of two types. When the misrepresentation relates to the contents of the will or purported will, the fraud is in the execution of the will. When the misrepresentation relates to facts that cause the testator to want to include a provision in a will (or refrain from including a provision in a will, or revoke a provision already in a will, or refrain from revoking a provision already in a will) the fraud is in the inducement. **Answer (b), therefore, is not correct.** Constructive fraud, also known as technical fraud, may arise even without an intent on the part of the speaker to mislead. Constructive fraud arises where one speaks of a supposed fact that is susceptible of knowledge as though one has actual knowledge of the fact, but in fact the speaker does not have actual knowledge of the supposed fact and the supposed fact turns out not to be true. **Answers (c) and (e), therefore, are not the best answers.**

- Additional reference: See William M. McGovern, Jr. and Sheldon F. Kurtz, Wills, Trusts and Estates § 6.1 (3d ed. 2004).

13. **The best answer is (b).** "A fiduciary relationship with respect to property in which one person manages the property for the benefit of another" is a definition of a trust. A postponement of enjoyment trust is one type of such trust. With a postponement of enjoyment trust, property is held in trust until the time or event specified by the settlor. (E.g., "Said property to be held in trust until my nephew reaches the age of 35, at which time my nephew shall receive the corpus.") The other answer choices to the question should impress upon the student that there are several instances in which inheritance law or property law use the appellation "trust" to describe property arrangements that are not true trusts. **Answer (a) is not correct.** Where the donor transfers property and expresses his "desire," "hope," or "wish" (or uses similar precatory language) that the transferee use the property to benefit a third party, the court will have to decide if the donor intended to impose a legal obligation on the transferee to hold the property in trust (in which case a true trust arises), or whether the donor merely intended to impose at most a moral obligation on the transferee. In the latter case, the donor has created a mere "precatory trust." Despite the name, this is no trust at all, as it is not a fiduciary relationship with respect to the property. **Answer (c) is not correct.** An honorary trust is a trust-like gift that is not intended to benefit the transferee and does not have any specific beneficiary who can enforce the trust as a gift, but has a specific

non-charitable purpose. The honorary trust lacks the "for the benefit of another" element of a trust. **Answer (d) is not correct.** When a trust fails or terminates of its own terms and the settlor has not directed what is then to happen to the property (or the settlor's direction cannot be carried out) a resulting trust arises by operation of law channeling the property back to the settlor (or the settlor's estate). A resulting trust does not involve the on-going management of property or a fiduciary relationship with respect to property. **Answer (e) is not correct.** A constructive trust is really not a trust at all in the sense of contemplating an on-going fiduciary relationship between the "constructive trustee" and the beneficiary. Rather, a constructive trust is a remedy a court imposes in order to prevent unjust enrichment, particularly in cases of fraud, duress, or undue influence. Commonly, the court orders as a constructive trust remedy that the holder of certain property transfer the property to another.

14.   **The best answer is (a).** Michael created a vested remainder in Jackie. The remainder is not defeasible and more specifically is not subject to the condition that Jackie survive Anna or anyone else to take. The holder of a future interest (one that has already been created) need not survive until the time of possession in order to take unless the grantor conditions taking on survival. Jackie, did not need to survive Anna, therefore, in order to take possession of the property. Moreover, remainders (as well as executory interests and reversions) are both devisable and descendible. Jackie had the ability, therefore, to devise his future interest. He did devise that interest to Edward. Edward will take the property, therefore, when Jackie's interest becomes possessory (at the expiration of Anna's life estate). **Answer (b) is not correct.** Michael gave away a vested remainder in fee simple to Jackie. Michael, therefore, did not retain a reversion. **Answer (c) is not correct.** Anna never possessed a contingent remainder. **Answer (d) is not correct.** Lapse is a concept that traditionally has been applied only with respect to a devise where a devisee has predeceased the testator. Anti-lapse statutes, it follows, generally apply only to devises and only where the devisee has predeceased the testator. UPC § 2-707 is contrary.

15.   **The best answer is (e).** The land is community property because it was acquired during marriage with marital wages. In Texas (and most community property states), all property is community if it is acquired during marriage except for property that is acquired by gift, bequest, or devise (and certain other limited exceptions). The stock was inherited so it is not community property. It is Harold's separate property. The estate tax rule is that only half of the value of community property at death is included in the decedent's gross estate. So, $1.0 million in value of the land is included together with the $1.0 million in stock. The gross estate is

thus $2.0 million and that makes **answers (a) and (b) both incorrect. Answer (c) is true and so is answer (d)**. The federal estate tax allows a 100% deduction for any property that is left to the surviving spouse. This is known as the unlimited marital deduction. **Since both answers (c) and (d) are true, the best answer is (e)**.

16. **The best answer is (b). Answer (a) can't be true**. There are numerous cases, many of them from Texas, in which a Testator or Witness neglected to sign the will, but did sign the self-proving affidavit along with everyone else. If answer (a) were true, then those cases could have easily been dismissed on the theory that the self-proving affidavit proved the execution. Instead, most of these cases were litigated on the question of whether or not the signing of the affidavit could count as the signing of the will. Early cases held that signing the affidavit was insufficient to constitute the signing of the will. Those cases demonstrate that in many states the presumption of valid execution can be no more than rebuttable.

Answer (c) is wrong. The affidavit, even with a duly executed will, cannot establish an irrebuttable presumption that the will is valid. If it did, there would be no will contests based on mental competence or undue influence or any of the grounds for challenging a will. Nor does the affidavit create even a rebuttable presumption about validity. Thus, **answer (d) is wrong**. Will contests on grounds of undue influence and mental competence are controlled by the same substantive and procedural rules, whether or not there was an affidavit. Witnesses and notary publics signing an affidavit are not swearing to the absence of undue influence. Nor are they swearing to the mental competency of the testator. They may swear that the testator appeared to be of sound mind, and that might create a presumption of competence (since the testator appeared sane at the time), but that presumption would not be irrebuttable. Thus, **answer (e) is wrong**.

17. **The best answer is (e). Both (b) and (c) are correct**. Their combined estate is $5.5 million. In 2006, the estate tax exemption is only $2.0 million. It increases to $3.5 million in 2009. So if both of them were to die in the next three years, their combined estates (i.e., one estate stacked onto the other one since they each intend to leave everything outright to the survivor) at the time of the second to die would exceed the exemption. That means answer (c) is correct. Even if the deaths do not occur until 2009, their combined estate of $5.5 million exceeds the $3.5 million exemption. And (b) is also correct. No matter when they die, there will be no estate tax at the time of the first death because the marital deduction will reduce the taxable estate to zero. Thus, **both (b) and (c) are true statements and so option (e) is the correct answer**.

18.   **The best answer is (b)**. The gift to Amir is valid because it vests immediately upon Ursula's death, but the contingent remainder "may" vest too remotely. As a result it is void. The remainder is not to Sam, if he graduates from college. It is to the first child of Amir to graduate. That may or may not be Sam. It is possible that it will be to another child of Amir, a child yet to be born. Let's call him Seth. Since Seth cannot be used as the measuring life to validate the gift to him, the only way a gift to him would be valid would be if it were necessarily to vest within 21 years of the death of someone who was a life in being at the time the interest was created. We only have two possibilities, Amir and Sam. Yet it is hypothetically possible that both will die and Seth will graduate from college more than 21 years later. As a result the remainder interest is void under the rule. It is void even it turns out that Sam is the first child to graduate from college and even if it turns out that Amir has no more children. The rule looks at what is possible from the time of creation of the contingent future interest. If there is a possibility, no matter how slight or absurd, that the interest will vest too remotely, then the interest is void.

19.   **The best answer is (e)**. Since Amir is dead, he can have no more children. That means the remainder to Sam is valid under the rule. But **answer (c) cannot be the correct answer** because it says that Sam will in fact get the trust corpus. We won't know whether he will actually get the corpus until he has met the condition: graduation from college. **Answer (b) can't be correct** because Amir was given only a life estate. Since he is now dead, his estate cannot collect anything. **Answer (d) is not correct** because the gift to Sam does not violate the rule. If he graduates from college it will necessarily happen during his own lifetime and he can be the validating life, since he was alive at time of creation of the interest (i.e., at Ursula's death). **Thus answer (e) is correct.** His interest is valid and so he will collect the corpus provided he graduates from college.

20.   **The best answer is (a)**. The question is whether Mick intended to exercise the power even though he did not specifically make reference to it. Mick has a general power and the creator/donor of the power did not provide for takers in default. UPC §2-608 provides that in such a case a general residuary clause expresses an intent to exercise the power. Of course if Nick's will had required that the power be mentioned, then the residuary clause standing along would be insufficient. But his will says nothing about how the power should be exercised. Thus any action by Mick indicating an intent to exercise is sufficient and in this case, the residuary clause does that.

21.   **The best answer is (d)**. The power of appointment was not exercised and since it is not a general power, it cannot be exercised by the residuary

clause. **Thus answer (a) is wrong**. Also, since it is not a general power, it cannot go to Mick's estate. **That means answer (b) is wrong**. And since there are no takers in default or implied takers in default, the interest passes as a reversionary interest retained by Nick. Nick owned the property at his death subject to being divested if Mick exercised the power. Since Nick was never divested, whatever he owned at death passes to his successors in interest. The residuary clause in Nick's will is broad enough to capture the reversionary interest and it existed at that time since it was created in the specific devise of the trust property. Thus the property goes to Yale. Also, since the gift was in trust, any beneficiary who takes after Mick's life estate would have to be alive at that time to take. See UPC §2-707. That means Mick is not a possible option even as the intestate heir of Nick and so **answer (c) is wrong**. That makes answer (d) the best option. See Restatement (Second) of Property: Donative Transfers at §24.2. See also Restatement (Third) of Property: Wills and Other Donative Transfers (Tentative Draft No. 5) §19.23. The trick is to determine who those successors are and following the general rule that a failed gift in a specific devise falls into the residuary, the conclusion is that the property goes to Yale.

22.   **The best answer is (a)**. This is not a charitable trust. Gino's purpose is admirable in support of college educations, but these scholarships are really just private gifts to the children of his employees. That is not a sufficient enough public purpose to qualify as a charitable trust. As a result, the trust is subject to the rule against perpetuities and will likely be struck down. It is difficult to see how "wait and see" or the 90 year statutory provision will help this trust. We know that Gino's intent was to set up a perpetual trust fund, something that you can't do under the rule against perpetuities. The trust provides that only income will be distributed to beneficiaries and so we can't wait and see whether the assets will vest within the period of the rule. We can't really wait 90 years to see whether they vest either because we know from the beginning that they won't. If there is a *cy pres* statute in the jurisdiction that can be applied to rewrite an interest that violates the rule against perpetuities, a court might construe the trust as lasting only for the period of the rule. That means some future gifts of income would be possible, but they would have to stop once the period of the rule had run its course and the trust assets would have to be distributed to someone at that time – either the then living potential beneficiaries (if the court construed the trust solely for the benefit of future issue of the three managers) or as a reversionary interest in Gino. In any event, the rule would prevent future generations from receiving scholarships. **Answer (b) is not correct**. The issue of three individuals may grow to be a large class, but they are certainly identifiable and so the trust will not fail for lack of identifiable beneficiaries. **Answer**

(c) is not correct. A trust never fails for want of a trustee. The court will appoint a successor.

23.   **The best answer is (b)**. Under UPC §2-507 tearing up the will is sufficient to revoke the will provided the testator so intended and provided further that the testator was the one doing the tearing. The testator can ask someone else to perform the act of tearing, but the act will not revoke the will unless it is done in the "conscious presence" of the testator. "Conscious presence" is discussed further at §2-502. It includes an act that is done within one of the senses of the testator. Thus it need not be within the testator's line of sight if it is close enough for the testator to hear what is going on. Here, however, the act was done at Blanche's home, miles away from the hospital, and thus not within her conscious presence. Thus, the will was not property revoked and may be probated.

24.   **The best answer is (a)**. The estate tax allows each person to transfer a certain amount at death free from tax. In 2006 (and 2007-2008), that amount is $2.0 million. It increases to $3.5 million in 2009. The plan suggested by the estate planner is for Husband to transfer at least $2.0 million (i.e., the amount of the current exemption) in trust for the benefit of wife for life, then to the children. The wife can enjoy the income from the trust and can be given the power to invade corpus so long as the power is limited by an ascertainable standard (e.g., health, education, support, and maintenance). As a result the $2.0 million will not be taxed at either Husband's death or at the death of Wife because she owns no taxable interest in the trust at her death. At wife's death, assuming no increase in value and no increase in the exclusion amount, she will leave the remaining $8.0 million to the children and will be taxed on $6.0 million (because she too gets a $2.0 million exclusion). The net result is that the children get the full $10.0 million at the death of the second parent, but only $6.0 million has been subject to tax. By contrast, if he leaves the entire $10.0 million to her outright, there will be no tax at his death, but at her death, $8.0 million of the $10.0 million will be subject to tax. The purpose of the by-pass is to get more money to the kids free of tax. The problem is described as "over-qualifying for the marital deduction" because Husband only needs the $8.0 million marital deduction, together with his $2.0 million exclusion, to produce no tax liability at his death.

       Answer (b) is incorrect. There is no way to use the gift tax exclusion at death. It must be used during lifetime. **Answer (c) is incorrect**. There is no generation-skipping tax problem in this fact situation. That problem would only arise at the time the property passes to the grandchild generation. **Answer (d) is incorrect** because the by-pass trust does not reduce taxes at Husband's death, but rather at Wife's death.

25.   **The best answer is (b).** If Marvin adopts Samantha, she becomes his sole intestate heir. That would prevent his other heirs from having standing to challenge the will.

Answer (a) is not the best answer even though it might look like a good option, because it will cause some tax problems. Transferring current ownership to himself and Samantha is one way to protect against a will contest because none of the joint tenancy property will be in the probate estate. Samantha will take as the surviving joint tenant. There are, however, several tax downsides to this option, which make it less attractive. Marvin's estate is valued at more than $5.0 million. If he puts more than $2.0 million of his current assets in joint tenancy, he will have to pay gift taxes. Creation of a joint tenancy is a completed gift of 50% of the value of the property because Samantha as joint tenant has the power to unilaterally sever the tenancy and vest 50% of the property in herself as a tenant in common. If Marvin transfers the full $5.0 million, he will have made a taxable gift of $1.5 million and will pay a hefty gift tax. Answer (a) is also not as fool-proof as answer (b) because if Marvin were to die in the next few years, his heirs would have standing to challenge the inter vivos transfer on the same grounds they might have to challenge a testamentary transfer (e.g., lack of capacity, fraud, duress, undue influence). Answer (a) only works to defeat the claims of the heirs if Marvin lives beyond the statute of limitations for those claims. So while answer (a) is not wrong, it is not as attractive and complete a solution to the problem as answer (b).

Answer (d) is not the best answer for the same reasons that answer (a) is not the best answer. The current transfer of the remainder interest to Samantha is a completed inter vivos gift. The transfer could be challenged by the other heirs if Marvin were to die before the relevant statutes of limitations for possible claims by the heirs had run. The transfer is also a completed gift for gift tax purposes. The fair market value of a remainder interest in $5.0 million worth of property, when the life tenant is already 80 years old, is clearly higher than the $1.0 million lifetime exemption from the gift tax. The gift tax liability makes this option less attractive.

Answer (c) is of no help. The only way to draft an effective no-contest clause is to provide that the challenger will lose a bequest in the will. If the challenger challenges and wins, he/she will claim his/her intestate share. If he challenges and loses, then the will will be probated. And if the will doesn't make any provision for the challenger – e.g., a gift that will be lost – then the challenger has nothing to lose in pursing the challenge.

Answer (e) is not the best answer. While it may seem helpful for a testator to explain in detail why he is disinheriting certain family members, that tactic carries some risks. One of the heirs might be angered by the explanation and be more inclined to challenge the will. And sometimes explanations, if they are particularly detailed or emotional, are used by the challengers to prove that the testator was not of sound mind. In any event, including the reasons will not absolutely protect the will from challenge by the disinherited heirs.

**ANSWER KEY
EXAM 6**

Wills, Trusts, and Estates
Answer Key and Explanations

Exam Six

1. **The best answer is (e).** In general, a will substitute is subject to challenge on grounds of undue influence to the same degree as is a will and a court will adjudicate that challenge using the same standards it would use to adjudicate a claim of undue influence with respect to a will. If undue influence causes the settlor to purport to revoke the inter vivos trust, the purported revocation is not valid even if the settlor is the sole beneficiary of the trust during her lifetime. The argument that the settlor has retained control of the property subject to the revocable trust and, therefore, should be allowed to revoke the trust for any reason should be rejected. The theory of undue influence is that the revocation does not reflect the intent of the settlor, but rather reflects the will of the person who has exerted the undue influence.

    *   Additional reference: See William M. McGovern, Jr. and Sheldon F. Kurtz, Wills, Trusts and Estates §§ 7.2, 9.1 (3d ed. 2004) ("Living trusts may be challenged for incapacity or undue influence just like wills, and the standards are virtually the same.").

2. **The best answer is (c).** This is a specific gift. A specific gift is a gift of a particular thing that can be identified as part of the estate. The house at 627 Canal View Drive is a gift of a particular thing that can be identified as part of the estate. This is not a residuary gift. A residuary gift is a gift of whatever remains in the estate after the payment of specific, general and demonstrative gifts. **Answer (a), therefore, is not correct.** This is not a general gift. A general gift is a gift of a certain quantity or type of property, but it does not refer only to, and is not payable only out of property found in the estate at T's death. **Answer (b), therefore, is not correct.** This is not a demonstrative gift. A demonstrative gift is a quantity or type (but not a specific item) of property to be satisfied out of a specific asset if available, otherwise from general assets of the estate. **Answer (d), therefore, is not correct.**

3. **The best answer is (c).** The acts of independent significance doctrine allows a testator to specify who takes a particular piece of property or what property a particular person takes by referring to an event that has a significance independent of its effect on a will. Thus, only if the sole purpose of the event that the testator refers to is to determine who takes under the will will the designation (of who takes or what property) be invalid. The theory behind this doctrine is that the purposes that the will formalities serve will not be undermined by the designation provided that the event referred to has a significance independent of its effect on the

will. **Answer (a) is not correct.** First, we do not know from the facts given who the decedent's intestate heirs are. More importantly, the testator has died with a valid will that passes his estate to his sister. The intestate heirs, therefore, will not take, regardless of who they are. **Answer (b) is not correct.** The anti-lapse statute would not apply in this case since, for one reason, the testator's description of the beneficiary itself suggests that the testator would not want it to apply when a sister survives. **Answer (d) is not correct.** There is nothing inherently invalid about a gift conditioned on the beneficiary surviving.

- Additional reference: See William M. McGovern, Jr. and Sheldon F. Kurtz, Wills, Trusts and Estates § 6.2 (3d ed. 2004).

4.   **The best answer is (d).** The rationales set out in answers (a), (b), and (c) each is a commonly given justification for a slayer statute. With respect to answer (a), the desire to deter a wrongful killing is arguably the weakest of the rationales. One might argue that if the prescribed criminal penalties do not deter the homicide, the possibility of forfeiture of inheritance rights is not likely to add much deterrent effect.

- Additional reference: See William M. McGovern, Jr. and Sheldon F. Kurtz, Wills, Trusts and Estates § 2.7 (3d ed. 2004).

5.   **The best answer is (e).** It is true that ademption by satisfaction in the vast majority of cases applies to general gifts. **Answers (a), (c), and (d), therefore are not the best answer.** And if a testator has given a specific piece of property inter vivos to the devisee of that property, we might conclude that ademption by extinction rather than satisfaction is the relevant doctrine. However, satisfaction can apply to gifts other than general gifts (whether they be residuary, specific, or class gifts). For example, UPC § 2-609(a) provides that "[p]roperty a testator gave in his [or her] lifetime to a person is treated as a satisfaction of a devise . . . if . . . the testator declared in a contemporaneous writing that the gift is in satisfaction of the devise or that its value is to be deducted from the value of the devise . . . ." This UPC provision on ademption by satisfaction is not limited to general gifts. Thus, if the testator makes an inter vivos gift of his gold watch and declares in a contemporaneous writing that the gift is meant to satisfy a devise to the recipient of the testator's silver watch, the testamentary gift of the silver watch should be deemed satisfied.

6.   **The best answer is (d).** Answers (b) and (c) accurately describe features of the Uniform Probate Code's elective share and contrast those features with certain general principles relating to community property systems. Only a surviving spouse can assert an elective share against the decedent

spouse's estate: The elective share is not available to a spouse who does not survive the other spouse. In contrast, community property rights vest as property is acquired during the marriage: Each spouse has an interest in community property as it is acquired. Community property rights relate only to property acquired during the marriage and, in general, do not include claims against property acquired by gift or devise. In contrast, the UPC's elective share calculation focuses upon the augmented estate, which includes property acquired prior to the marriage as well as property acquired by gift or devise. **Answer (a) is not the best answer.** In general, a decedent spouse is entitled to devise his or her share of the community property free of the claims of the surviving spouse.

- Additional references: See William M. McGovern, Jr. and Sheldon F. Kurtz, Wills, Trusts and Estates § 3.7 (3d ed. 2004); UPC §§ 2-201 through 2-208.

7. **The best answer is (e).** A secret trust exists when a will purports to make an absolute gift, but there is an undisclosed agreement between T and the legatee that the latter will hold the property in trust for another. In most jurisdictions in the United States, in the case of a secret trust, the court will impose a constructive trust in favor of the intended beneficiaries. This is thought to prevent unjust enrichment of the intended trustee who, if the court did nothing, would appear on the face of the will to be entitled to keep the intended trust property as his own. **Answer (a) is not correct.** A provision in a will that purports to devise property to a devisee who shall hold the property as trustee, but which fails to specify the beneficiary of the trust or the important terms of the trust is a semi-secret trust. **Answer (b) is not correct.** When a trust fails or terminates of its own terms and the settlor has not directed what is then to happen to the property (or the settlor's direction cannot be carried out) a resulting trust arises by operation of law channeling the property back to the settlor (or the settlor's estate). A resulting trust is the usual outcome in the case of a semi-secret trust. **Answer (c) is not correct.** To create a trust, a settlor must manifest an intent that one person hold the property for the benefit of another. Where the donor transfers property and expresses his "desire," "hope," or "wish" (or uses similar precatory language) that the transferee use the property to benefit a third party, the court will have to decide if the donor intended to impose a legal obligation on the transferee to hold the property in trust (in which case a true trust arises), or whether the donor merely intended to impose at most a moral obligation on the transferee. In the latter case, the donor has created a mere "precatory trust." Despite the name, this is no trust at all. **Answer (d) is not correct.** An honorary trust is a trust-like gift that is not intended to benefit the transferee and does not

have any specific beneficiary who can enforce the trust as a gift, but has a specific non-charitable purpose.

8. **The best answer is (a).** The omitted spouse doctrine is concerned principally with carrying out the (unexpressed) intent of the testator. The theory underlying the doctrine is that the testator who executed a will prior to marriage would have amended or revoked that will after marriage to provide for his or her spouse had he or she thought about it and effectively implemented his or her desires. The doctrine does not apply, therefore, in the face of sufficient evidence that the decedent would not have wanted it to apply. **Answer (d) is not correct.** The omitted spouse doctrine applies only to wills executed prior to the testator's marriage. See UPC § 2-301.

   - Additional reference: See William M. McGovern, Jr. and Sheldon F. Kurtz, Wills, Trusts and Estates § 3.6 (3d ed. 2004).

9. **The best answer is (c).** The "rule of convenience" provides that for the purposes of a class gift, the class closes when any one member of the class has satisfied all conditions for the gift and is entitled to demand payment. In this fact pattern, the first person who has satisfied all conditions for the gift is Judy who turns 21 in year 25. Judy can demand payment in year 25 and so the class closes at that time. **Answer (e) is not correct.** No persons can be added to the class after the class closes, but persons can drop out of the class after the class closes. We need not wait to see if Greg will reach age 21 in year 50 in order to close the class.

10. **The best answer is (d).** If Dorothy had died in year 2, no members of the class would have been born at Dorothy's death. There is an exception to the "rule of convenience" (the rule that a class closes when any one member of the class has satisfied all conditions for the gift and is entitled to demand payment) in cases in which no members of the class have been born at the death of the testator. In such cases, the class will close when it closes naturally. In the hypothetical in the problem, the class will close physiologically when Dorothy's last surviving child dies. That is when we can be sure that Dorothy will have no more grandchildren. Patty, who was Dorothy's last surviving child, died in year 39.

11. **The best answer is (e).** Dorothy conditioned her gift to each grandchild on the grandchild reaching the age of 21. She did not condition any gift on a child surviving until the class closed or until the time of distribution. Moreover, the law of future interests does not impose a requirement that the holder of a future interest survive until possession. Each of the grandchildren who was born before the class closed and who reached the age of 21 is entitled, therefore, to an equal share of the $1,000,000. Judy

was born before the class closed. Judy died at the age of 23. Judy is entitled, therefore, to a share of the $1,000,000. (At the age of 21, Judy had a vested remainder in the $1,000,000 subject to partial divestment if other grandchildren born before the class closed reached the age of 21. Her interest was not, however, subject to divestment based on any failure to survive until the class closed or until possession.) **Answers (a), (b), and (c), therefore, are not correct. Answer (d) is not correct.** Kathy failed to live until age 21. Therefore, she will not share in the gift.

12. **The best answer is (e).** In general, inheritance law today treats a parent and child by adoption the same as it treats a parent and child by birth. Thus, the adoptive child inherits from his intestate adoptive parent the same as he would if he were a child of that parent by birth. The adoptive parent inherits from his intestate adoptive child the same as he would if he were a parent of that child by birth. The adoptive child also inherits through the adoptive parent the same as if he were a relative of the decedent by birth. Thus, if the adoptive parent predeceases the adoptive child, the adoptive child will stand in the shoes of the adoptive parent for the purposes of intestacy law. UPC § 2-114(b) provides that "[a]n adopted individual is the child of his [or her] adopting parent or parents and not of his [or her] natural parents, but adoption of a child by the spouse of either natural parent has no effect on (i) the relationship between the child and that natural parent or (ii) the right of a child or a descendant of the child to inherit from or through the other natural parent."

   • Additional reference: See William M. McGovern, Jr. and Sheldon F. Kurtz, Wills, Trusts and Estates § 2.10 (3d ed. 2004).

13. **The best answer is (d).** The amount of savings generated through the use of a revocable trust will vary from state to state, with the greatest savings occurring in those states that have high probate fees. In some states the savings may be minimal. Client, however, owns realty in several different states. If she puts all of her realty in a revocable trust, she should be able to avoid the costs of ancillary probate proceedings in those states. She will not avoid any estate taxes because property in a trust that is subject to a power to revoke is included in the gross estate of the person who has the power. The power to revoke is tantamount to outright ownership. At any moment, she can revoke and revest the ownership of the property in herself. Section 2038 of the Internal Revenue Code specifically includes in the gross estate property which the decedent has transferred, but has a power to revoke.

   Answer (a) is wrong because the power to revoke prevents any estate tax savings. **Answer (b) is wrong** because the revocable trust will save some money. The second half of answer (b) is correct, i.e., that a trust is easier to amend than a will. **Answer (c) is incorrect** because all assets in a revocable trust will be included in the gross estate for tax purposes. To avoid estate taxes on life insurance policies, the policy would have to be transferred to an irrevocable trust in which Client had no incidents of ownership. **Answer (e) is wrong** because revocable trust cannot save her anything in estate taxes.

14.   **The best answer is (a). Answer (b) is clearly wrong** because UPC 2-504(c) says that signatures affixed to the affidavit will be considered affixed to the will if needed to prove due execution of the will. **Answer (c) is clearly wrong** because, if Clarence was merely filling in blanks on a will form, it is likely that many of the essential terms were printed and not in Clarence's handwriting. Answers (d) and (e) are possible in jurisdictions that recognize substantial compliance and probable intent. But **answers (d) and (e) are not the best answers in a UPC state** because UPC 2-503 states clearly that if a document was not executed correctly, it will nonetheless be probated as the Testator's will if the proponent (Bob) can establish by clear and convincing evidence that the decedent (Clarence) intended the document to be his will. We don't have to question whether or not Bob can establish that intent because the question assumes he can. Since he can prove intent, yes, the will can be probated.

Non-UPC states have not generally adopted substantial compliance as a possible way to comply with Wills Act formalities. Substantial compliance nonetheless is a valid legal argument in such states in cases in which the formalities have not been followed precisely. The UPC rejects substantial compliance in favor of the harmless error rule of 2-503. Thus, **answer (a) is preferable to answer (d)**.

Probable intent is a doctrine that may have been adopted by the Supreme Court of New Jersey, but it has not been accepted broadly. The UPC's harmless error rule is not a probable intent rule. The UPC says if you can prove intent with clear and convincing evidence, then the document can be probated. UPC 2-503 is thus more of a "clear and convincing evidence of intent" rule. That makes **answer (a) the preferable answer to (e)**.

Finally, it may be argued that the will is validly executed under the UPC because 2-504(c) appears to count signatures on the self-proving affidavit as signatures on the will. However, we have only Clarence and one witness signing the affidavit. Whether the notary public can be counted as the second witness when the notary public was witness to the swearing and not the signing or adoption of the will by Clarence is not clearly answered by UPC 2-504(c). In any event, even if the will is considered executed correctly because of the signatures on the affidavit, **answer (a) is still the best choice** of the options provided.

15.   **Answer (a) is best.** The farm should not be included in her gross estate because it is not property she owns at death. **Answers (b) and (c) are wrong** because a life estate terminates at death and so she owns nothing of value to be included in the estate. The value of the life estate is not included in her gross estate. Nor is the value of the remainder interest. The transfer that occurs at Michelle's death is from grandfather to the grandkids. While this may be a generation skipping transfer, if a tax is due, it will not be paid by her estate, but rather by the transferee, the grandkids, out of the trust property. Also, there is a $1.0 million exemption, so if this is the only skipping transfer made by the grandfather, no generation-skipping tax should be due. Thus **answer (d) is wrong.**

16.   **The correct answer is (a).** Under UPC 2-103, the lineal descendants take by representation. UPC 2-106 defines representation to require dividing the estate at the first generational level where there are surviving descendants entitled to take. In this fact situation, that is at the grandchild level. The estate is to be divided into as many shares as there are descendants alive and able to take (that would be three) and deceased descendants who left descendants who can take as their representatives (that would two additional shares, one for William, who is the parent of Kim and one for the unnamed grandchild who was the parent of Kathy). Thus the estate should be divided into five shares. Each of the grandchildren takes his or her one-fifth share and William's one-fifth goes to Kim and the other grandchild's one-fifth, goes to Kathy.

Note that Gary had two children and both children left issue. A strict per stirpes distribution, as opposed to the UPC approach, would have divided the estate at the child level so that Kathy would have ended up with one-half and the issue of Joan would have had to split the other half. However, the UPC approach treats descendants at the same generational level equally. Thus **answer (c) is incorrect**.

17.   **The best answer is (a).** The common law rule against perpetuities is applied at the time of the transfer, at which time it is possible that Susan can have more children. The rule presumes fertility until death so whether she intends to have more children or even is incapable of having more children is irrelevant. The class of potential takers (children of Susan who reach age 25) will close at Susan's death. It is possible that she will have a fourth child who could be only one year old at her death. All other lives in being (Ralph and the three other kids) might all die. Then we'd be left with one potential taker, child number four, who will not vest by reaching

the required age within 21 years. The kid is only 1 year old. It will take 24 years for us to learn whether or not that kid will take. Since this is a class gift and one member of the class vests too late – more than 21 years after all lives in being at time of creation of the interest – the gift to the entire class fails and thus there is a reversion in Ralph. The fact that one child of Susan has already reached age 25 does not help in this fact situation because the class will not close until Susan's death. The case of *Jee v. Audley*, decided by the English courts in 1787 established the class gift rule that voids the gift to a class if there is any potential member of the class who might vest too remotely. This was a lifetime gift from Ralph. We are not told whether Ralph is alive at Susan's death. The reversion will go to his estate if he is not alive – or to whoever inherited from him. But since we don't know those additional facts, answer (a) is the best answer because it is the only one that recognizes that the remainder is void and thus Ralph had a reversion.

Answer (b) is incorrect because Susan was given a mere life estate and it cannot be enlarged simply because the remainder is void.

Answer (c) is incorrect because at the very least, even in the absence of the rule against perpetuities, the children would have to reach age 25 in order to take.

Answer (d) is incorrect because of the violation of the rule against perpetuities. Otherwise, it would be correct.

Answer (e) is incorrect because even though the oldest child appears vested, the class is not yet closed. It will not close until Susan's death, at which time the hypothetical existence of a fourth child under the age of 4 makes the gift to all members of the class, including the 25-year-old, void. The rule regarding class gifts is that the class must close within the period of the rule (that happens here since the class closes at Susan's death) AND every member of the class must become vested within the period of the rule. It is this latter condition that cannot be met in this case because the hypothetical fourth child, if under the age of 4, will not necessarily become 25 within 21 years of lives in being at time of creation of the interest.

18.   **The best answer is (b)**. A will does not need to use the magic language "and his heirs" to create a fee simple interest. Thus each of the sons is given an immediate fee simple interest by the language that says "to Bob and Jim." The "but" clause following the gift creates a condition subsequent which could divest either of them at their respective deaths if they have no "then living" children. We won't know whether that

condition occurs until their deaths. There is no rule against perpetuities problem here because the divesting and vesting in someone else, if it occurs at all, will necessarily occur no later than the deaths of Bob and Jim (both lives in being).

It is not possible to have a remainder following a fee simple interest. So **answer (a) is incorrect.**

The contingent gift over (if Bob dies with surviving children) is an executory interest in Jim. (And the contingent gift over if Jim dies without children is an executory interest in Bob.) The executory interest is not contingent on the recipient of that interest having children at the time or even being alive at the time. One might infer that there is an implied condition that the property only goes to Bob and Jim if they have children surviving them. But literally, if the condition (not having children at time of death) occurs, the gift over to the other son is absolute. One could view answer (c) as correct in that each of them has a vested fee simple that is subject to divestment, but **answer (c) is not the best answer** because they also each have an executory interest.

Answer (d) is incorrect because they can be divested of the fee simple if the condition subsequent occurs.

Answer (e) is incorrect because they each have an interest that may last longer then their own lives. If Bob has children surviving him then his title turns into a fee simply absolute at his death. The same is true for Jim. Thus, they do not have mere life estates.

> Note: There is only one condition to be met in order for Jim to take Bob's interest or for Bob to take Jim's interest. That condition is "death with no surviving children." If both of them die with children surviving, it will turn out that their fee interests stay vested and each's 50% interest will pass to his estate. If both of them die without children surviving, then Bob's interest (50%) will shift to Jim and Jim's interest (50%) will shift to Bob. If one dies without surviving children and the other had surviving children at death, 100% of the property will end up in the estate of the son who had surviving children.

19.   **The best answer is (a).** Gary's life interest is immediately vested. The gift to the first child to graduate from high school is void because it is possible, judged from time of creation, for it to vest too remotely under the rule against perpetuities. Applying the "what might happen" approach of the common law rule, Gary might have another child years later, Cliff

might die before graduating from high school, Trudy and Gary might die as well, and then more than 21 years later the later-born child might graduate from high school. It is irrelevant that Cliff, a life in being, actually becomes the first child of Gary to graduate from high school. **Answer (b) is wrong** because the gift over was not to Cliff and thus the gift violates the rule against perpetuities under the "what might happen" analysis of the facts. The "what might happen" approach also invalidates the gift over to Gary's then living issue since it might vest at the death of the unborn child. Thus **answer (c) is wrong.** Since only answer (a) is correct, both **answers (d) and (e) are wrong.**

20.   **The best answer is (e).** UPC §2-901 applies a 90 year wait and see period to save otherwise invalid future interests. Gary vests immediately under the rule so his interest is valid. Cliff vests 16 years later so his interest vests within the 90 year period. But the gift to his issue is not saved by the UPC rule because his issue do not vest until his death, which occurs 95 years after creation of the interests. Thus, **answer (c) is incorrect.** And that makes **answer (d) incorrect.**

This fact pattern presents a situation in which the traditional "wait and see" approach, which allows future interests to vest once we learn whether they will in fact vest within the period of the rule, would validate the gift to the issue, but the 90 year limit on vesting does not validate the gift to issue because they vest at year 95. As it turns out, we know 16 years after the interests are created that all interests will vest within the period of the rule because once we learn that Cliff takes the life estate at Gary's death, we know that the gift to issue will vest either at Gary's death or at Cliff's. (Note: if Cliff predeceases Gary, the gift to his issue will vest at the end of Gary's life estate.) Since both Gary and Cliff were in fact lives in being at time of creation, they can be used as the validating measuring lives. But under the 90 year rule of the UPC, measuring lives are irrelevant. The future interests must vest, if at all, within 90 years of creation.

21.   **The best answer is (b).** While T may have added X's name and the bank may even have changed the records on the account to reflect the change, T has done nothing to deliver the gift to X. Under the common law an inter vivos gift requires intent plus delivery (and some would say acceptance by the donee). The intent is clear, but there is no delivery. **Answer (a) is not the best answer** because there is no gift of anything when T purchases the policy. Thus there is nothing to attack. This is a valid contract between T and the life insurance company to pay money to X at T's death. T pays the life insurance company for its service. The arrangement is valid as a contract. **Option (c) is not subject to attack** as a testamentary substitute. It is valid because legal title is transferred to T and X, who become

fiduciaries for the benefit of the beneficiaries. It doesn't matter that the trustees and beneficiaries are the same people. This is a real transfer of a present interest in property. **Option (d) is not subject to attack.** It is an effective transfer of title because T delivered the deed to X. Recording is not necessary to complete the gift, but delivery of the deed is. **Option (e) is not as susceptible to attack as option (b).** Option (e) creates a present gift of the dog because the intent is clear and there is constructive delivery. The letter is written in present tense ("I am giving you my dog"). Enclosing the photo might serve as constructive delivery and offering possession at the instigation of the donee is evidence of transferring control to the donee. This should be a completed gift as compared with option (b), where there is no delivery, constructive or otherwise.

22.   **The best answer is (c). Answer (a) is incorrect** because they can name each other as beneficiary whether or not they create a life insurance trust. **Answer (b) is incorrect** because they should have both documents. They will want to execute a durable power of attorney for health care to enable the partner to make decisions if that is possible. A living will is a directive to the physician about end of life decisions and if they want to be sure that their wishes are carried out in that regard they should have a living will as well as the power of attorney in the event the partner is not available to make decisions. Consider, for example, the fact that both of them might be critically injured in the same accident. And, the living will is not enough because it addresses only the end of life issue. There are many other medical decisions that might need to be made by one partner for the benefit of the other, e.g., whether or not to try experimental drugs or whether to have a risky surgery. They need both documents. Thus **answer (c) is the only correct answer.**

23.   **The best answer is (c). Answer (a) is incorrect** because in the absence of default takers, the court will imply a gift in default to the permissible objects of the power. There are currently three permissible objects of the power. This is a small enough group to justify implying a gift in default to them. **Answer (b)** is incorrect because such a deal constitutes a fraud on the power and will be ruled an invalid exercise of the power if discovered. It is certainly likely that the descendant who did not benefit from the appointment would discover any transfer to George and complain about the arrangement. **Answer (c)** is incorrect for the same reason that answer (a) is incorrect. **Answer (d)** is not likely to work because Paula, the person who created a gift to Clarence's issue, is a stranger to this adoption and a gift to George is not likely the result she had in mind when she used those words. There may be no harm in trying this but there can be no guarantee that it will work. That makes answer (e) the best answer.

24.   **The best answer is (c).** The UPC provides that upon divorce the gift to
the wife in the will is revoked. The probate property will pass instead to
the alternative beneficiaries, the children. The UPC further provides that
payable on death beneficiary designations, such as the life insurance
designation and the pension plan designation, will also be revoked upon
divorce. See UPC §2-804. But the Supreme Court has held that ERISA
(Employee Retirement Insurance and Security Act) pre-empts state law on
this question. Under ERISA, the designations that are made in the
documents of the employer's plan must be followed. The pension plan and
the life insurance are part of the employer's plan. See *Egelhoff v. Egelhoff*,
532 U.S. 141 (2001). Thus the wife must take the pension plan and life
insurance proceeds. Thus **answers (b), (d), and (e)** are wrong because
they all give the children part of these non-probate assets.

Some state probate courts have avoided the effect of *Egelhoff* by holding
that a property settlement at divorce in which a wife allows the husband to
keep the pension plan serves as a waiver of the wife's rights to the death
benefits. Waiver, they explain, is part of federal common law and so they
are following the ruling in *Egelhoff* by relying on federal law rather than
state law to determine who should receive the benefits. The Supreme
Court has not yet ruled on this point. Nonetheless, that argument is not
available here because the divorce documents are silent as to the pension
plan and life insurance.

Answer (a) is incorrect because the UPC prevents the wife from
receiving the probate assets. (The UPC also prevents her from receiving
the non-probate assets, but as explained, ERISA trumps that provision of
state law.) **Answer (b) is incorrect** because of ERISA. It would have been
correct if the UPC had applied and not been pre-empted by ERISA.
Answer (d) is incorrect because ERISA gives life insurance, as well as
the pension plan, to the ex-wife, since she was the one designated in the
plan documents. **Answer (e) is totally incorrect** and there is no
justification for it.

25.   **The best answer is (b).** The clause creates a spendthrift trust. The general
rule is that a grantor cannot create a spendthrift trust for himself or herself
because it would be against public policy to allow a person to unilaterally
protect himself or herself from creditors. But the grantor can transfer
property into a trust for the benefit of third parties and restrict the rights of
those creditors to reach the interest in the trust. **Answer (a) is incorrect**
because the trust provision will be enforced as to third party beneficiaries.
Answer (c) is incorrect because the provision can be enforced even to
prevent pre-existing creditors from reaching the property. Those creditors
would have had no claim against the property of the Grantor and so the

Grantor is perfectly free to transfer an interest in that property to someone and provide that the person's creditors can't reach the property. Of course whenever the trust property is distributed to a beneficiary, a creditor could reach the property at that time because at that point in time title is in the beneficiary rather than the trustee. **Answers (d) and (e) are incorrect** because they include a correct option, B, as well as incorrect options.

**ANSWER KEY
EXAM 7**

Wills, Trusts, and Estates
Answer Key and Explanations

Exam Seven

1. **The best answer is (d).** A discretionary trust is one in which the trustee is given discretion to decide who shall receive trust funds or discretion to decide how much of the trust funds a beneficiary shall receive. In this case, the trustees have discretion to decide how much of the trust funds Andy shall receive. **Answer (a) is not correct.** A spendthrift trust is a trust in which the beneficiary's interest may not be attached by his creditors and the beneficiary may not assign his interest in the trust. **Answer (b) is not correct.** The fact that the trust is a discretionary trust means that it is not a mere successive-interest trust. **Answer (c) is not correct;** the trust is not a support trust because the amount of trust property that the beneficiary receives is not measured by his need for the property. **Answer (e) is not the best answer.** The term "postponement-of-enjoyment trust" typically is used to describe a trust in which an event in the life of the beneficiary triggers the beneficiary entitlement to enjoy an interest in the trust property. An example would be a trust that distributes principal to the beneficiary when he attains the age of 35.

2. **The best answer is (d).** Under the harmless error principle (*see* UPC § 2-503), a document that has not been executed with the formalities prescribed in a jurisdiction for execution of a will may nonetheless be probated as a will if the court finds that there is clear and convincing evidence that the testator intended the document to be his will. The writing on the back of the will and on the back of the codicil should be considered subsequent instruments that revoke the will and codicil, respectively. True, these writings are not executed with the formalities generally prescribed for execution of a will. Nor do these writings qualify as valid holographic wills because the material provisions ("null and void") are not in the handwriting of the testator. Moreover, these notations do not qualify as "cancellations" (revocations by physical act) under the majority approach because the marks of cancellation ("null and void") do not touch the words of the will. Nevertheless, if a court concludes that there is clear and convincing evidence that the testator intended for the signed notations to be her last will (revoking the earlier will and codicil), the court should find that the will and codicil are revoked by subsequent instrument. The testator's signature immediately below the notations "null and void" arguably should be sufficient for a court to find by clear and convincing evidence that the testator intended these notations to be her will. **Answers (a), (b), and (e), therefore, are not the best answers.** The words of cancellation do not touch the words of the will. The UPC's harmless error principle does not apply to acts of revocation and, therefore, is not a means to cure this defect. The will and codicil,

therefore, are not revoked by physical act. **Answer (c), therefore, is not the best answer.**

3.   **The best answer is (e).** In general, American courts will not correct a will on grounds of mistake of fact. There are exceptions, such as under the doctrine of dependent relative revocation. Still, **answer (a) is not the best answer.** The traditional doctrine of dependent relative revocation ("DRR") provides that where the testator labored under a mistake of fact or law in revoking a testamentary gift and where the testator would not have revoked the gift had he known of the mistake of fact or law, the court may disregard the revocation. However, where the testator labored under a mistake of fact, traditional DRR doctrine requires that the mistake appear on the face of the revoking instrument. The testator's mistake of fact in believing that Paul had died does not appear on the face of the revoking instrument and, therefore, DRR should not be applied to undo the revocation. **Answer (b) is not the best answer.** A constructive trust could be imposed in favor of Paul to prevent fraud or unjust enrichment. To find fraud, the court must find, among other elements, that the friend intended to mislead the testator. A finding that the friend labored under a mistake about Paul having died would prevent a finding of fraud. Moreover, in general, a court will not impose a constructive trust to remedy mistake of fact. **Answer (c) is not the best answer.** An anti-lapse statute would have no application in the case of a revoked gift, and cannot be applied to the gift to Paul in any event given that Paul has not predeceased the testator.

Note that UPC § 2-302 (c) provides that "[i]f at the time of execution of the will the testator fails to provide in his [or her] will for a living child solely because he [or she] believes the child to be dead, the child is entitled to share in the estate as if the child were an omitted after-born or after-adopted child."

•   Additional reference: See William M. McGovern, Jr. and Sheldon F. Kurtz, Wills, Trusts and Estates § 6.1 (3d ed. 2004).

4.   **The best answer is (d).** When applied, the doctrine of republication by codicil brings the date of the execution of the will up to the date of the execution of the codicil. The doctrine of republication by codicil can be applied only to a prior validly executed will. If the prior document was not executed properly, it is not a will (rather, it is an invalid attempt at a will) and it cannot have a codicil (which, by definition, is a will that partially supplants an earlier will). (The doctrine of incorporation by reference may work to validate the devises contained in the earlier document by incorporating them into the "codicil".) Further, the doctrine

of republication by codicil is rightly applied only if doing so will carry out the intent of the testator. The doctrine is intended to be an intent-effectuating doctrine. The theory is that it is appropriate to presume that the testator, at the time she executes her codicil, has reviewed her earlier will and intends to reaffirm its contents to the extent that codicil does not disavow the earlier will. It is appropriate, therefore, to bring the date of the earlier will up to the date of the codicil. The doctrine should not be applied, however, if doing so will defeat the testator's intent.

5.   **The best answer is (a).** The UPC's elective share provisions are grounded on two principles. The first principle is the marital sharing theory, which asserts that the marital union gives rise to an economic partnership, and that both partners are entitled to share in the fruits of that partnership regardless of how title to the property is held. The UPC implements this theory principally through the augmented estate, which seeks generally to base the elective share calculation on the sum of property owned by either spouse, and also through the accrual schedule, which increases the elective share percentage as the duration of the marriage increases. See UPC § 2-202 and §§ 2-203 through 2-207. The second principle is that spouses in a marriage owe each other a duty of support during their lifetimes and that duty continues, to some extent, after the death of a spouse. The UPC implements this theory principally through the "supplemental elective share amount" which is a minimum amount that a surviving spouse is entitled to take under the elective share. See UPC § 2-202(b). **Answer (b) is not correct.** In a jurisdiction in which non-probate assets generally are not subject to the elective share, a court might utilize the "illusory transfer" test to subject certain non-probate assets to the claims of the surviving spouse. Such a maneuver is not necessary under the UPC as the UPC includes non-probate assets within the augmented estate upon which the elective share calculation is performed. **Answer (c) is not correct.** The UPC's elective share is not available to non-marital partners.

   • Additional reference: See William M. McGovern, Jr. and Sheldon F. Kurtz, Wills, Trusts and Estates § 3.7 (3d ed. 2004).

6.   **The best answer is (d).** An honorary trust is a trust-like gift that is not intended to benefit the transferee and does not have any specific beneficiary who can enforce the trust as a gift, but has a specific non-charitable purpose. **Answer (a) is not correct.** To create a trust, a settlor must manifest an intent that one person hold the property for the benefit of another. Where the donor transfers property and expresses his "desire," "hope," or "wish" (or uses similar precatory language) that the transferee

use the property to benefit a third party, the court will have to decide if the donor intended to impose a legal obligation on the transferee to hold the property in trust (in which case a true trust arises), or whether the donor merely intended to impose at most a moral obligation on the transferee. In the latter case, the donor has created a mere "precatory trust." Despite the name, this is no trust at all. **Answer (b) is not correct.** When a trust fails or terminates of its own terms and the settlor has not directed what is then to happen to the property (or the settlor's direction cannot be carried out) a resulting trust arises by operation of law channeling the property back to the settlor (or the settlor's estate). **Answer (c) is not correct.** A constructive trust is really not a trust at all in the sense of contemplating an on-going fiduciary relationship between the "constructive trustee" and the beneficiary. Rather, a constructive trust is a remedy a court imposes in order to prevent unjust enrichment, particularly in cases of fraud, duress, or undue influence. Commonly, the court orders as a constructive trust remedy that the holder of certain property transfer the property to another.

- Additional reference: See William M. McGovern, Jr. and Sheldon F. Kurtz, Wills, Trusts and Estates § 9.7 (3d ed. 2004).

7.   **The best answer is (d).** This is a demonstrative gift. A demonstrative gift blends an element of a general gift (a gift of a certain quantity or type of property) with an element of a specific gift (a gift of a particular thing that can be identified as part of the estate). This is not a residuary gift. A residuary gift is a gift of whatever remains in the estate after the payment of specific, general and demonstrative gifts. **Answer (a), therefore, is not correct.** This is not a general gift. A general gift is a gift of a certain quantity or type of property, but it does not refer only to, and is not payable only out of property found in the estate at T's death. **Answer (b), therefore, is not correct.** This is not a specific gift. A specific gift is a gift of a particular thing that can be identified as part of the estate. **Answer (c), therefore, is not correct.**

8.   **The best answer is (d).** Both answers (b) and (c) are not true. The judicial doctrine of equitable adoption provides that for the purposes of intestacy, under certain facts, a person who is not the legal child of the intestate decedent may inherit from the intestate decedent as though if a child of the intestate decedent. Most jurisdictions that recognize equitable adoption hold that the doctrine of equitable adoption will not apply unless the decedent had contracted to adopt the child with a person legally capable of consenting to the child's adoption. The decedent must have acted as a parent to the child even though the decedent failed to legally adopt the child. Equitable adoption allows the child to inherit from the intestate equitable adoptive parent. The doctrine, however, does not allow

the equitable adoptive parent to inherit from the equitable adoptive child who dies intestate. The rationale is that given that the equitable adoptive parent failed to perform the adoption contract, the equitable remedy should not be available to him. Equitable adoption does not allow the child to inherit through the equitable adoptive parent from a relative of the equitable adoptive parent. The rationale is that because the relative of the equitable adoptive parent was not a party to the adoption contract, it is not appropriate to apply an equitable remedy against the relative's estate.

- Additional reference: See William M. McGovern, Jr. and Sheldon F. Kurtz, Wills, Trusts and Estates § 2.10 (3d ed. 2004).

9.   **The best answer is (c).** Because Peter and Paul have predeceased Tom, the gift of the residue to Peter and Paul lapses. A residuary gift that lapsed at common law passed by intestacy. The residue of Tom's estate, therefore, will pass by intestacy. Mary is Tom's sole intestate heir. It is of no moment that Tom's will expressed his intent that Mary not take any of his property. At common law and in most American jurisdictions today, the only way to disinherit an heir with respect to probate property is to effectively devise that property to someone else. The UPC, in contrast, provides for a "negative will." UPC § 2-101(b) provides that "[a] decedent by will may expressly exclude or limit the right of an individual or class to succeed to property of the decedent passing by intestate succession. If that individual or a member of that class survives the decedent, the share of the decedent's intestate estate to which that individual or class would have succeeded passes as if that individual or each member of that class had disclaimed his [or her] intestate share." Thus, if the jurisdiction had adopted UPC § 2-101(b), Mary would be treated as having disclaimed her intestate inheritance and her share would pass instead to her daughter Louise.

- Additional reference: See William M. McGovern, Jr. and Sheldon F. Kurtz, Wills, Trusts and Estates § 3.10 (3d ed. 2004).

10.   **The best answer is (c).** The putative spouse doctrine is not accepted in all jurisdictions. In those jurisdictions that do recognize a putative spouse doctrine, a court may award property to a person who in good faith believed that she was married to the property owner. The doctrine may be applied when the parties break up or at the death of the property owner. The doctrine is an equitable remedy and the court has discretion to apportion the property at issue at the court believes justice requires. Some courts have given the putative spouse all of the marital property and some have split the property between the putative spouse and the legal spouse. Applying equitable principles, it is hypothetically possible that a judge

would decide to give no property to the putative spouse. However, once a court recognizes the doctrine, it is likely that at least some of the property will go to the putative spouse. See Uniform Marriage and Divorce Act § 309.

- Additional reference: See William M. McGovern, Jr. and Sheldon F. Kurtz, Wills, Trusts and Estates § 2.11 (3d ed. 2004).

11. **The best answer is (d).** At common law B has a vested remainder. There is no express or implied condition of survivorship attached to B's interest. Thus B does not have to survive A in order to take. At B's death, the vested remainder will pass to B's estate. If B died intestate, the estate, including this vested remainder, would pass to B's heirs, which may or may not be B's issue. If B died testate, the estate, including this vested remainder, would pass to the named beneficiaries in the will, which may or may not be B's issue. Thus, **answer (c) (B's issue) is not correct.** A had only a life estate. At A's death his interest in Blackacre ceases so that there is nothing to pass either to A's issue or to A's estate. **Thus, answers (a) and (b) are both incorrect. Answer (e) is also incorrect** because the Testator devised her entire fee simple interest in Blackacre. Thus, there is no interest retained by the Testator's estate.

12. **The best answer is (c).** UPC §6-213(b) specifically states that a POD designation may not be altered by will. That means **answer (a) is incorrect. Answer (b) is also incorrect** because a codicil has the same power as a will and can therefore pass any kind of property. **Answer (d) is incorrect.** Although the $100,000 will pass outside of probate, it was nonetheless owned by the decedent at death and so will be included in his gross estate for estate tax purposes. **Because answer (d) is false, answer (e) is necessarily incorrect.**

13. **The best answer is (a).** The gift to Sam and John is a residuary gift. John's death causes the gift to John to lapse. The antilapse statute does not apply to save the gift for John's daughter because Tony and John are not related. The antilapse statute only applies when the lapsed gift is a gift to certain relatives. See UPC §2-603. **That makes answer (b) incorrect.** There are only two possible places John's lapsed gift can go. It will either go to the remaining residuary taker, Sam, or it will go to Tony's intestate heirs as property that was not disposed of under the will. Most states adopt a rule that a lapsed gift in the residuary clause goes to the other residuary clause beneficiaries. **That makes answer (a) the best answer.** A handful of states still apply the "no residue of a residue" rule and treat the lapsed residuary gift as one that falls outside of the residuary, which means outside of the will, and thus must pass as intestate property. **In such a state, answer (d) would be the correct answer. Answer (e) is another**

possibility in such states. The argument is that a gift to a class never lapses unless all class members predecease the testator. Thus, if Sam and John were a class, Sam would take the full gift as the only living member of the class. However, it is highly unlikely that a gift to two friends would qualify as a class gift.

Answer (c) is wrong because John predeceased the testator. Thus neither he nor his estate can take anything. **Answer (a) is the best answer** because it reflects the majority rule that a lapse in the residuary will pass to the remaining residuary takers.

14.   **The best answer is (b).** Under UPC §2-607, a specific devise passes subject to any existing mortgage on the property. Thus, **answers (a) and (c) are wrong** since they say that Sally takes the property free and clear of the mortgage. After distributing the home to Sally, the executor should distribute the stock to Pat. The gift of the Rockwell stock is a specific bequest and so Pat should take the 100 shares of stock regardless of what the value is. **Answer (d) is incorrect** because the gift was of the stock, not of the value of the stock. A will speaks at death. At death, the 100 shares were worth less. Pat takes the stock owned at death, not additional stock.

Answer (e) is incorrect because the Rockwell stock, being specific, would only abate after the $100,000 general legacy to Josh. Pat should take the stock and Josh should take $50,000 in cash, which is all the cash that would be left after paying off the mortgage.

15.   **The best answer is (e).** Frank is not obligated to support his mother by state law. State law obligations of support are imposed only upon spouses (and in some states, domestic partners) and parents of minor children. Gifts of support to other family members do constitute taxable gifts. Thus, **answers (a) and (b) are wrong.** A taxable gift is any gift made to any single donee in a tax year to the extent the value of the gift exceeds the annual exclusion. The annual exclusion in 2006 was $12,000 ($10,000 adjusted upward for inflation). Thus, the amount of the taxable gift is the value of the gift ($25,000) minus the annual exclusion of $12,000, or $13,000.

If you chose **answer (c)**, you may have been thinking about the lifetime exemption from the gift tax. Frank will not have to pay any gift tax until his cumulative gift-giving exceeds $1.0 million. But he will have to file a tax return each time he makes a taxable gift. This gift is taxable because it exceeds the annual exclusion amount. But no tax will be due because it does not exceed the $1.0 million exemption, provided Frank has not used up his lifetime exemption. You can't tell that from the facts given since the only facts relate to the current tax year. In any event, **answer (c) is wrong** because whether or not a tax is due, Frank must file a return reporting the taxable gift.

16.　　**The best answer is (a)** because all the other answers involve fairly well-settled issues of law. **Answer (b) is not the best answer** because it does not raise a challenging question. If a city enforces a private trust, the city is a state actor, and the trust becomes subject to the equal protection clause. See *Evans v. Newton.* **Answer (c) is not the best answer** because it does not raise a challenging question. This is clearly a charitable trust (housing for the homeless) and so the *cy pres* doctrine can certainly be applied to this trust. Whether it *will* be applied depends on whether the trust's purpose is found to be illegal (e.g., unconstitutional), impossible (e.g., no homeless men in the city), or, in some cases, impractical. But, in any event, cy pres "may" be applied to a charitable trust. **Answer (d) is not the best answer** because Rich Testator is clearly not a state actor. If he were, then every testator whose will is probated or whose private trust is enforced by a court would be a state actor. Case law holds otherwise. See *Shapira v. Union National Bank* (Ohio 1974). **Answer (e) is not the best answer** because the trust clearly does not violate the rule against perpetuities since it is a charitable trust. Such trusts are not subject to the rule against perpetuities. By process of elimination, that leaves answer (a), whether Hannah has standing to sue the city, as the most interesting and challenging question. As a general rule, only the attorney general of the state has the authority to enforce a charitable trust. But Hannah is an individual who is homeless and may be harmed by the enforcement of the specific restriction of providing housing only for men. Likelihood of harm may be sufficient to give her standing. Individuals have pursued similar cases in several states and been allowed to continue their challenges even though technically the attorney general is the proper party to bring the challenge. She would want to contest the restriction on several grounds: violation of the equal protection clause because of the unjustified gender discrimination, possible violation of the Fair Housing Act which prohibits gender discrimination, or violation of a well-established public policy against gender discrimination.

17.　　**The best answer is (b). Answer (a) is not the best answer** because that option will only work if all 15 of the nieces and nephews are able to process the checks before Doris dies. Since she is "on her deathbed," this option is risky. A gift must be completed before death to qualify as a gift that qualifies for the annual exclusion. The rule that checks must be presented and paid before the death of the person writing the check reflects the underlying rule that a person can always stop payment on a check before it is submitted to the bank for payment. Thus, it is a revocable gift until that time and is not a completed gift at the time the payee receives the check. Transfers that are revocable are included in the decedent's estate for tax purposes under IRC §2038. **Answer (c) is incorrect** because including these gifts in the will means that the amounts will be part of her taxable estate at death. **Answer (d) is not the best answer** because it raises the same issue as Answer A. Deposits to a joint account are not completed gifts because the depositor can always withdraw the amount. Thus, such deposits are revocable gifts and subject to inclusion in the estate under § 2038. If the nieces and nephews actually withdrew the funds before her death the gifts would be complete, but that would take time. By process of elimination, **answer (b) is the best option.** Trust formalities are simple. In most states, she can declare herself trustee of the savings account and no additional transfer of funds would be required to complete the trust. She should be clear that the terms of the trust are irrevocable. If she dies before the amounts are distributed, then a successor trustee can carry out the terms of the trust and distribute the amount to each niece and nephew. The key here is that before they get the cash they each have a vested $1/15^{th}$ interest in the trust fund, which means they are all entitled to slightly over $13,000 at the time the trust is created. $12,000 of that amount is free of the gift tax and also escapes the estate tax. The key here is to make it clear that her intent is to complete a gift immediately of the $200,000 fund.

One can argue that delivery of a check for $12,000 to a donee should count as symbolic delivery of the $12,000 and thus count as a completed gift at the time of delivery, but the cases do not adopt this theory and instead generally apply the rule that delivery of a check is not a completed gift.

18.   **The correct answer is (e).** A distribution per stirpes means that the initial division is made at the first generational level below the deceased – i.e., at the level of Fred's children. Fred had three children. But Evan predeceased Fred, leaving no children to take his share so his share disappears. That leaves only Barbara and Steve. So the estate is cut into halves at the children level. Since Barbara is still alive she takes her half. Steve's half is then distributed to his lineal descendants. The "per stirpes" distribution requires a further division at the level of Steve's children. He had two children. Thus, his half share should be cut in half. One half of his half (or one-fourth of the total) will go to his daughter, Betsy. The other half of his half (one-fourth of the total) would have gone to the other daughter, but in her stead (since she is deceased), it will be split between her two children, Jeff and Jim. Thus they each take half of their mother's one-fourth share for a final distribution to each of them of one-eighth of the total estate.

Answer (a) is wrong because it calls for a per capita distribution. The applicable statute calls for a per stirpes distribution. None of the other options are correct because the estate must be divided in half at the child level. Barbara must receive her one-half of the estate.

19. **The best answer is (a).** The gift of a life estate to Dorothy's children does not violate the rule against perpetuities. She could have an afterborn child, of course, but the life estates in all of Dorothy's children (existing and hypothetical afterborn ones) vest completely at Dorothy's death. Thus, the life estate in Ames and Allen is valid and the trustee should continue to pay income out to them.

    Answer (b) is incorrect because the gift over to Dorothy's then living grandchildren (or descendants of grandchildren) does violate the rule against perpetuities. That interest is a contingent remainder because as of Larry's death we do not know who the then living grandchildren or descendants of grandchildren will be. Judged from Larry's death, there is a possibility that the contingent remainder might vest too remotely – i.e., more than 21 years after the death of lives in being as of Larry's death. Dorothy is still alive at Larry's death and thus is capable of having afterborn children. If she did have such a child and if that child lived for more than 21 years after the deaths of Dorothy, Ames, Allen, George, and Mitch, and all other lives in being connected with this gift, then the gift over to grandchildren would vest at the death of that unborn child – an event that could occur more than 21 years after lives in being at time of creation of the interest. The remainder is void, so Cindy can't take the remainder interest as a grandchild. In any event, based on the facts given, there is no way to know at Dorothy's death whether Cindy will in fact survive Ames and Allen, which would have to happen in order for her to become vested. So **that is another reason why answer (b) cannot be the best answer.**

    Since the remainder is void, at common law, the testator, Larry, retained a reversionary interest in the trust assets. That interest should pass to his heirs, who were Dorothy and George. He may have intended to disinherit George, but if he failed to make an effective gift of his entire estate, whatever interest is left over will pass via intestacy and George will be one of his intestate heirs. Thus, **answer (e) cannot be correct.**

    Answers (c) and (d) are both incorrect because the question asks what will happen to the trust property at Dorothy's death. While the trust will ultimately terminate and the property will revert to Larry's estate due to the violation of the rule against perpetuities, there is no need to terminate the trust until Ames and Allen have enjoyed their currently vested life estates. The trust should terminate at the death of the survivor of Ames and Allen and the assets should then vest in Larry's intestate heirs, Dorothy and George, or in their estates. **Answer (c) is also incorrect** because Ames and Allen are not the intestate heirs of Larry. Dorothy and George are his intestate heirs.

20. **The best answer is (c).** The remainder interest in the three children is a contingent remainder because it is based on a condition precedent, surviving until age 25. Judged from the time the trust was created, it was possible for Thomas to have additional children. The remainder interest in that possible afterborn child cannot be validated by any of the existing lives in being. All of those people could die at a time when the new child is only one year old. That means the afterborn child will not necessarily become 25 (or not become 25) within 21 years of any of their deaths. Thus, the contingent remainder in that hypothetical child is void. As a result the remainder interest to all children is invalid because the rule voids the gift to a class if there is one hypothetical member of the class whose interest could vest too late. *Jee v. Audley*, an English case, decided in 1787, established this class gift rule as part of the common law rule of perpetuities. Since the gift over to the children was void from the time it was created, Thomas was left with a reversionary interest in the trust property. The reversionary interest would have been property that Thomas owned at death. Since he didn't know he owned it, he would not have bothered to mention it in his will, but the residuary clause is drafted broadly enough to cover all his property interests. As a result the reversionary interest in the trust property passes to the residuary taker in the will: the Second Methodist Church.

Answer (b) is not the best answer. According to the facts all three of the children did in fact become vested, even before Thomas died. He lived for another 20 years after creating the trust, which was sufficient time for all of his children to reach age 25. Nonetheless, the validity of the remainder under the rule against perpetuities must be judged from the time the future interest was created and not at some later point in time. "But for" the hypothetical afterborn child and the rule against perpetuities, the answer would be answer (b) since there is no requirement that the three children survive Abigail in order to take. In a jurisdiction that applied "wait and see" as a common law exception to the rule against perpetuities, answer (b) would be the best answer.

Answer (a) is incorrect because the gift over to the children violates the rule against perpetuities. And, even if it did not, all three children would take rather than just Arthur and Carolyn since all three children met the condition precedent, attaining the age of 25.

Answer (d) is incorrect because the reversion retained by Thomas was owned by him at death and thus would have passed as testate property to the named residuary taker rather than to his intestate heirs. **Answer (e) is also incorrect.**

21.   **The best answer is (c).** At common law the will would be invalid because it was not subscribed by two disinterested witnesses. But the state statute saves the will by voiding gifts to interested witnesses. Voiding the interest makes the witness competent. Thus, the will can be probated. That makes **answer (a) incorrect** since the will is valid.

The next issue to determine is whether daughter's gift under the will must be voided. Under the will she gets half the estate. Without the will, under the intestacy statute, she gets half the estate. She receives no benefit from the will. One could argue even in the absence of a purging statute that she is not really an interested witness since she receives no benefit from the will. The statute specifically says that she can receive so much of the gift as she would have received in the absence of the will. Thus, under the purging statute, she can receive half the estate, which is her entire gift under the will. The more difficult issue is to determine where the stepson's purged legacy goes. Most states with statutes like this would consider his gift a lapsed gift that should pass via intestacy. The only problem with that solution is that under these facts anything that passes via intestacy will benefit the daughter since she is entitled to a portion of the intestate estate. Applying the letter of the statute, daughter gets half the estate as her legacy under the will and another 25% of the estate as an equal intestate heir with her stepmother. This makes **answer (c) the best answer.**

One might argue, however, that the combined result of saving her gift in the will and allowing her to take via intestacy means that she does get a benefit from the establishment of the will. Without the will, she would only receive 50% of the estate. With the will established, she will receive 75% of the estate. The attractiveness of answer (d), which limits the daughter to 50% of the estate, is that it seems to produce the desired aim of the statute (a subscribing witness cannot benefit from the establishment of the will). The problem, however, is that **the current statutory language, construed literally, cannot produce the result in answer (d).** Thus answer (c) remains the best answer. To get the result provided in answer (d), the statute would need to be amended to provide that when a subscribing witness's gift in the will is saved and a different voided gift passes to that witness via intestacy or in any other fashion, the subscribing witness's total portion of the estate should not exceed what she would have received if the will had not been established.

Answer (b) is clearly wrong because the statute does not say that witnesses cannot take a portion of the estate, just that they cannot take under the will.

Answer (e) is wrong although daughter does have a creative argument in favor of this outcome. She could argue that she and stepson were the only residuary beneficiaries. Her residuary share was saved by the statute and stepson's voided share of the residuary (the other half of the estate) should pass to her as the only valid residuary taker. This argument fails because it would give her a gift of 100% of the estate under the will, half of which would have to be voided by the statute because the benefit is greater than her intestate share.

22.   **The best answer is (d). Answers (a), (b), and (c) all give the surviving spouse more protection** because they would give the surviving spouse in a community property state at least 50% of the community property. In answer (a) that is probably all of the property acquired during marriage. In answer (b) the community estate would include all separate property acquired before moving to the state, which by agreement is converted to community property and all property acquired after moving to the state. In answer (c) the spouse gets at least half the community and, depending on how long they've been married a portion of any separate property. **Answer (e) also offers more protection** because under the UPC this surviving spouse would receive 50% of all property in the augmented estate.

Answer (d) clearly offers the least amount of protection to the surviving spouse. First of all, the surviving spouse can only claim one-third of the deceased spouse's estate. And, unlike the augmented estate concept of the UPC, this statute appears on its fact to apply only to property that is owned by the deceased spouse at death. In most states with this sort of statute, that means the claim is against the probate estate and would not include property that had been transferred into a living trust, or into a bank account with a POD beneficiary, or a life insurance policy that named a beneficiary other than the wife. Some states, through judicial decision, have expanded the rights of disinherited spouses by allowing them to make claims against property that was transferred out of the probate estate in fraud of the spouse's rights or in an illusory transfer. But the problem remains that the statute only gives a right to a one-third claim against property that is actually owned at death.

23.   **The best answer is (d).** The memorandum is valid under UPC §2-513, but it can only be effective to pass tangible personal property. Thus the gift of the stock to Steve is not valid because stock is intangible property. The rest of the gifts are of tangible personal property and they all seem

sufficiently identified. Artwork on the walls versus artwork in the studio would seem to be covered by the doctrine of Acts of Independent Significance. An artist's own work would be in the studio and a different standard would be applied to determine what would be hung on the walls. But putting stock certificates in a desk drawer may not be an Act of Independent Significance and even if it was, there was no provision in the will giving the stock to Steve. So he'd still lose under the rule that memorandums can only pass tangible property. Nor can the doctrine of incorporation by reference help Steve since the codicil refers to a memorandum that was not in existence at the time the codicil was signed.

Answer (a) is wrong because we don't have to rely on holographic wills to give effect to the memorandum. **Answer (b) is wrong** because incorporation by reference can't save the gift of the stock to Steve. Incorporation by reference can only apply to a writing that was in existence at the time the codicil was executed. The codicil was executed on May 2, 2005 and the memorandum was dated June 1, 2006. **Answer (c) is wrong** because the doctrine of Acts of Independent Significance can't save the gift of stock to Steve. For that doctrine to come into play there would have to be a valid testamentary writing giving the stock in the drawer to Steve. **Answer (e) is wrong** because only the gift of the stock to Steve fails under UPC §2-513.

24. **The best answer is (b).** At common law, lapsed gifts in the residuary would fall outside the will and pass by intestacy to the testator's heirs. In this problem, the gifts to Clark's sister and to Clark's wife both lapse. In the absence of an applicable anti-lapse statute, the options are for these lapsed gifts to pass either to the residuary taker or by intestacy. The no residue of a residue rule at common law would give the lapsed gifts to Clark's heirs, Sam and Sally. **Answer (a) is irrelevant. Answer (c) is clearly wrong** since repeal of the rule would allow the lapsed gifts in the residuary to pass to the remaining residuary taker, the University. **Answer (d) will not help Sam and Sally** because the lapsed gifts were to a sibling and a spouse, not to a descendant. **Answer (e) also cuts against their claim** because the only way they can take 75% of the estate is through intestacy.

25. **The best answer is (d).** One must have capacity to revoke, which is similar to testamentary capacity. The mental ability needed both to execute a will and to revoke one is less than is needed to deal with one's everyday affairs. A person who has been adjudicated incompetent is presumptively not capable to execute or revoke a will. But that presumption can be rebutted if it can be proved that Vicki was in a lucid moment. Thus, **answer (a) is not the best** answer because the

presumption about lack of capacity is rebuttable. **Answer (b) is simply incorrect.** Destroying a will by tearing it up, even if other documents are torn at the same time, is a sufficient revocatory act so long as Vicki has sufficient capacity and intent. **Answer (c) is not the best answer** because will #1 was revoked by will #2 and not by physical act.

1.   **The best answer is (c).** The statute of frauds requires that a trust for land be in writing. **Answer (a) is not correct.** In a large majority of American jurisdictions, a trust of personal property may be created orally. Restrictions on the oral creation of trusts may come from the statute of frauds, which requires that trusts of land be in writing, or from the statute of wills, which requires that testamentary trusts be in writing. But the law of trusts generally allows the oral creation of trusts. **Answer (b) is not correct.** One need not use the word "trust" to create a valid trust. One merely must sufficiently manifest an intention to create a trust. The words used in the hypothetical would seem sufficient to manifest such an intent. **Answer (d) is not correct.** The farm itself is property; therefore, the farm may serve as the trust res regardless of whether it ever produces any profits. **Answer (e) is not correct.** This answer choice states the general prerequisites for creation of a trust. And the purported trust in the hypothetical does meet each of these prerequisites. Nevertheless, the statute of frauds requires that trusts for land be in writing. Omar has, therefore, failed to create a valid trust.

   - Additional reference: See William M. McGovern, Jr. and Sheldon F. Kurtz, Wills, Trusts and Estates § 4.6 (3d ed. 2004).

2.   **The best answer is (b).** The trust the settlor has created is a mere successive interest trust. Adam will enjoy an interest in the trust for his life. At Adam's death, the trust property will revert back to the settlor, or to the settlor's estate. **Answer (a) is not correct.** The trust is not a spendthrift trust. A spendthrift trust is one in which the beneficiary may not assign his interest and the beneficiary's creditor's may not attach his interest. The question gives no indication that such is the case with the instant trust. **Answer (c) is not correct.** The trust is not a support trust regardless of the language "to be used for Adam's support." To be a support trust, the amount of income or principal that the beneficiary receives from the trust must be measured against the beneficiary's need for such support. In the instant case, Adam will receive all of the income from the trust, regardless of the degree to which he needs support from the trust and even if he lacks a need for the income. The trust, therefore, is not a support trust.

3.   **The best answer is (b).** The law will not enforce, as against public policy, a testamentary condition intended to encourage divorce. (In contrast, a court may enforce a condition relating to divorce if it concludes that the testator's motive was to provide for the devisee in the event of a

divorce, as opposed to encouraging the divorce.) Nor will the law enforce a testamentary condition that constitutes an unreasonable restraint on marriage, as there is a public policy favoring marriage. Thus, were the testamentary condition in answer (d) "provided that Daniel does not marry," courts would not enforce the condition. Courts have tended to enforce bequests conditioned upon the beneficiary marrying within a certain religion, however, as courts have not tended to see such a condition as an unreasonable restraint upon marriage. See Shapira v. Union National Bank (Ohio 1974). **Answer (d), therefore, is not the best answer. Neither answer (a) nor answer (c) is the best answer** because the law is far less hostile to conditional bequests that do not relate to future behavior at the time of the testator's death. The conditions in answers (a) and (c) either will have been met at the time of the testator's death or they will not have been. There is no danger, therefore, that these conditional bequests will influence Daniel's behavior after the testator's death. Finally, **answer (e) is not the best answer** because the law generally allows a property owner to withhold a gift during life unless and until the donor's condition is met. In support of this approach treating inter vivos gifts differently from testamentary gifts is the notion that the potential inter vivos donor must bear the consequences of his actions during his life (for example, Daniel might be quiet unhappy with him and act accordingly) and might change his mind during his life due to new information or others trying to talk the property owner out of his position. In contrast, the testator who makes a conditional bequest has no chance to change his mind after death and does not have to bear the consequences of his actions after death.

- Additional reference: See William M. McGovern, Jr. and Sheldon F. Kurtz, Wills, Trusts and Estates § 3.10 (3d ed. 2004).

4.   **The best answer is (b).** An honorary trust is a trust-like gift that is not intended to benefit the transferee and does not have any specific beneficiary who can enforce the trust as a gift, but has a specific non-charitable purpose. The devise in the hypothetical is trust-like in that it leaves property to May, not to be used for May's benefit but to be used for the benefit of another. The other in this case, however, is not human. A valid private trust must have a definite human beneficiary. **Answer (a), therefore, is not correct.** The purported trust is not a valid charitable trust because it lacks a charitable purpose. A trust for the benefit of animals, such as to prevent cruelty to animals, would have a charitable purpose. A purported trust for the benefit of a specific animal, however, lacks a charitable purpose. **Answer (c), therefore, is not correct.** An honorary trust must not violate the jurisdiction's rule against perpetuities.

In the hypothetical, the gift is limited to 21 years after the testator's death. The gift, therefore, will not violate the RAP.

- Additional reference: See William M. McGovern, Jr. and Sheldon F. Kurtz, Wills, Trusts and Estates § 9.7 (3d ed. 2004).

5.   **The best answer is (c)**. Under UPC §2-707, a future interest in a trust is contingent on the beneficiary surviving until the time of distribution. Here, the time of distribution is at A's death, so B must survive A in order to take the future interest. UPC §2-707(b)(1) applies to this fact situation because the future interest is to a named individual, not to a class, and the instrument does not create an alternative taker. This statute creates a substitute gift in B's descendants. Thus "B's issue" is the best answer. There is no requirement that B be related to the Testator in any way. Thus **answer (b) is incorrect**. If you opted for answer (b), perhaps you were thinking of the antilapse statute, UPC 2-603, which creates a substitute testamentary gift in the event of a beneficiary's failure to survive the Testator, but only in cases in which the Testator and the beneficiary are related. In a state that has not adopted UPC 2-707, the correct answer would be answer (d). B's estate would take because B has a vested remainder interest. But applying the UPC, **answer (d) is incorrect.**

6.   **The best answer is (e)**. UPC 2-707 requires B to survive A in order to take. Thus **answer (b) cannot be right**. At B's death, B has no surviving descendants. Thus, 2-707(b)(1) cannot be used to create the substitute gift. Instead UPC 2-707(d) applies to create a substitute gift of the remainder interest in Blackacre in T's residuary taker if the testamentary gift to B was not a residuary gift. The facts do not tell you whether the devise was a specific one or in the residuary, but you can safely assume that this is a specific devise since it is a gift of a specific piece of property. In addition, if the gift had been in a residuary clause, the substitute taker would have been T's heirs, not T's estate. Thus, in any event, **answer (c) is incorrect. Answer (a) is incorrect** because A was given no more than a life estate. That leaves only options (d) and (e). **Answer (d) is not the best answer** because if the residuary taker fails to survive, the residuary taker will not take. See UPC §2-707(d)(1) which provides that the interest in the residuary taker is to be treated as a future interest. That means that the general rule of 2-707(b) applies to require that the residuary taker survive to time of distribution in order to take.

7.   **The best answer is (a).** Willa predeceased Ivan and so she is not entitled to anything. Her estate cannot take and Karl cannot take on her behalf. Thus, **answer (d) is clearly wrong.** Nor can the estates of Eva and Joan take. They both predeceased their father and so they take nothing. Thus,

answer (e) is also clearly wrong. UPC 2-103 applies and names the decedent's descendants as the intestate heirs. No one except the descendants will take. That narrows the choices down to answers (a) and (b). The question now becomes how much each of the grandchildren will take. The UPC says that descendants take by representation, which suggests that they are taking as representatives of their parents. UPC 2-106 defines "by representation" in such a way that if all of the descendants are related to the deceased in the same degree (e.g., if all are grandchildren, which is the case here), they take equal shares. The UPC "by representation" scheme is known as the "per-capita-at-each generation" scheme of distribution. All descendants at the same generation will take equal shares of whatever share is assigned to that generation. Here, the only takers are the three descendants related at the grandchild level and so they each take one-third of the estate.

8.   **The best answer is (b).** Dan is the named beneficiary, but in order to take at Tom's death, Dan must survive Tom. Since he fails to survive, the gift to Dan lapses. UPC 2-603, the antilapse statute, does not apply to create a substitute gift because Dan is not related to Tom. Since the gift fails, Tom dies intestate. Under UPC 2-103(2), the property goes to Tom's sole surviving parent. **Answer (a) is clearly wrong** because Dan must survive in order to take anything. **Answer (c) is wrong** because the UPC clearly provides that the intestate heir is the surviving parent and does not include step-parents. **Answer (d) is wrong** because father Joe's right to inherit as intestate heir cuts out any rights of inheritance that would have gone to Tom's siblings. Half-siblings can inherit and under UPC 2-107 they inherit the same share as whole-blood siblings. But no siblings inherit in this case because Tom has a surviving parent who can inherit. **Answer (e) is wrong** because Dan cannot take and no one can take through him as his substitute since the antilapse statute only applies to certain relatives (e.g., grandparents or descendants of grandparents of the deceased). Furthermore, even if the antilapse statue applied, the substitute taker would be the beneficiary's surviving descendants, not the beneficiary's heirs.

9.   **The best answer is (e) because both (a) and (c) are true.** Lost wills can be probated, but when the evidence shows that the will was in the possession of the deceased at the time of her death, a presumption arises that the deceased destroyed the will with the intent to revoke it. Since the facts offer no information to suggest that something different happened to the will (e.g., that Alice threw it away by mistake or that someone else took it after Alice's death), it is true that Sara will have a tough time overcoming the presumption of revocation. **Answer (b) is not true** because Alice's sole intestate heir is her mother. Thus, **both answers (b) and (d) are incorrect.** Option (c) is true because if both Agnes and Susan

renounce (or disclaim) their intestate shares, they will both be treated as predeceasing Alice. That would leave Sara as the only intestate heir. **Since only (a) and (c) are true, the best answer is (e).**

10.   **Answer (b) is the best answer.** The language on the signature card does not explicitly say whether or not there are any survivorship rights. Because the account is identified as a joint tenancy account, Moe can argue that the survivorship feature of joint tenancies should be presumed. If he wins, all the funds will go to him. See UPC 6-212. But the form they used does not comply with the forms provided in UPC 6-204 so there can be no conclusive presumption about survivorship. UPC 6-203 says that Article 6 applies to all joint accounts, but to determine whether 6-212 applies, you must first determine what sort of account this is. Martha's estate will want to argue that since Martha made all the deposits, she intended to open an account that could be accessed by Moe during Martha's life, for Martha's benefit or for their joint household expenses, but that Moe's rights should end at Martha's death. Some states call this a "convenience account" and will allow extrinsic evidence to prove that was the intent of the parties even if the signature card indicates that the account is a joint and survivorship account. Under the UPC, only if the signature card is ambiguous as to survivorship can extrinsic evidence be submitted. Once the evidence is submitted, the court will determine which of the account types listed in 6-204 is closest to the intent of the parties. The "convenience account" is most like the "agency (power of attorney) account." If the court were to agree that this was an "agency account," the agency would end at Martha's death and the funds on deposit would go to Martha's estate, not to Moe.

Answer (a) is not correct because the only time a conclusive presumption exists is when there is no ambiguity as to the survivorship nature of the account.

Answer (c) is not the best answer. Yes, Martha's estate can argue that the funds belong to her because they were all deposited by her. But that fact alone is not enough to counter Moe's argument that the account was a survivorship account. If it is a survivorship account, the funds will belong to Moe even though all the deposits were made by Martha.

Answer (d) is not the best answer. Yes, Martha's estate can argue that this looks like a lifetime gift to Moe since the account was opened during their joint lives. Delivery is needed before a gift can be effective. But signing the signature cards together with the evidence that Moe was able to withdraw funds, weakens the "no delivery" argument. In addition, although some states used to accept this argument as a valid challenge to survivorship arrangements through bank accounts, the argument is not generally recognized today.

(e) is not correct. If there were no state statute on this point, the estate could make the "no testamentary formalities" argument. But UPC 6-101 clearly makes this argument a loser because it provides that arrangements such as this bank account are nontestamentary. Thus, no testamentary formalities are required.

11.   **The best answer is (d). Answer (a) is technically correct, but not the best answer.** Terry, as a surviving spouse, can elect against the will and claim her elective share under UPC 2-202. Since they've only been married four years, however, she will be entitled to only 12% of the augmented estate. Based on these limited facts, the augmented estate appears to total approximately $2.3 million because it includes not only the assets Dexter owned at death (valued at $2.1 million) but also the life insurance proceeds that went to Terry at his death ($200,000). Terry's 12% share of the augmented estate is $276,000. She is already receiving $200,000 from the insurance and so her claim against the probate assets is only $76,000. While answer (a) is correct it is not the best answer, because Terry's claim as an omitted spouse, if successful, entitles her to the full probate estate.

Answer (b) is not correct because the will is not revoked upon marriage under the UPC.

Answer (c) is correct in that Terry can claim as an omitted spouse. **But it is not the best answer** because UPC 2-301(a)(3) creates a problem for Terry. At the time of the marriage, Dexter took out an insurance policy in a substantial amount, from which one might infer that he intended to provide for Terry via the insurance rather than via the will. Thus she might lose the omitted spouse claim. Because that is a possibility, **answer (c) is not the best answer.**

Answer (d) is the best answer because Terry should first claim as an omitted spouse under UPC 2-301 since that claim will yield her the most value (i.e., the entire probate estate plus the $200,000 insurance proceeds). But in the event she is not successful in that claim, she should be prepared to argue, in the alternative, for a spousal elective share, which would at least yield her an additional $76,000.

Answer (e) is not correct because even if Terry loses her omitted spouse claim and Sandra takes under the will, she will not take the entire estate since the spousal share will claim at least $76,000 out of the estate.

12. **The best answer is (b).** As a general rule a trust can be terminated so long as the settler and all beneficiaries agree. This rule is codified in the Uniform Trust Code at §411, which provides for termination even if the termination is inconsistent with a material purpose of the trust. §411 also provides that the existence of a spendthrift clause does not constitute a material purpose, but that provision has little bearing here if the settler and all beneficiaries agree to the termination. Thus **answer (a) is not as good an answer as (b)**. Since Both Sam and Gloria want to terminate the trust, the only thing they need is consent from Tom. Upon termination, the assets will be distributed as Sam and Gloria agree.

They don't need the assent of the trustee. Thus **answer (b) is better than answer (d). Answer (c) is incorrect** because the trustee's agreement alone is not enough to terminate the trust.

13. **The best answer is (d).** The $10,000 gift to Devon was intended to be an advancement on his inheritance. Since Devon and Jamail are each entitled to half of the estate, they should get equal amounts. To figure out how much each one gets, you add the $10,000 early distribution to Devon to the $50,000 that is available for distribution at death. The total is $60,000. Each son should receive $30,000. Since Devon has already received $10,000, he is entitled to $20,000 from the estate and Jamail is entitled to the balance of $30,000.

Answer (a) is incorrect. The UPC has altered the common law rule regarding advancements by repealing the presumption that all inter vivos gifts were intended to be advancements. Under the UPC, an inter vivos gift will only be treated as an advancement if there is some contemporaneous writing evidencing that intent. The letter from Devon should be sufficient to prove that the gift was an advancement. Thus, the $50,000 estate will not be split equally.

Answer (b) is incorrect. Devon does not have to actually pay the $10,000 to the estate. He just gets a smaller distribution from the estate to account for the fact that he already has $10,000 of the full $60,000 amount that Ella had available to gift to her sons.

Answer (c) is incorrect because a verbal statement is insufficient to prove that the $10,000 was an advancement.

Answer (e) is incorrect for two reasons. First, using a disclaimer to renounce part of the inheritance is not the only way to even up the estate since we can use the doctrine of advancements, even as modified by the UPC, to accomplish that task. Second, if Devon renounced $10,000 of his inheritance that would literally mean that his $25,000 inheritance would be reduced to $15,000 and Jamail, as the only other heir, would take his own $25,000 plus the $10,000 that Devon renounced. Jamail's total share of the $60,000 available would then be $35,000 and Devon would end up with only $25,000. They would not be equal.

14. **Answer (d) is best.** It includes the $1.0 million exclusion from the gift tax plus the $12,000 annual exclusion. Jane will have to file a gift tax return and on it, she will show a taxable gift of $1.0 million. The $12,000 gift is not a taxable gift since it is covered by the annual exclusion. On the tax return she will report a taxable gift of $1.0 million, but will owe no tax on that gift.

15. **Answer (d) is best.** Sam should take out the policy on Damon. If Sam owns the policy, it will not be included in Damon's estate under §2042. Damon could take out the policy and gift it to Sam, but then §2035 would be triggered. If Damon lives for more than three years past the date of the gift, the value of the policy at death will not be included in the estate, but if he dies before that time, it will be included. **Answer (a) is wrong** because §2042 includes the policy if Damon is the owner and **answer (b) is wrong** because §2042 also includes the value of the policy in the estate if the estate is the beneficiary of the policy.

16. **The best answer is (c).** The concern about the little green men might be an insane delusion but it did not cause her to leave her money to William. Thus **answer (a) is not the best answer.** Both the sons and William helped her overcome that fear. There is no evidence in the statement of facts that William unduly influenced her. **Thus answer (b) is not the best answer.** Children are often presumed to be the natural objects of a parent's bounty in the absence of a spouse, but these days it is often true that a close friend or paramour would be the intended beneficiary. Thus **answer (d) is not the best answer.** That leaves answer (c) as the most likely choice. The brain tumor and the bouts of fear about little green men suggest that she might not have had mental capacity at the time she signed the will in favor of William. In that event, the earlier 1974 will would still be valid and, under it, the sons would take.

17. **The best answer is (d).** There is no doctrine of common law adoption. Adoption is totally a creature of statute and so the statute must be followed to create a parent/child relationship by adoption. One exception to strict

compliance is the doctrine of equitable adoption. That doctrine probably is not available on these facts because there is no evidence that Florence and David promised to adopt Delores, which is a requirement for application of the doctrine. Even if it did apply, the doctrine is one that estops the adoptive parents (in this case Florence and David) from claiming that Delores is not their adoptive child. In other words, if the doctrine applied, it would help Delores inherit from Florence and David, but it would not help Florence and David to inherit from Delores. Since there is no possible parent/child relationship and since Delores died intestate, we need to determine who her heirs are. She is survived only by collateral relatives, her aunt Florence and her uncle Willy. David is her uncle only by marriage and cannot inherit on that basis. Thus Florence and Willy her only two blood relatives will inherit equally.

18.   **The best answer is (b).** Peggy can disclaim under UPC 2-1105. She may disclaim "in whole or in part." Thus there is nothing wrong with her keeping $200,000 of her intestate share and disclaiming the rest. UPC 2-1106(b)(3) provides that the disclaimed interest (here the $800,000) passes as though the disclaimant had predeceased. However, the disclaimant cannot use the disclaimer to effect a change in the division of the intestate's estate. Doug's estate passes half to Peggy and half to Bonnie. If Peggy had actually predeceased Doug, then the estate would have been divided equally among the three grandchildren under the UPC's per capita at each generation rule. To prevent the application of the per capita rule in this case, UPC 2-1106(b)(3) further provides that if the descendants of the disclaimant are to share in the estate, then "the disclaimed interest passes only to the descendants of the disclaimant." Thus, Peggy's disclaimed $800,000 interest in the estate passes to her two children and Bonnie keeps her $1.0 million intestate share.

19.   **The best answer is (a).** The divesting event (the Cubs winning the series) is obviously something that might occur long beyond lives in being plus 21 years (the period of the rule). Since the divesting event may occur too late to vest the University within the period of the rule, that leaves Stuart with a vested fee simple interest. **Answer (c) is incorrect.** The charitable exception is not available in this fact situation. A charitable gift can be subject to conditions without violating the rule and a divesting event that divests from one charity and gives it to another is not subject to the rule. But here we have an interest vested in a private individual and so the rule applies with full force. The University cannot take.

20.   **The best answer is (c).** Son has a vested life estate at T's death, but the gifts over to his widow and to his "then living children" are contingent. Thus, we need to apply the rule against perpetuities to determine whether

either of these interests are valid. The gift to Norm's widow is valid because if it vests at all, it will vest at Norm's death and since Norm is a life in being that vesting event takes place within the period of the rule. This hypothetical raises the classic common law problem of the unborn widow. There is no guarantee as of T's death that Nora will be Norm's widow. She is not named. Nora could die before Norm and Norm could marry someone who was not a life in being at T's death. While the gift to the widow is valid because it vests (if at all) at Norm's death, the gift over to the children is not valid because it will vest (if at all) only upon the death of the widow (who conceivably could die more than 21 years after Norm and other lives in being at time of creation of the interest). **Answers (a) and (b) are both wrong** because Susan is not vested and will not become vested. The gift to the class of "then living" children is completely void. Once you strike the remainder in the children you are left with a life estate in Norm, a contingent life estate in Norm's widow, and a reversionary interest in Testator. Since the gift of Blackacre was a specific devise, the retained interest passes along with all of the rest of Testator's property in the residuary clause. As a result Norm ends up with a vested remainder following the two life estates. Some people might view Norm as taking Testator's reversionary interest. But the effect of the will is to transfer the future interest to Norm as a third party and future interests created in third parties are usually remainders (or executory interests). In any event, answer (c) remains the best answer.

21.   **The best answer is (e).** The UPC applies. UPC §2-901 validates the remainder interest at the time of Testator's death only if the common law rule of perpetuities is satisfied at that time. The rule is not satisfied because of the unborn widow problem and so the remainder interest in the children is invalid under 2-901(a)(1). But then 2-901(a)(2) provides that otherwise invalid interests will be given a 90 year period to vest. If they vest within 90 years of their creation, they will become valid. In the meantime, they are in limbo, not invalid and not valid. The future interests were created at Testator's death. Six years later, according to the facts, Norm dies. So we'll have to wait another 84 years to see whether or not Nora dies within that time since the interests in the children will not vest until her death. Note that this 90 year rule is different from basic "wait and see." Under "wait and see," the interests in the children would be validated at the time that Nora becomes Norm's widow. At that time we would learn that the interests, if they vest at all, will vest within the period of the common law rule. But under the 90 year rule, we have to wait 90 years to determine whether or not the interests do in fact vest. It is highly unlikely that Nora's death will occur more than 90 years after Testator's death. Thus, in all probability the children's interests will be valid, but we can't know that under the UPC until Nora dies.

22.   **The best answer is (e).** The UPC does not invalidate a will solely because the subscribing witnesses are also beneficiaries. Nor does the UPC void the interest of such witnesses in order to make them competent. See UPC §2-505. The underlying issue in these cases is whether the witnesses did anything wrong to gain a benefit under the will, such as unduly influence the Testator or lie about his state of mind. The UPC approach is to assume that if an interested witness actually did anything wrong, including fraud, duress or undue influence, the will should be challenged on those grounds. Given the facts in this hypothetical, there is no evidence of any wrongdoing. Absent the will, the daughter and the stepson's mother would be beneficiaries as intestate heirs. The will should be valid and the estate distributed as the Testator provided, half to the daughter and half to the stepson.

23.   **The best answer is (d).** All of the property looks like community property from the statement of facts, but if Herman can trace ownership of the investment property to the separate property that he owned before the marriage, then that property, unless co-mingled with community property, retains its characterization as separate property. **Answer (a) is incorrect** because record title produces strong but rebuttable evidence as to ownership. Thus it is not conclusive. **Answer (b) is incorrect** because spousal agreements that change the characterization of community property must be in writing. **Answer (c) is irrelevant.** If the will is valid, the property owned by Wanda will pass under the will and not via intestacy.

24.   **The best answer is (c).** Walter had a nongeneral power to appoint to his children. Had he exercised the power while all of his children were alive, he could have appointed to Ann, Amy and Dan. The fact that Dan failed to survive him would have caused his gift to lapse, but the anti-lapse statute would have saved the gift for his children. The Restatement (Second) of Property: Donative Transfers at §18.6 says "Statutes, commonly referred to as antilapse statutes, provide substituted takers in the event a devisee or legatee dies before the will takes effect, unless a contrary intent is manifested. Those statutes, if not made expressly applicable, should nevertheless have their purpose and policy applied: (1) To an appointment to an object of a power as if the appointive property were owned by either the donor or the donee, and (2) So that the substituted takers are regarded as objects of the power." The Restatement (Third) is consistent and even more explicit. It provides: "The donee of a nongeneral power is authorized to appoint to the descendants of a deceased permissible appointee..." See Restatement of the Law (Third) Property: Wills and Other Donative Transfers (Tentative Draft No. 5) at §19.12(c). Thus, as of Walter's death, the permissible appointees of the power were Ann, Amy and Dan's two children. Both the Second and Third Restatements provide that in the absence of a clause specifying takers in default, the property subject to a lapsed nongeneral power will pass to the permissible objects of the power, who in this case are Ann, Amy, and Dan's two children. See Restatement Second at §24.2 and Restatement Third (Tentative Draft) at §19.23.

Answer (a) is incorrect because the policy of the state's antilapse statute, even though it doesn't mention powers of appointment, should apply to allow Dan's children to take along with Ann and Amy. **Answer (b) is incorrect** because the antilapse statute would give Dan's gift to his children and if it goes to his estate, his wife will take as beneficiary of his will. **Answers (d) and (e)** are incorrect because they are based on the assumption that the property will revert to Grandfather's estate and the clear modern position is to avoid reversions whenever possible.

25.   **The best answer is (d).** To be effective as an inter vivos gift, there must be a delivery of the deed to the donee or at least to an agent of the donee. You are Elaine's lawyer and so cannot possibly be considered the agent of Jess. If there is no valid delivery of the deed then the transfer of title is not effective. Recording can constitute delivery, but this deed is not being recorded. All of the other options are wrong because they assume that the deed does transfer title. It does not. The property is still owned by Elaine at her death.

WILLS, TRUSTS, AND ESTATES
ANSWER SHEETS

EXAM ONE

1. (A) (B) (C) (D) (E)	10. (A) (B) (C) (D) (E)	18. (A) (B) (C) (D) (E)
2. (A) (B) (C) (D) (E)	11. (A) (B) (C) (D)	19. (A) (B) (C) (D) (E)
3. (A) (B) (C) (D) (E)	12. (A) (B) (C) (D) (E)	20. (A) (B) (C) (D) (E)
4. (A) (B) (C) (D) (E)	13. (A) (B) (C) (D) (E)	21. (A) (B) (C) (D) (E)
5. (A) (B) (C) (D) (E)	14. (A) (B) (C) (D) (E)	22. (A) (B) (C) (D)
6. (A) (B) (C) (D) (E)	15. (A) (B) (C) (D) (E)	23. (A) (B) (C) (D) (E)
7. (A) (B) (C) (D) (E)	16. (A) (B) (C) (D)	24. (A) (B) (C) (D) (E)
8. (A) (B) (C) (D) (E)	17. (A) (B) (C) (D) (E)	25. (A) (B) (C) (D) (E)
9. (A) (B) (C) (D) (E)		

EXAM TWO

1. (A) (B) (C) (D)	10. (A) (B) (C) (D) (E)	18. (A) (B) (C) (D) (E)
2. (A) (B) (C) (D) (E)	11. (A) (B) (C) (D)	19. (A) (B) (C) (D) (E)
3. (A) (B) (C) (D) (E)	12. (A) (B) (C) (D) (E)	20. (A) (B) (C) (D)
4. (A) (B) (C) (D) (E)	13. (A) (B) (C) (D) (E)	21. (A) (B) (C) (D)
5. (A) (B) (C) (D) (E)	14. (A) (B) (C) (D) (E)	22. (A) (B) (C) (D)
6. (A) (B) (C) (D) (E)	15. (A) (B) (C) (D) (E)	23. (A) (B) (C) (D) (E)
7. (A) (B) (C) (D) (E)	16. (A) (B) (C) (D)	24. (A) (B) (C) (D) (E)
8. (A) (B) (C) (D) (E)	17. (A) (B) (C) (D) (E)	25. (A) (B) (C) (D) (E)
9. (A) (B) (C) (D) (E)		

EXAM THREE

1. (A) (B) (C) (D) (E)	10. (A) (B) (C) (D) (E)	18. (A) (B) (C) (D) (E)
2. (A) (B) (C) (D) (E)	11. (A) (B) (C) (D)	19. (A) (B) (C) (D) (E)
3. (A) (B) (C) (D)	12. (A) (B) (C) (D) (E)	20. (A) (B) (C) (D)
4. (A) (B) (C) (D) (E)	13. (A) (B) (C) (D) (E)	21. (A) (B) (C) (D) (E)
5. (A) (B) (C) (D) (E)	14. (A) (B) (C) (D) (E)	22. (A) (B) (C) (D) (E)
6. (A) (B) (C) (D)	15. (A) (B) (C) (D)	23. (A) (B) (C) (D) (E)
7. (A) (B) (C) (D)	16. (A) (B) (C) (D) (E)	24. (A) (B) (C) (D) (E)
8. (A) (B) (C) (D)	17. (A) (B) (C) (D) (E)	25. (A) (B) (C) (D) (E)
9. (A) (B) (C) (D) (E)		

EXAM FOUR

1.	(A)	(B)	(C)	(D)	(E)	10.	(A)	(B)	(C)	(D)	(E)	18.	(A)	(B)	(C)	(D)	(E)
2.	(A)	(B)	(C)	(D)	(E)	11.	(A)	(B)	(C)	(D)		19.	(A)	(B)	(C)	(D)	(E)
3.	(A)	(B)	(C)	(D)	(E)	12.	(A)	(B)	(C)	(D)	(E)	20.	(A)	(B)	(C)	(D)	(E)
4.	(A)	(B)	(C)	(D)	(E)	13.	(A)	(B)	(C)	(D)	(E)	21.	(A)	(B)	(C)	(D)	(E)
5.	(A)	(B)	(C)	(D)	(E)	14.	(A)	(B)	(C)	(D)	(E)	22.	(A)	(B)	(C)	(D)	(E)
6.	(A)	(B)	(C)	(D)	(E)	15.	(A)	(B)	(C)	(D)	(E)	23.	(A)	(B)	(C)	(D)	(E)
7.	(A)	(B)	(C)	(D)	(E)	16.	(A)	(B)	(C)	(D)		24.	(A)	(B)	(C)	(D)	(E)
8.	(A)	(B)	(C)	(D)	(E)	17.	(A)	(B)	(C)	(D)	(E)	25.	(A)	(B)	(C)	(D)	
9.	(A)	(B)	(C)	(D)	(E)												

EXAM FIVE

1.	(A)	(B)	(C)	(D)	(E)	10.	(A)	(B)	(C)	(D)	(E)	18.	(A)	(B)	(C)	(D)	(E)
2.	(A)	(B)	(C)	(D)	(E)	11.	(A)	(B)	(C)	(D)	(E)	19.	(A)	(B)	(C)	(D)	(E)
3.	(A)	(B)	(C)	(D)	(E)	12.	(A)	(B)	(C)	(D)	(E)	20.	(A)	(B)	(C)	(D)	(E)
4.	(A)	(B)	(C)	(D)	(E)	13.	(A)	(B)	(C)	(D)	(E)	21.	(A)	(B)	(C)	(D)	(E)
5.	(A)	(B)	(C)	(D)	(E)	14.	(A)	(B)	(C)	(D)	(E)	22.	(A)	(B)	(C)	(D)	(E)
6.	(A)	(B)	(C)	(D)	(E)	15.	(A)	(B)	(C)	(D)	(E)	23.	(A)	(B)	(C)	(D)	(E)
7.	(A)	(B)	(C)	(D)	(E)	16.	(A)	(B)	(C)	(D)	(E)	24.	(A)	(B)	(C)	(D)	
8.	(A)	(B)	(C)	(D)	(E)	17.	(A)	(B)	(C)	(D)	(E)	25.	(A)	(B)	(C)	(D)	(E)
9.	(A)	(B)	(C)	(D)	(E)												

EXAM SIX

1.	(A)	(B)	(C)	(D)	(E)	10.	(A)	(B)	(C)	(D)	(E)	18.	(A)	(B)	(C)	(D)	(E)
2.	(A)	(B)	(C)	(D)	(E)	11.	(A)	(B)	(C)	(D)	(E)	19.	(A)	(B)	(C)	(D)	(E)
3.	(A)	(B)	(C)	(D)	(E)	12.	(A)	(B)	(C)	(D)	(E)	20.	(A)	(B)	(C)	(D)	(E)
4.	(A)	(B)	(C)	(D)	(E)	13.	(A)	(B)	(C)	(D)	(E)	21.	(A)	(B)	(C)	(D)	(E)
5.	(A)	(B)	(C)	(D)	(E)	14.	(A)	(B)	(C)	(D)	(E)	22.	(A)	(B)	(C)	(D)	(E)
6.	(A)	(B)	(C)	(D)	(E)	15.	(A)	(B)	(C)	(D)		23.	(A)	(B)	(C)	(D)	(E)
7.	(A)	(B)	(C)	(D)	(E)	16.	(A)	(B)	(C)	(D)	(E)	24.	(A)	(B)	(C)	(D)	(E)
8.	(A)	(B)	(C)	(D)	(E)	17.	(A)	(B)	(C)	(D)	(E)	25.	(A)	(B)	(C)	(D)	(E)
9.	(A)	(B)	(C)	(D)	(E)												

EXAM SEVEN

1. (A) (B) (C) (D) (E)
2. (A) (B) (C) (D) (E)
3. (A) (B) (C) (D) (E)
4. (A) (B) (C) (D) (E)
5. (A) (B) (C) (D) (E)
6. (A) (B) (C) (D) (E)
7. (A) (B) (C) (D) (E)
8. (A) (B) (C) (D) (E)
9. (A) (B) (C) (D) (E)

10. (A) (B) (C) (D) (E)
11. (A) (B) (C) (D) (E)
12. (A) (B) (C) (D) (E)
13. (A) (B) (C) (D) (E)
14. (A) (B) (C) (D) (E)
15. (A) (B) (C) (D) (E)
16. (A) (B) (C) (D) (E)
17. (A) (B) (C) (D)

18. (A) (B) (C) (D) (E)
19. (A) (B) (C) (D) (E)
20. (A) (B) (C) (D) (E)
21. (A) (B) (C) (D) (E)
22. (A) (B) (C) (D) (E)
23. (A) (B) (C) (D) (E)
24. (A) (B) (C) (D) (E)
25. (A) (B) (C) (D)

EXAM EIGHT

1. (A) (B) (C) (D) (E)
2. (A) (B) (C) (D) (E)
3. (A) (B) (C) (D) (E)
4. (A) (B) (C) (D) (E)
5. (A) (B) (C) (D) (E)
6. (A) (B) (C) (D) (E)
7. (A) (B) (C) (D) (E)
8. (A) (B) (C) (D) (E)
9. (A) (B) (C) (D) (E)

10. (A) (B) (C) (D) (E)
11. (A) (B) (C) (D) (E)
12. (A) (B) (C) (D) (E)
13. (A) (B) (C) (D) (E)
14. (A) (B) (C) (D)
15. (A) (B) (C) (D)
16. (A) (B) (C) (D)
17. (A) (B) (C) (D) (E)

18. (A) (B) (C) (D)
19. (A) (B) (C) (D)
20. (A) (B) (C) (D) (E)
21. (A) (B) (C) (D) (E)
22. (A) (B) (C) (D) (E)
23. (A) (B) (C) (D)
24. (A) (B) (C) (D) (E)
25. (A) (B) (C) (D) (E)

EXAM SEVEN

1. (A) (B) (C) (D) (E)
2. (A) (B) (C) (D) (E)
3. (A) (B) (C) (D) (E)
4. (A) (B) (C) (D) (E)
5. (A) (B) (C) (D) (E)
6. (A) (B) (C) (D) (E)
7. (A) (B) (C) (D) (E)
8. (A) (B) (C) (D) (E)
9. (A) (B) (C) (D) (E)
10. (A) (B) (C) (D) (E)
11. (A) (B) (C) (D) (E)
12. (A) (B) (C) (D) (E)
13. (A) (B) (C) (D) (E)
14. (A) (B) (C) (D) (E)
15. (A) (B) (C) (D) (E)
16. (A) (B) (C) (D) (E)
17. (A) (B) (C) (D)
18. (A) (B) (C) (D) (E)
19. (A) (B) (C) (D) (E)
20. (A) (B) (C) (D) (E)
21. (A) (B) (C) (D) (E)
22. (A) (B) (C) (D) (E)
23. (A) (B) (C) (D) (E)
24. (A) (B) (C) (D) (E)
25. (A) (B) (C) (D)

EXAM EIGHT

1. (A) (B) (C) (D) (E)
2. (A) (B) (C) (D) (E)
3. (A) (B) (C) (D) (E)
4. (A) (B) (C) (D) (E)
5. (A) (B) (C) (D) (E)
6. (A) (B) (C) (D) (E)
7. (A) (B) (C) (D) (E)
8. (A) (B) (C) (D) (E)
9. (A) (B) (C) (D) (E)
10. (A) (B) (C) (D) (E)
11. (A) (B) (C) (D) (E)
12. (A) (B) (C) (D) (E)
13. (A) (B) (C) (D) (E)
14. (A) (B) (C) (D)
15. (A) (B) (C) (D)
16. (A) (B) (C) (D)
17. (A) (B) (C) (D) (E)
18. (A) (B) (C) (D)
19. (A) (B) (C) (D)
20. (A) (B) (C) (D) (E)
21. (A) (B) (C) (D) (E)
22. (A) (B) (C) (D) (E)
23. (A) (B) (C) (D)
24. (A) (B) (C) (D) (E)
25. (A) (B) (C) (D) (E)